Durkheimian
sociology:
cultural studies

Durkheimian sociology: cultural studies

Edited by Jeffrey C. Alexander

University of California, Los Angeles

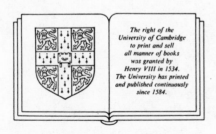

The right of the
University of Cambridge
to print and sell
all manner of books
was granted by
Henry VIII in 1534.
The University has printed
and published continuously
since 1584.

Cambridge University Press
Cambridge
New York   Port Chester
Melbourne   Sydney

Published by the Press Syndicate of the University of Cambridge
The Pitt Building, Trumpington Street, Cambridge, CB2 1RP
32 East 57th Street, New York, NY 10022, USA
10 Stamford Road, Oakleigh, Melbourne 3166, Australia

First published 1988
Reprinted 1989

Printed in Great Britain at
the University Press, Cambridge

British Library cataloguing in publication data

Durkheimian sociology: cultural studies.
1. Durkheimian school of sociology
I. Alexander, Jeffrey C.
301   HM22.F79

Library of Congress cataloguing in publication data

Durkheimian sociology: cultural studies
Includes index.
1. Durkheimian school of sociology.
2. Durkheim, Emile, 1858–1917.
3. Social change.
I. Alexander, Jeffrey C.
HM24.D985   1988   301'.092'4   87–24912

ISBN 0 521 34622 3

For Robert Bellah

Contents

Contents

Contributors

JEFFREY C. ALEXANDER is Professor and Director of Graduate Studies in the Department of Sociology at UCLA. His books include *Theoretical Logic in Sociology, Twenty Lectures: Sociological Theory since World War II*, and *Action and Its Environments: Toward a New Synthesis*. Past chair of the Theory Section of the American Sociological Association, he has been a Guggenheim Fellow and, most recently, a member of the School of Social Science at the Princeton Institute for Advanced Studies.

LYNN HUNT taught at the University of California, Berkeley from 1974 to 1987 and is now Professor of History at the University of Pennsylvania. She also has been a visiting professor at the École des Hautes Études in Paris and Beijing University. Her publications include *Revolution and Urban Politics in Provincial France* and *Politics, Culture and Class in the French Revolution*. She has been awarded both ACLS and Guggenheim fellowships.

EDWARD A. TIRYAKIAN is Professor of Sociology at Duke University. He has published on a wide variety of sociological topics, from Durkheim and existential phenomenology to the sociology of religion and comparative problems of modernity. Recently, he has edited a volume *The Global Crisis* (1984) and coedited *New Nationalisms of the Developed West* (1985). He has served as president of the American Society for the Study of Religion (1981–84), as chair of the Theory Section of the American Sociological Association (1974–75, 1985–86), and is currently vice-president of the International Association of French-Speaking Sociologists (AISLF).

ERIC W. ROTHENBUHLER is currently Assistant Professor in the Department of Communication Studies at the University of Iowa. His interests are in the mass communication process, defined as any instance of public symbolic action. His research has focused on media events as festivals of social solidarity, the structure of commercial culture industries, and their audiences. He is currently working on a series of essays generalizing about the functions of mass communication processes in social systems.

RUTH A. WALLACE is currently Professor of Sociology at George Washington University in Washington, DC. Her publications include *Contemporary Sociological*

Theory (with Alison Wolf), *Contemporary Sociological Theory: Continuing the Classical Tradition* (with Alison Wolf), and *Gender in America* (with Patricia Lengermann). She has been elected chair of the Theory Section of the American Sociological Association for 1988.

SHIRLEY FOSTER HARTLEY is Professor of Sociology at the California State University, Hayward. She has published three books and numerous articles in subjects as diverse as illegitimacy, population, the status of women internationally, research ethics, the multiple roles of clergy wives, reproductive engineering, and, most recently, the race between food and population, and friendship. She has served for three years as Associate Editor of *Contemporary Sociology*. She was also elected to the Board of Directors of the Population Association of America and was invited to serve the Population Research Study Section of the National Institute of Health, DHEW.

RANDALL COLLINS is Professor of Sociology at the University of California, Riverside. He is the author of a number of books and articles, including *Conflict Sociology: Toward an Explanatory Science*; *The Credential Society*; *Three Sociological Traditions*; *Weberian Sociological Theory*; and, most recently, *Theoretical Sociology*.

HANS-PETER MÜLLER is an assistant at the Institute for Sociology and Social Politics at the University of the Federal Armed Services in Munich. His publications include *Herrschaft und Legitimität in modernen Industriegesellschaften* (with Manfred Kopp), *Wertkrise und Gesellschaftsreform: Emile Durkheims Schriften zur Politik*, and *Gerechtigkeit, Diskurs oder Markt? Die neuen Ansätze in der Vertragstheorie* (edited with Lucian Kern). From 1986 to 1987 he was John F. Kennedy Fellow at Harvard University.

DANIEL DAYAN is an adjunct professor at the Annenberg School of Communications, and a visiting professor at the school of Cinema and Television, University of Southern California. He has taught cinema and television at the Hebrew University, Jerusalem, Tel Aviv University, the American Interuniversity Center for Film and Cultural Studies (Paris), the University of Paris II, and Stanford University. Besides his current work on television, his writings on the semiotics of film include "The tutor code of classical cinema" (in Nichols, B., ed., *Movies and Methods*), and *Western Graffiti: Jeux d'Image et Programmation du Spectateur*.

ELIHU KATZ is Professor of sociology and communications at the Hebrew University of Jerusalem and Distinguished Visiting Professor at the Annenberg School of Communications at the University of Southern California. He has previously been affiliated with Columbia University and the University of Chicago. His work has concentrated on the sociology of mass communications, and he is co-author of *Personal Influence* (with Paul F. Lazarsfeld), *The Secularization of Leisure* (with Michael Gurovitch), *Broadcasting in the Third World* (with E. G. Wedell), and *Mass Media and Social Change* (with Tamas Szecsko). His current work is with Daniel Dayan on "media events" and with Tamar Liebes on the decoding of American popular culture overseas.

Acknowledgements

This volume was conceived amidst the effervescence of a small and lively conference on "Emile Durkheim's Sociology of Religion," sponsored by the Werner-Reimers-Stiftung in June 1983, which took place on the foundation's handsome grounds in Bad Homburg. Werner Gephart amicably hosted the meeting, organizing it specifically around the "later Durkheimian" theme. That only two of the original conference participants have contributed to the present book – Hans-Peter Müller and myself – detracts in no way from the value of those early discussions. To both Gephart and the Werner-Reimers-Stiftung, therefore, I would like to record my thanks.

I would also like to note with appreciation the intellectual and organizational advice of Sue Allen-Mills, my editor at Cambridge University Press. Her persistence certainly has made this a better book.

Initially an outside reviewer of this manuscript, Charles Lemert played an exceptional role. He fast assumed the guise of house critic and became intimately involved in decisions about not only the book's structure but its intellectual frame. For his perceptive and extremely helpful feedback on my introductory statement I would like to express my particular thanks.

It has now been seventy years since Emile Durkheim's death, and it is one of the fundamental premises of this volume that his intellectual bequest – the legacy of his later years – has yet fully to be claimed. In the years intervening, of course, a number of important scholars and theorists have pointed the way. For me personally, the most important has been Robert Bellah. A sensitive and life-long student of the great French master, Bellah communicated to his students the unique symbolic emphasis that separates Durkheim from the other classics and that constitutes such an important challenge for contemporary sociology. The present volume takes up this challenge, even if it represents only one small step along the way.

Jeffrey C. Alexander

Introduction: Durkheimian sociology and cultural studies today

Jeffrey C. Alexander

This book is designed to bring the analysis of symbolic phenomena more directly into the discourse of sociology. The human studies are in the midst of an explosion of cultural interest. In diverse disciplinary orientations throughout Europe and in literary studies in the United States, semiotics and structuralism – and the poststructuralist movements which have followed in their wake – have fundamentally affected contemporary understandings of social experience and ideas. In American social science there has emerged over the last twenty years a complementary movement within anthropology. This symbolic anthropology has begun to have powerful ramifications on related disciplines, especially on American and European social history.

In the discipline of sociology, however – particularly but not only in its American guise – researchers and theorists are still fighting the last war. In the 1960s there was a general mobilization against the hegemony of structural–functional theory in the "idealist" form associated with Parsons. This challenge has triumphed, but theorizing of an equally one-sided sort has taken its place. The discipline is now dominated by micro and macro orientations which are either anti-systemic, anti-cultural or both. The anti-cultural macro approach, which emphasizes conflict and social "structures," made positive, innovative contributions in the early phase of the fight against functionalism. It helped stimulate, for example, the reaction against the reigning consensus perspective in history. But the new social history, as it has been called for two decades, is by now old hat; it is in the process of being overtaken by a different kind of social history, one which has a pronounced cultural bent. Sociology, meanwhile, remains mired in presymbolic thought. It is as if in this small corner of the intellectual world the Reformation and Renaissance have been reversed. Sociologists are still trying to reform the Parsonian church. For them the cultural renaissance has yet to come. In sociology there is, as yet, scarcely any cultural analysis at all.

The irony is that important intellectual roots of this cultural revival can actually be traced to one of sociology's own founders, Emile Durkheim. Sociologists know Durkheim primarily through the works he published in the middle 1890s, *The Division of Labor in Society*, *The Rules of Sociological Method* and *Suicide*. On the basis of these works, as Collins suggests later in this volume, sociologists have identified "Durkheimianism" – and to some extent sociology as such – with an emphasis on external constraints and "coercive social facts" on the one hand, and with positivistic, often quantitative methods on the other.

But it was only after the completion of these works that Durkheim's distinctively cultural program for sociology emerged.[1] It is true, of course, that even in his earlier works there is an unmistakable concern with subjectivity and solidarity. But only in the studies which began in the later 1890s did Durkheim have an explicit theory of symbolic process firmly in hand. It was at this time that he became deeply interested in religion. "A great number of problems change their aspects completely," Durkheim (1960 [1899]:351) wrote, "as soon as their connections with the sociology of religion are recognized." Durkheim came to believe, indeed, that theories of secular social process have to be modelled upon the workings of the sacred world. This turn to religion, he emphasized, was not because of an interest in churchly things. It was because he wanted to give cultural processes more theoretical autonomy. In religion he had discovered a model of how symbolic processes work in their own terms.

In scattered essays in the late 1890s, and in the monographs and lectures which followed until his death in 1914, Durkheim developed a theory of secular society that emphasized the independent causal importance of symbolic classification, the pivotal role of the symbolic division between sacred and profane, the social significance of ritual behavior, and the close interrelation between symbolic classifications, ritual processes and the formation of social solidarities. It was an unfortunate if largely fortuitous fact that the published work in which Durkheim announced and systematically developed this new theory – which he called his "religious sociology" – was devoted to archaic religion and to what would today be seen as anthropological concerns. Only in his unpublished lectures did Durkheim elaborate this new perspective in regard to the secular phenomena of modern life.

If Durkheim had lived beyond the First World War, the perspective of these lectures would be much more widely known today, for he would no doubt have converted them into published scholarly works. We would then have available to us systematic explorations of the "religious" structures and processes that continue to inform contemporary life. The posthumous publication of the lectures (Durkheim 1956, 1958a [1928],

1958b [1950], 1961 [1925], 1977 [1938] has certainly made his ambition and preliminary thinking in this regard perfectly clear. In a series of profound and probing discussions of education, politics, professional organization, morality and the law, Durkheim demonstrated that these modern spheres must be studied in terms of symbolic classifications. They are structured by tensions between the fields of the sacred and profane; their central social processes are ritualistic; their most significant structural dynamics concern the construction and destruction of social solidarities. These lectures demonstrate the truth of Durkheim's remonstrance in the opening pages of *The Elementary Forms of Religious Life*, the late masterpiece in which he outlined his "religious sociology." He has not devoted himself to "a very archaic religion," Durkheim declares, "simply for the pleasures of telling its peculiarities." If he has taken Aboriginal religion as his subject, he argues (Durkheim 1912:1), this is only "because it has seemed to us better adapted than any other to lead to an understanding of the religious nature of man, that is, to show us an essential and permanent aspect of humanity." His point, he insists, is that it is not only archaic man who has a religious nature, but also the "man of today."

The problem, however, is not only that Durkheim failed to enunciate this new and quite radical view of secular society in his published work. It is also that this late Durkheimian perspective eventually ceased to be articulated at all. For some years after his death, Durkheim's closest students, and those whom they influenced, continued to carry out studies that forcefully demonstrated the power of his later cultural approach. Halbwachs' (e.g. 1913, 1950) research on working-class consumption and collective memory, Simiand's (1934) on money, Mauss' (1967 [1925]) on exchange, Bouglé's (1908) on caste – these are merely the best known illustrations of how "late Durkheimianism" was carried into practice by the Durkheim school.

The possibilities that these studies opened up, however, were never extensively mined. In the aftermath of the First World War, the influence of the Durkheim school waned. The movements that sought to carry forward its legacy, moreover, distorted key elements of its thought. The *Annales* school of history began with a Durkheimian thrust, but its "sociological" emphasis soon tilted toward demographic and socio-political structures and away from consciousness. On the other hand, under Mauss' influence, what was left of the school proper veered increasingly toward ethnography (see Vogt 1976). Because of these and other developments, the theoretical ambitions manifest in Durkheim's later program gradually faded away. By the 1930s, the French intellectual community viewed Durkheimianism either as apolitical, archaicizing ethnography or as scientistic sociological determinism. It was rejected on both grounds.

As Durkheimian ideas made their way beyond French borders they were pushed in directions equally opposed to the symbolic interests of his later work. Radcliffe-Brown founded British social anthropology in Durkheim's name, but his mechanistic functionalism might be better identified with the theorizing against which Durkheim's later writing had been aimed. When Parsons initiated sociological functionalism in the late 1930s, he (Parsons 1937) declared Durkheim to be one of its founders. But while Parsons saw more of the cultural Durkheim than most interpreters, he explicitly criticized the later focus on autonomous symbolic processes. Rather than symbolic systems, Parsons insisted that sociology be concerned with social values and their institutionalization. He tied this value emphasis (e.g. Parsons 1967), moreover, to his search for the foundations of consensual social order.[2] In the post-Parsons period, sociologists who have conspicuously taken up Durkheim's mantle (e.g. Bloor 1976, Douglas and Wildavsky 1982, Traugott 1985) have tended to conceptualize culture in an even more reductive way.[3]

Yet, while the challenge of Durkheim's later writings has not been taken up by sociology, in other branches of the human studies it has been actively pursued. The relationship has often been indirect and the influence subterranean. Those who are pursuing a "late Durkheimian" program are often unaware that such a link exists. When the possibility is recognized, moreover, it has often been denied. Nonetheless, a compelling case can be made that, more than any other classical figure, it is to Durkheim that the contemporary cultural revival to which I earlier referred is most deeply in debt.

Consider, for example, Ferdinand Saussure, whose centrality is widely acknowledged because it was he who first conceived of modern structural linguistics and conceptualized "semiotics" as the science of signs. While Saussure never cites Durkheim directly – his major work, too, consisted of posthumously published lectures – parallels between his intellectual system and Durkheim's are striking indeed. In contrast with his linguistic contemporaries, Saussure (1916:107) insisted on the "institutional" character of language. He called language a social fact (*un fait social*, p. 21) that emerged from the *conscience collective* (p. 104) of society, the linguistic elements of which were "consecrated through use" (Godel 1957:145). Saussure depended, in other words, on a number of key concepts that were identical with the controversial and widely discussed terms of the Durkheim school. Most linguistic historians (e.g. Doroszewski 1933:89–90, Ardener 1971:xxxii–xiv), indeed, have interpreted these resemblances as evidence of Durkheim's very significant influence on Saussure. In doing so, moreover, they have conceived of Durkheim in his later, more symbolical guise.[4]

Whether a direct relationship can actually be demonstrated, however, is not the most important concern. The echoes in Saussurian linguistics of Durkheim's symbolic theory are deep and substantial. Just as Durkheim insisted that religious symbols could not be reduced to their interactional base, Saussure emphasized the autonomy of linguistic signs *vis-à-vis* their social and physical referents. From his own insistence on cultural autonomy Durkheim was led to an interest in the internal dynamics of symbolic and ritual systems. From Saussure's emphasis on the arbitrariness of words there followed a similar concentration on the structures of symbolic organization in and of themselves.

Similar parallels exist between later Durkheimian theory and Lévi-Strauss' structural anthropology. Lévi-Strauss insists that societies must be studied in terms of symbolic classifications, that these symbolic systems are patterned as binary oppositions, and that social action (at least in premodern societies) is expressive and cultural rather than instrumental and contingent. Here is another influential cultural program, in other words, that bears a striking similarity to the late Durkheimian program I have outlined above. Once again, moreover, while direct linkage is impossible to establish, a compelling case for significant influence can be made. In linguistics, Lévi-Strauss acknowledges the influence not only of Jakobson but also of Saussure. In anthropology, he recognizes primarily his debt to Marcel Mauss, whose earlier work on symbols he (Lévi-Strauss 1968) praises for emphasizing the autonomy of classification and the antipathies and homologies of which it is composed. That Lévi-Strauss often takes sharp issue with Durkheim cannot, therefore, be taken at full face value. In the first place, such denials (e.g. Lévi-Strauss 1945) associate Durkheim with an anti-symbolic "sociologism" that is at odds with the emphasis of his later work. In the second place, not only was Mauss himself Durkheim's closest student, but the work of Mauss that Lévi-Strauss (e.g. 1968: xxxi) most applauds, the essay translated as *Primitive Classification*, was co-authored with Durkheim and represents only one of many exemplifications of the later Durkheimian program.

From Saussure and Lévi-Strauss some of the most important contemporary cultural movements have been derived. It was structural thinking more than any other current that stimulated Roland Barthes to elaborate his enormously influential studies in social and literary semiotics. Over the last thirty years Barthes and other semioticians have explicated the codes – the systems of symbolic classification – that regulate a wide array of secular institutions and social processes, from fashions (1983) and food production (Sahlins 1976) to civil conflict (Buckley 1984). Poststructuralists like Foucault have carried this emphasis on the structuring power of symbolic patterns, or discourses, even further into the social domain.

On occasion these thinkers have made their relation to Durkheim explicit. These acknowledgements, however, often serve to emphasize
rather than to reduce the distance between Durkheim's later program and
sociology as it has come to be conventionally understood. Barthes
(1983:10) insists in his methodological introduction to *The Fashion
System*, for example, that while "the sociology of Fashion is entirely
directed toward real clothing[,] the semiology of Fashion is directed
toward a set of collective representations." He follows with the extraordinarily revealing statement that his own, semiotic emphasis leads "not to
sociology but rather to the *sociologics* postulated by Durkheim and
Mauss" (original italics), footnoting the same essay on primitive classification cited by Lévi-Strauss.

In most cases, however, these Durkheimian roots are simply not recognized at all. In *A History of Sexuality*, Foucault devotes a major section of
his argument to demonstrating the religious roots of the modern
"rational" insistence on exposing the sexual basis of various activities.
This contemporary discourse, he insists (1980:68), has "kept as its
nucleus the singular ritual of obligatory and exhaustive confession, which
in the Christian West was the first technique for producing the truth of
sex." Secularization, then, consists in "this rite [having] gradually
detached itself from the sacrament of penance." A more clear-cut exemp-
lification of Durkheim's later program for sociology would be hard to
find. It was Durkheim (1960 [1899]:350) who insisted that religious
phenomena "are the germ from which all others . . . derived" and the
treatment in his late lectures of such secular phenomena as contract and
exchange find their echoes in Foucault. That Foucault himself never en-
tertained the possibility of a Durkheimian link is in a certain sense beside
the point. His work rests on an intellectual base to which late Durkheimian thought made an indelible contribution.

Both as theory and empirical investigation, poststructuralism and
semiotic investigations more generally can be seen as elaborating one of
the pathways that Durkheim's later sociology opens up. Indeed, they
have demonstrated the importance of his later theory more forcefully
than any discipline in the social sciences more narrowly conceived. As
such, they constitute primarily theoretical resources from which the
effort to create a cultural sociology will have to draw.

In emphasizing this extra-sociological Durkheimianism, however, I do
not want to suggest that within the social science disciplines there has
been no work related to late Durkheimian theory at all. There have, in
fact, been some interesting developments, and even if they have not been
of comparable scope or influence they point in similar ways. Without, for
the most part, explicitly acknowledging Durkheim's work, these efforts

have joined his emphases to other theoretical frameworks in order to develop a more symbolic kind of discourse about secular life.

It is ironic, perhaps, that the most important developments of this type emerged from the dissolution of the Parsonian camp. As disaffection with structural-functionalism increased, three of Parsons' most important students and co-workers tried to push his framework toward a distinctively Durkheimian emphasis on symbolism, sacredness and ritual. Shils (1975) argued that secular, differentiated societies have symbolic "centers" which inspire awe and mystery and that it is the proximity to these sources of sacredness which allocates such "structural" qualities as social status. In a series of critical essays in the 1960s, Geertz (1973a, 1973b) argued that whether cultural systems are "religious" has nothing to do with their supernatural quality, and everything to do with the degree to which they are sacralized, inspire ritual devotion, and mobilize group solidarity. Since that time, Geertz has interpreted secular phenomena from Balinese cockfighting (Geertz 1973c) to American political campaigns (Geertz 1983) in more or less similar symbolic and culturalist terms.

Shils and Geertz never acknowledged their debt to Durkheim. It is true, of course, that they drew widely from cultural theory, and in this sense their failure to make the reference explicit merely reflects the permeation of later Durkheimian thinking into the general intellectual milieu. It also, however, reflects the resistance toward, and misunderstanding of, late Durkheimian ideas within social science itself. The result is that, while Geertz's work especially has been enormously influential outside the field of sociology, this turn toward cultural theorizing from within the social sciences has had only a limited impact on traditional sociological work (for exceptions, see Stivers 1982, Zelizer 1985 and Prager 1986).[5] It is only the third disaffected Parsonian, Robert Bellah, who openly acknowledged the link to Durkheim; indeed, he has made this connection the lynchpin of his newly cultural work.

Bellah (1970, 1980a) has argued that secular nations have "civil religions." These are symbolic systems that relate national political structures and events to a transcendent, supra-political framework that defines some "ultimate" social meaning. Bellah calls this framework religious not because it must refer to God, but rather in order to emphasize the sacredness of its symbols and the ritual power it commands. In these terms, even atheistic, communist nations possess civil religions. Not ontological properties but historically determined social conditions determine the effect of a civil religion on society.

More than any other social scientific formulation, the civil religion concept promised to open sociology to the power of Durkheim's later work. In the years since Bellah's original formulation, the concept has, indeed, been used to explain a wide variety of political and cultural situations (e.g. Coleman 1970, Moodie 1974, Wolfe 1975, Bellah 1980b, c, Hammond 1980a, b, Rothenbuhler 1985). Yet civil religion has not, in fact, entered the language of social science in a central and powerful way. Rather, it has been taken up primarily in "religious studies" by sociologists who specialize in religion (e.g. Hammond 1983a, b) and by theologians (e.g. Lynn 1973, Marty 1974, Wilson 1979) with a special interest in society. The reasons, I think, have to do not only with the resistance of social science to embracing cultural work but also with central ambiguities in the original concept itself.

Bellah first conceived the civil religion idea in a discussion which argued for the close relation between American politics and Protestant religiosity. He suggested that, while the connection was not necessary in principle, in practice the American civil religion did in fact center on traditional Christian symbols. Indeed, he argued that growing agnosticism could undermine the status of American civil religion *vis-à-vis* secular power. Moreover, the most significant expositor of Bellah's concept, the sociologist of religion Phillip Hammond (1983a, b), has sought to limit civil religion explicitly to the kind of formation that exists in the American case. A nation has a civil religion, in his view, only if it has institutionalized a cultural system that ties politics to churchly symbols but is independent of an established Church. But such an argument, while certainly illuminating particular empirical issues (cf. Thomas and Flippen 1972 and Wimberly et al. 1976), narrows the more far-reaching and general implications of the concept, for it effectively cuts the concept off from its late Durkheimian base (*contra* Hammond 1974). Ironically, it was against precisely this kind of narrowing that Durkheim launched his later arguments, which in turn formed the basis for Bellah's original conception of the term.

Shils and Bellah, of course, are sociologists, and while Geertz is not – he is an anthropologist – he was trained by Parsons, a theorist who was. Taken together, their work certainly constitutes another major resource from which cultural analysis must draw. The other source of significant ideas that has emerged from within the social sciences comes from anthropology. The Durkheimian sociologists pushed theories about modern society to incorporate concepts previously applied only to premodern ones. Late-Durkheimian anthropologists have used Durkheim's theories of premodern society to move to a study of modern life. While beginning from opposite directions, in other words, they have ended up in much the same place.

Of these anthropological developments, Turner's work on the ritual process is undoubtedly the most important (see, e.g. Moore and Myer-hoff 1975). Turner (1969) argues that the basic components of ritual can be abstracted from the specific situations of archaic societies and treated as fundamental aspects of social behavior as such. Because all rituals involve transitions from one patterned position or structure to another, he suggests that ritual can be seen as possessing not simply an integrative but an "anti-structural" dimension. During this anti-structural or "liminal" phase, he suggests, participants experience intense solidarity, or "communitas." Since this condition of liminal solidarity constitutes a deviant status, it often provides an opening for social change. In his later work, Turner (e.g. 1974) tried to separate these elements from an association with actual ritual events. He demonstrated that liminality and communitas could be seen as central features of such widely divergent secular phenomena as political confrontations, athletic contests and counter-cultures.

Once again, the relationship between this new development in cultural theory and Durkheimian thought is never explicitly made. For his specific teminology, indeed, Turner drew on the work of van Gennep, the contemporary of Durkheim's who criticized his explanation of Aboriginal religion. But the similarities between Turner's ideas and Durkheim's later project are too obvious to overlook (see, e.g. the discussions in Dayan and Katz and Rothenbuhler below). This is not to say, of course, that Turner did not go beyond Durkheim in valuable ways. Indeed, he has shown more clearly than Durkheim how rituals can depend on contingent behavior and can be deeply involved in social change.

Much the same can be said for the work of Mary Douglas, the other anthropologist whose work has contributed significantly to broader currents in cultural studies. She has documented the classifying and symbolic functions of what are usually taken to be merely physical and adaptive activities (e.g. Douglas and Isherwood 1979). Most particularly, she (1966) has shown that pollution is a form of social control that societies use against symbolically deviant, profane things. Even in such clear efforts to generalize from religious to secular activity, however, Douglas dissociates her efforts from Durkheimian work. Still, it is the "Durkheimian-ism" of Radcliffe-Brown that she is fighting, not the symbolic theory of Durkheim's own later work. Her conception of pollution expands Durkheim's notion of profanation by relating it directly to issues of social control.[6]

My argument in this Introduction has been that, even while references to Durkheim's later theory have virtually disappeared, his "religious sociology" has significantly influenced the developments in cultural studies that are invigorating the intellectual world today.[7] Two conclusions follow, both of which have to do with the benefits of making this framework explicit. The first relates to cultural studies more generally. By making this Durkheimian framework explicit, the inner connections between these different developments can much more easily be seen. Only if these inner connections are established can the theoretical basis for contemporary cultural analysis be accurately portrayed. The full array of theoretical resources is necessary if a general and comprehensive social scientific understanding of culture is finally to emerge (see Alexander, forthcoming).

The second conclusion is more limited. It has to do with cultural studies in a more disciplinary sense, specifically with the prospects for a cultural sociology. Disciplinary practice is defined by its classics, and for sociology Durkheim's work is arguably the most classic of all. At the present time, "Durkheim" is perceived largely in terms of the structural concerns of his middle-period work. Insofar as the Durkheimian reference of contemporary cultural studies becomes explicit, however, this narrow understanding becomes increasingly difficult to sustain. If it cannot be sustained, if the understanding of Durkheim shifts towards the later work, then there will be increasing pressure to bring cultural analysis squarely into the practice of sociology. This, I have argued, was precisely the ambition of Durkheim himself.

It is certainly not coincidental that it has been in the midst of this outpouring of Durkheim-inspired cultural work that a new and much more sophisticated phase of Durkheim scholarship has emerged. The scope of Durkheim's lectures in the later period was evident only after Lukes (1972) published the first fully annotated account of Durkheim's life and work. Lukes' research also brought to light biographical material which underscored not only the existence of Durkheim's turn to religion but the personal significance it may have had for him. Later in the 1970s there emerged a group of scholars around Phillip Bésnard and *La Revue française de sociologie*, who initiated a new wave of historical explorations of Durkheim and his school. Once again, these historical investigations revealed the importance of the religious turn, not only for Durkheim himself but for the direction of his students' work (e.g. Birnbaum 1976, Bésnard 1979, 1983). Neither Lukes nor the French group argued that there emerged a later "religious sociology" more generally conceived. The interpretations that succeeded these pioneering studies, however (e.g. Filloux 1977, Jones 1977, Lacroix 1981, Alexander 1982), not only followed up on these leads but on the basis of this new understanding read the extant Durkheim material in an altered way. Gradually, a more general perspective did begin to emerge. While some interpreters still do not accede (e.g. Giddens 1977 and Traugott 1978), there is increasing agreement today that in the later period Durkheim's sociology underwent a decisive shift. It is, of course, the recognition of the crucial distinctiveness of this later work which has allowed the Durkheimian roots of contemporary cultural studies to be traced.

The chapters that follow, published here for the first time, are informed by this new reading of Durkheim's work. They make their late Durkheimian framework explicit, even as they draw upon the full repertoire of cultural theorizing I have described. As such, they not only contribute to reintegrating the cultural field but demonstrate the possibility of a cultural approach within the discipline of sociology more narrowly defined.

For all these chapters, the major point of departure is *The Elementary Forms of the Religious Life*, which functions as a model for explaining central processes in secular social life.[8] The other shared emphases follow naturally from this. They concentrate, first, on what might be called motivated expressive behavior as compared with conscious strategic action. This emotionally charged action, moreover, is not seen psychologistically, but instead as the basis for ritualization. It is conceived as action organized by reference to symbolic patterns that actors – even if they have a hand in changing them – did not intentionally create (cf. Wuthnow 1987. ch. 1). Sacredness is conceptualized as a focal point for such symbolic patterns and, hence, for ritual activity as well. It is treated as a natural outgrowth of the human anxiety about meaning and order and, simultaneously, as a focal point for the institutionalization of power and social control. None of this conceptual emphasis, finally, is connected to an emphasis on social consensus or psychological conformity. Indeed, such a relationship is usually explicitly disputed. The authors use a late Durkheimian framework to analyze phenomena which are disruptive, contingent, and related to social change.

Yet, while these chapters bring the late Durkheim to cultural analysis, they also bring contemporary cultural analysis to Durkheim. The language of structuralism and semiotics is omnipresent, and connections to the models developed by symbolic anthropology and sociology are frequently made. Just as pervasive is the connection of cultural analysis to theorizing of a much more social-structural sort. In this respect there is general agreement on the limitations of Durkheim's later work.[9] In various chapters the religious model is nested in Marxist, Weberian, functionalist, and even psychoanalytic theory.

I have organized the first chapers under the rubric, "Social Change and Sacralization." In her chapter "The Sacred and the French Revolution," Lynn Hunt shows that historical actors themselves are aware of the powers of sacrality and ritual. New sacred objects and ritual forms are invented, she argues, in periods of semiological crisis. To deal with the critique of authority in a more satisfactory way, Hunt adds to her cultural account a psychoanalytic theory of family dynamics writ large. On this basis, she argues that violence and the sacred are intertwined; indeed, that in periods of social crisis the sacred often becomes the site for conflict, violence and change.

In "From Durkheim to Managua: Revolutions as Revivals," Edward Tiryakian begins by setting Durkheim's late theory apart from conservative and functional thought. His aim is to push the later model beyond the confines of explicitly anthropological or religious concerns and into the realm of political sociology. States are related to nations, Tiryakian suggests, much as the profane is related to the sacred. "Nation" refers to an ideal, primordial solidarity which is rarely institutionalized in the actual state structure. Revolutions are attempts to revive the sacredness of the nation against the profanation of the state. Tiryakian compares the heightened energy and extraordinary, ritualistic qualities so evident in revolutions to religious revivals, and he shows that the typical structural causes of revolutions can also be treated as the necessary conditions for upheavals in this religio-cultural sense.

Eric Rothenbuhler's "The Liminal Fight: Mass Strikes as Ritual and Interpretation" takes up similar themes but emphasizes different elements of the later theory and connects these to different auxiliary traditions. Like Tiryakian, he begins by criticizing the traditional limitation of symbolic analysis to anthropological themes. He is equally critical, however, of the typical restriction of secular Durkheimian analysis – for example in the work of Bellah and Shils – to "official" events and politically legitimated symbolic centers. He suggests that the model must also be applied to conflict at the margins of established societies. Drawing on Turner, he describes how anti-establishment social conflict poses a symbolic challenge to the cultural underpinnings of everyday life. *Vis-à-vis* established institutions and lifestyles these liminal activities present alternative models of how institutions should be read and, indeed, of how society should be organized. What is involved, therefore, is not simply an institutional conflict but a symbolic, or liminal, fight. Social responses to such activities constitute a continuum. They range from repression, to constituting it as deviant and tolerating it, to legitimating it and coopting it through social reform, to promoting it through revolution. Rothenbuhler interprets the famous IWW strike in Lawrence, Massachusetts, in terms of the late Durkheimian framework he has evolved.

I have organized the second group of chapters under the title "Micro and Macro in Symbolic Context." Since Durkheim is, of course, usually taken to have crystallized an anti-micro approach, this is definitely a context which goes beyond the Durkheim of the middle-period work. In "Religious Elements in Friendship," Wallace and Hartley take up the voluntarism which Durkheim's later perspective provides. They show that sacredness is not only a quality of symbolic systems but a goal within interpersonal activity. Close friendships sacralize the participants for one another and, in the process, the relationship as such. Ritualization and sacredness are intertwined, because the transcendental qualities of sacred feelings must have spatial and temporal manifestation. They must be separated from the profane world and acted out in special arenas. Conversations and activities between close friends, moreover, reproduce the solidarity of the ritual process; they confirm the experience of we-ness in a repetitive and standardized way. These ritual activities also, Wallace and Hartley show, provide the participants with typically "religious" experiences of transformation and rebirth.

Because conflict sociology has been almost exclusively concerned with strategic action and divisions between groups, the Durkheimian claims by Randall Collins in "The Durkheimian Tradition in Conflict Sociology" might come as a surprise. Collins argues, in fact, that the model of *The Elementary Forms* must be placed at the center of every analysis of social conflict. In order to do so, the ritual theory must be analytically abstracted from Durkheim's functionalism and from his concern with consensus. It must be connected, in turn, not only with Marxist, Weberian and interactionist ideas of social process and structure – which allow its microscopic as well as its macroscopic relevance to be seen – but with the theory, which appeared in Durkheim's earlier work, about the differential organization of solidarity and civic culture in simple versus complex societies.[10] Such a Durkheimian conflict theory provides, in Collins' hands, principles for the formation of class consciousness and ingroup solidarity. He also uses it to bring into powerful focus a wide range of other empirical phenomena – the relation between work experience and child-rearing, problems of order-giving and the maintenance of authority, political symbolization and election campaigns, gender and power in the family.

Where Collins uses the later theory to sociologize the micro and subjective realm, Müller uses it to subjectivize massive state structures which are usually treated without any symbolic reference at all. From the perspective of Durkheim's later thought, he criticizes discussions of legitimacy crisis in late capitalist societies, on both explanatory and moral grounds. The problem with neo-Marxist, systems-theoretic, realpolitik, and communicative accounts of legitimacy, in Müller's view, is that they conceive of the state and its critics as acting without reference to symbolically constituted moral frameworks. Only if the symbolic dimension of states is acknowledged can the real tension that surrounds social-structural and political activities be conceived. Müller takes Bellah's civil religion concept as a vast improvement because it opens up this normative realm and also because it introduces the possibility for moral criticism. He finds it wanting, however, both because it is abstract and insufficiently related to social-structural features of late capitalist societies and also because, paradoxically, it ties the concept of civil religion too closely to the particular features of certain extant societies. In response, Müller outlines more systematically than ever before Durkheim's own ideas of a morally justifiable and socially relevant civil religion.

In the third section of this book, "Ritualization and Public Life," I have included Dayan's and Katz's chapter and my own. In "Articulating Consensus: The Ritual and Rhetoric of Media Events," Katz and Dayan use Turner's concept of anti-structure to describe anomalous, unscripted televised ceremonies as events which are outside of everyday routine. They see them, however, in a thoroughly Durkheimian way. As "symbolic gestures presented ceremonially to enlist consensus," television events are composed of three ritual subgenres – contests, conquests and coronations. How these rituals actually proceed depends not only on ritual expectations but on social structure and individual contingency. Communist and democratic countries, for example, exert very different kinds of constraints. It is only in open societies that contingency is allowed much play. In these situations, semiotics becomes a way of life, for every event is systematically open to multivalent and ambiguous readings. Drawing on speech-act theory, Dayan and Katz emphasize that such televised events have a subjunctive mood. Their process depends on performances, on negotiations between organizers, participants, spectators and television audience. Once again, the fact of ritual process is separated from any expectations about consensual outcome.

In my own contribution, "Culture and Political Crisis: 'Watergate' and Durkheimian Sociology," I argue many of the same points. Making use of phenomenological and interactionist perspectives, I elaborate the contingent aspects of modern rituals. Using Weber and Parsons, I try to connect Durkheim's later ideas to a broader theory of social structure. Rituals, I suggest, are simultaneously effects and causes of social crises; they open up these liminal periods to symbolic and moral issues of the most profound kind. After laying out a relatively schematic model of the factors upon which the resolution of such crises depends, I devote most of the chapter to analyzing the Watergate crisis. Here I make broad use of Bellah and Shils, and try to link a dynamic account of changing social process with a structuralist analysis of symbolic relationships in themselves. This chapter doubles, in part, as a conclusion for the volume as a whole. I frame the Watergate case study within some general reflections on the late Durkheimian framework and try to suggest the place which such a framework might have in a general theory of culture and society today.

The chapters that follow certainly do not exhaust the range of social analysis which Durkheim's later sociology might inspire. Nor is this collection intended to suggest that Durkheimian analysis, whether in a direct or indirect form, exhausts the possibilities for cultural analysis itself. Hermeneutics is not the only theory for which such analysis must also find a place. There would have to be more specifically Weberian and Marxist elements as well (see Alexander, forthcoming). For all of this, Durkheim's later work contains a program which must be revived. In a fragmented way it has been at the heart of cultural analysis all along. In a more explicit form it can revitalize the practice of sociology today.

Notes

1 For an overview and explication of Durkheim's intellectual development which emphasizes the shift toward subjectivity in his thought, see Alexander (1982, 1986). In this volume, fuller discussion of these issues – particularly the question of how Durkheim's "religious sociology" relates to secular concerns – can be found in the chapters by Hunt, Tiryakian, Alexander and Collins.

2 In the work of the other major American expositor of functionalism, Robert Merton, this distortion of Durkheim's actual theoretical intention took an even more pronounced form. Merton's (1968 [1938]) influential essay, "Social Structure and Anomie," came to be regarded as a prototypical application of the Durkheimian perspective. Merton drew here, however, entirely from Durkheim's earlier work. The extent to which he ignores the later sociology can be seen from the fact that when he labels one of his four categories of deviance "ritualistic" he does so in a dismissive and pejorative way.

3 My reference here is to Douglas' grid/group theory, which she identifies as the basis for a general theory of culture (see Douglas and Wildavsky 1982). In other parts of her work (e.g. Douglas 1966, Douglas and Isherwood 1979), as I will note below, she has, in fact, made important contributions to cultural theory in a late Durkheimian vein. Similar ambiguities mark Traugott's position (compare, e.g. Traugott 1984 and 1985).

4 E.g.: "One sees, in sum, that the *langue* of Saussure not only corresponds exactly to the *fait social* of Durkheim, but, in addition, that this *langue*, half psychical and half social, exercising constraint on the individual and existing in the collective conscience of the social group, was in some way modelled on Durkheim's 'collective representations'" (Doroszewski 1933: 90).

5 In addition to the quite profound effect Geertz has had on the general intellectual milieu in the United States, his ideas have been closely associated with the cultural turn in American social history which I noted in the beginning of this Introduction. His influence can be seen directly, for example, in the work of Sewell (1980), Darnton (1984) and Wilentz (1985). That broader intellectual currents are also involved, however, is demonstrated by the more or less simultaneous development within France of more symbolic approaches to social history. Hunt discusses the most important of these contributions – most of which concentrate on the French Revolution – in her chapter in this volume, where she points out that they can be seen as elaborations of Mathiez (1904), who worked within a late Durkheimian program. Hunt's (1984) own work on the French Revolution represents an important combination of this French Durkheimian turn with Geertzian ideas and cultural theory. It is revealing of the lack of contact between sociology and this recent cultural turn in social history that Sewell's (1985) incisive culturalist critique of Skocpol's (1979) macro-structural theory of revolution appeared – along with Skocpol's response – not in a sociological review but in *The Journal of Modern History*.

6 The connection becomes more easily seen if the "correction" of Caillois (1959 [1939]) – one of the last productive members of the Durkheimian school – is taken into account. Caillois argued that Durkheim's contrast between sacred and profane must be expanded to include a third term, because profane implied for Durkheim both routine (as compared with effervescent and charismatic) and evil (as compared with good).

7 The only major contemporary current which is not at least indirectly indebted to Durkheim is the German hermeneutical tradition, which began its ambitious and distinctive program of cultural interpretation with Dilthey, whose writings (e.g. Dilthey 1976) emerged over roughly the same period as Durkheim's own. In the present period, however, the significance of hermeneutics has been more directed to providing a philosophical justification for cultural analysis than toward carrying it out (e.g. Gadamer 1975, Bernstein 1976, Taylor 1979). In this context I would have to take issue with Lukes (1982), who draws a sharp line between Durkheimian sociology and contemporary cultural analysis on the grounds that Durkheim took a positivist rather than hermeneutic position. While there is no doubt about the limitations of the formal methodology to which Durkheim adhered, for example in a middle-period work like *Rules*, his later writing demonstrated a clear commitment to the hermeneutic method in practice. If this were not true, his ideas could not have provided the basis from which so much of contemporary cultural analysis has drawn.

8 Even Wallace and Hartley, who express reservations about the sharpness of the shift in Durkheim's later work, take their conceptual bearings from the "religious theory" as it was articulated in *The Elementary Forms*.

9 And also, of course, about the limitations of semiotics and structuralism as social theories in and of themselves (see Archer, forthcoming). The effort, in other words, is not to transform social science into cultural analysis but to make the analysis of symbols a major focus of multidimensional social science.

10 For these last two addenda to later Durkheimian theory, Collins turns to the writings of Erving Goffman and Basil Bernstein. He considers both these authors to be Durkheimian in the sense in which I am defining it here. I can only partially agree; each, I think, emphasizes isolated parts of the later theory and, as a result, never makes use of interrelations suggested by the framework as a whole. In this sense, they resemble the various streams of cultural analysis I have earlier described more than they do the symbolic sociologists and anthropologists whose work I mentioned as well. In part because of the influence of Goffman and Bernstein, Collins' perspective interpenetrates the middle and later work of Durkheim more than most of the other work presented here.

References

Alexander, Jeffrey C. 1982. *The Antinomies of Classical Thought: Marx and Durkheim.* Berkeley and Los Angeles: University of California Press.

    1986. "Rethinking Durkheim's Intellectual Development." *International Sociology* 1 (1–2): 91–107, 189–201.

    Forthcoming. "Analytic Debates: Understanding the 'Autonomy' of Culture." In J. C. Alexander and Steven Seidman, eds., *Culture and Society: Contemporary Debates.* Cambridge and New York: Cambridge University Press.

Archer, Margaret. Forthcoming. *Culture and Agency.* Cambridge: Cambridge University Press.

Ardener, Edwin. 1971. "Introductory Essay: Social Anthropology and Language." In E. Ardener, ed., *Social Anthropology and Language*, pp. ix–cii. London: Tavistock.

Barthes, Roland. 1983 [1967]. *The Fashion System.* New York: Hill and Wang.

Bellah, Robert N. 1970. "Civil Religion in America." In R. N. Bellah, *Beyond Belief. Essays on Religion in a Post-Traditional World.* New York: Harper and Row.

    1980a. Introduction. In R. N. Bellah and Phillip Hammond, *Varieties of Civil Religion*, pp. vii–xv. San Francisco: Harper and Row.

    1980b. "The Japanese and American Cases." In R. N. Bellah and P. Hammond, *Varieties of Civil Religion*, pp. 27–39. San Francisco: Harper and Row.

    1980c. "The Five Religions of Modern Italy." In R. N. Bellah and P. Hammond, *Varieties of Civil Religion*, pp. 86–118. San Francisco: Harper and Row.

Bernstein, Richard J. 1976. *Restructuring Social and Political Theory.* Philadelphia: University of Pennsylvania.

Bésnard, Phillip. 1979. "La Formation de l'équipe de *L'Année sociologique.*" *Revue française de sociologie* 20: 7–31.

    1983. ed. *The Sociological Domain: The Durkheimians and the Founding of French Sociology.* Cambridge: Cambridge University Press.

Birnbaum, Pierre. 1976. "La Conception durkheimienne de l'état: L'Apolitisme des fonctionnaires." *Revue française de sociologie* 17: 247–58.

Bloor, David. 1976. *Knowledge and Social Imagery*. London: Routledge.

Bouglé, Célèstin. 1908. *Essais sur le régime des castes*. Paris.

Buckley, Anthony. 1984. "Walls within Walls: Religion and Rough Behaviour in an Ulster Community." *Sociology* 18: 19–32.

Caillois, Roger. 1959 [1939]. *Man and the Sacred*. New York: Free Press.

Coleman, John. 1970. "Civil Religion." *Sociological Analysis* 31: 67–77.

Darnton, Robert. 1984. *The Great Cat Massacre and Other Episodes in French Cultural History*. New York: Basic Books.

Dilthey, Wilhelm. 1976. *Selected Writings*. Cambridge: Cambridge University Press.

Doroszewski, W. 1933. "Quelque rémarques sur les rapports de la sociologie et de la linguistique: Durkheim et Saussure." *Journal de Psychologie* 30: 83–91.

Douglas, Mary. 1966. *Purity and Danger. An Analysis of the Concepts of Pollution and Taboo*. London: Penguin.

Douglas, Mary and Baron Isherwood. 1979. *The World of Goods: Towards an Anthropology of Consumption*. New York: Norton.

Douglas, Mary and Aaron Wildavsky. 1982. *Risk and Culture. An Essay on the Selection of Technical and Environmental Dangers*. Berkeley and Los Angeles: University of California Press.

Durkheim, Emile. 1956. *Education and Sociology*. New York: Free Press.

    1958a [1928]. *Socialism and Saint-Simon*. Yellow Springs, Ohio: Antioch University Press.

    1958b [1950]. *Professional Ethics and Civic Morals*. New York: Free Press.

    1960 [1899]. "Preface to *L'Année sociologique 2*." In Kurt Wolff, ed., *Emile Durkheim et al. on Sociology and Philosophy*, pp. 347–52. New York: Free Press.

    1961 [1925]. *Moral Education: A Study in the Theory and Application of the Sociology of Education*. New York: Free Press.

    1965 [1912]. *The Elementary Forms of the Religious Life*. Trans. Joseph Ward Swain. New York: Free Press.

    1977 [1938]. *The Evolution of Educational Thought*. London: Routledge and Kegan Paul.

Filloux, Jean-Claude. 1977. *Durkheim et le socialisme*. Geneva: Librairie Droz.

Foucault, Michel. 1980. *A History of Sexuality*. New York: Vintage.

Gadamer, Hans-Georg. 1975. *Truth and Method*. New York: Crossroad.

Geertz, Clifford. 1973a. "Ideology as a Cultural System." In C. Geertz, *The Interpretation of Cultures*. New York: Basic Books.

    1973b. "Religion as a Cultural System." In C. Geertz, *The Interpretation of Cultures*. New York: Basic Books.

    1973c. "Deep Play: Notes on a Balinese Cockfight." In C. Geertz, *The Interpretation of Cultures*. New York: Basic Books.

    1983. "Centers, Kings, and Charisma: Reflections on the Symbolics of Power." In C. Geertz, *Local Knowledge*, pp. 121–46. New York: Basic Books.

Giddens, Anthony. 1977. "The Individual in the Writing of Emile Durkheim." In A. Giddens, *Studies in Social and Political Theory*, pp. 273–91. New York: Basic Books.

Godel, Robert. 1957. *Les Sources manuscrites du Cours de linguistique generale*. Paris: Librairie Minard.

Halbwachs, Maurice. 1913. *La Classe ouvrière et les niveaux de vie*. Paris.
1950. *La Mémoire collective*. Paris.

Hammond, Phillip. 1974. "Religious Pluralism and Durkheim's Integration Thesis." In A. W. Eister, ed., *Changing Perspectives in the Scientific Study of Religion*, pp. 115–42. New York: John Wiley.
1980a. "The Conditions for Civil Religion: A Comparison of the United States and Mexico." In R. N. Bellah and P. E. Hammond, *Varieties of Civil Religion*, pp. 40–85. San Francisco: Harper and Row.
1980b. "The Rudimentary Forms of Civil Religion." In R. N. Bellah and P. E. Hammond, *Varieties of Civil Religion*, pp. 121–37. San Francisco: Harper and Row.

Hunt, Lynn. 1984. *Politics, Culture, and Class in the French Revolution*. Berkeley and Los Angeles: University of California Press.

Jones, Robert Alun. 1977. "On Understanding a Sociological Classic." *American Journal of Sociology* 83 (2): 279–319.

Lacroix, Bernard. 1981. *Durkheim et la politique*. Paris: PUF.

Lévi-Strauss, Claude. 1945. "French Sociology." In Georges Gurvitch and Wilbert E. Moore, eds., *Twentieth Century Sociology*, pp. 503–37. New York: The Philosophical Library.
1968. "Introduction à l'oeuvre de Marcel Mauss." In M. Mauss, *Sociologie et anthropologie*. Paris: PUF.

Lukes, Steven. 1972. *Emile Durkheim: His Life and Work*. New York: Harper and Row.
1982: Introduction. In S. Lukes, ed., *Durkheim: Rules of Sociological Method*. London: Macmillan.

Lynn, Robert Wood. 1973. "Civil Catechetics in Mid-Victorian America: Some Notes about Civil Religion, Past and Present," *Religious Education* 68: 5–27.

Marty, Martin. 1974. "Two Kinds of Civil Religion." In R. E. Richey and D. G. Jones, eds., *American Civil Religion*. New York: Harper and Row.

Mathiez, Albert, 1904. *Les Origines des cultes révolutionnaires (1789–1792)*. Paris.

Mauss, Marcel. 1967 [1925]. *The Gift*. New York: Free Press.

Merton, Robert. 1968 [1938]. "Social Structure and Anomie". In R. Merton, *Social Theory and Social Structure*, pp. 185–214. New York: Free Press.

Moodie, Dunbar. 1974. *The Rise of Afrikanerdom*. Berkeley and Los Angeles: University of California Press.

Moore, Sally F. and Barbara G. Myerhoff, eds. 1975. *Symbol and Politics in Communal Ideology*. Ithaca, NY: Cornell University Press.

Parsons, Talcott. 1937. *The Structure of Social Action*. New York: Free Press.
1967 "Durkheim's Contribution to the Theory of the Integration of Social Systems." In T. Parsons, *Sociological Theory and Modern Society*. New York: Free Press.

Prager, Jeffrey. 1986. *Building Democracy in Ireland: Political order and Cultural Integration in a Newly Independent Nation*. Cambridge and New York: Cambridge University Press.

Rothenbuhler, Eric. 1985. "Media Events, Civil Religion, and Social Solidarity: The Living Room Celebration of the Olympic Games." Unpublished Ph.D. Dissertation. University of Southern California.

Sahlins, Marshall. 1976. *Culture and Practical Reason*. Chicago: University of Chicago Press.

Saussure, Ferdinand. 1964 [1916]. *A Course in General Linguistics*. London: Owen.

Sewell, William, Jr. 1980. *Work and Revolution in France*. Cambridge and New York: Cambridge University Press.

   1985. "Ideologies and Social Revolutions: Reflections on the French Case." *Journal of Modern History* 57: 57–85.

Shils, Edward. 1975. *Center and Periphery: Essays in Macrosociology*. Chicago: University of Chicago Press.

Simiand, François. 1934. "La Monnaie, réalité social." *Annales sociologiques*, ser. D. (Paris): 1–86.

Skocpol, Theda. 1979. *States and Social Revolutions*. Cambridge and New York: Cambridge University Press.

Stivers, Richard. 1982. *Evil in Modern Myth and Ritual*. Atlanta: University of Georgia Press.

Taylor, Charles. 1979 [1971]. "Interpretation and the Sciences of Man." In Paul Rabinow and William M. Sullivan, eds., *Interpretive Social Science: A Reader*, pp. 25–72. Berkeley and Los Angeles: University of California Press.

Thomas, M. C. and C. C. Flippen. 1972. "American Civil Religion: An Empirical Study." *Social Forces* 51: 218–25.

Traugott, Mark. 1978. Introduction. In M. Traugott, ed., *Emile Durkheim on Institutional Analysis*. Chicago: University of Chicago Press.

   1984. "Durkheim and Social Movements." *European Journal of Sociology* 25: 319–26.

   1985. *Armies of the Poor*. Princeton: Princeton University Press.

Turner, Victor. 1969. *The Ritual Process: Structure and Anti-structure*. Chicago: Aldine.

   1974. *Dramas, Fields, and Metaphors: Symbolic Action in Human Society*. Ithaca, NY: Cornell University Press.

Vogt, W. Paul. 1976. "The Use of Studying Primitives," *Theory and Society* 4: 32–44.

Wilentz, Sean, ed. 1985. *Rites of Power*. Philadelphia: University of Pennsylvania Press.

Wilson, John F. 1979. *Public Religion in American Culture*. Philadelphia: Temple University Press.

Wimberly, R. C. et al. 1976. "The Civil Religious Dimension: Is It There?" *Social Forces* 54: 890–900.

Wolfe, James. 1975. "The Kennedy Myth: American Civil Religion in the

Sixties." Unpublished Ph.D. Dissertation. Graduate Theological Union, Berkeley, California.

Wuthnow, Robert. 1987. *Meaning and Moral Order: Explorations in Cultural Analysis*. Berkeley and Los Angeles: University of California Press.

Zelizer, Viviana. 1985. *Pricing the Priceless Child*. New York: Basic Books.

Social change and sacralization

1 The sacred and the French Revolution

Lynn Hunt

An idol is a very sacred object and sacredness the highest value ever recognized by man. An idol is often, however, nothing but a block of stone or a piece of wood, things which in themselves have no value.
Emile Durkheim, "Value Judgments and Judgments of Reality," in *Sociology and Philosophy*, trans. D. F. Pocock. (Glencoe, Ill., 1953), p. 86.

The metaphysical principles of Locke and Condillac should become popular, and the people should be accustomed to see in a statue only stone and in an image only canvas and colors.
From an article in the *Annales patriotiques* during year II of the French Revolution, as quoted by E. H. Gombrich, "The Dream of Reason: Symbolism of the French Revolution," *British Journal for Eighteenth-Century Studies* 2 (1979): 187–205, p. 190.

Emile Durkheim was never indifferent to what he called "the principles of 1789."[1] He singled out Rousseau and Montesquieu as the forerunners of sociology, but they were also the two chief inspirations for the revolutionaries of the 1790s.[2] Rousseau and Montesquieu initiated the discovery of society's laws of operation; the revolutionaries put these discoveries into practice. It was the task of sociology to reflect on this interaction. The revolutionaries learned from Montesquieu and Rousseau that social relations were based on convention. Because they were conventional – man-made – they could be remade. A people could learn that statues were only stone and that superstitious fanaticism could be given up for a more rational cult (even a Cult of Reason). Durkheim never went quite this far himself, yet informing his writings on religion was the positivist conviction that education and especially sociology could enable people to understand the social truths behind religion and perhaps eventually to move beyond religion to sociology pure and simple.

Durkheim's interest in the Revolution was most apparent in his writings on religion. In making the central argument of *The Elementary Forms of the Religious Life*, he cited the work of the socialist historian Albert Mathiez on revolutionary cults: "This aptitude of society for setting itself up as a god or for creating gods was never more apparent than during the first years of the French Revolution" (pp. 244–5). Along with

25

the Crusades, the Renaissance and the Reformation, the Revolution was regularly listed by Durkheim as one of the great creative periods in history.[3] Nevertheless, in his early writings, Durkheim struck a note of ambivalence about the Revolution. In a review published in 1890, he insisted that more needed to be known before it was possible to say whether the "principles of 1789" constitute "a pathological phenomenon or, on the contrary, simply represent a necessary transformation of our social conscience."[4]

The Revolution of 1789 intrigued Durkheim because it showed that the arguments he was making about primitive religion also applied to the modern world. In *The Elementary Forms of the Religious Life*, Durkheim set out to study the most primitive and simple religion known in order to get at "essential and permanent" aspects of humanity (p. 13). The Revolution revealed the same aspects: "society and its essential ideas become, directly and with no transfiguration of any sort, the object of a veritable cult . . . things purely laical by nature were transformed by public opinion into sacred things" (p. 245). As a result of this experience, the "principles of 1789" themselves became a religion: "In a word, they have been a religion which has had its martyrs and apostles, which has profoundly moved the masses, and which, after all, has given birth to great things."[5] As it became increasingly clear that scholarly debates over the significance of the Revolution overlapped with political struggles over the definition and even the survival of the Third Republic, Durkheim began to take more consistently the side of the republicans who looked back to 1789 for the origins of their political ideals.[6]

Central to Durkheim's work on religion and to his interest in the French Revolution was his notion of the sacred. His analysis of the sacred in "primitive" religion has been criticized on ethnographic, methodological, logical and theoretical grounds.[7] Yet, his conceptualization of the sacred has had enormous influence on sociologists and by way of anthropology and sociology has also had considerable influence on historical writing. The main analytical thrust of Durkheim's writing on the sacred is now in some sense taken for granted; no one doubts that religion can be related to society in a variety of ways. The question now is how they are to be related. It may be an "essential and permanent" aspect of human life that society has an aptitude "for setting itself up as a god or for creating gods," but many questions remain about the mechanisms and meaning of this kind of creation.

In this chapter, the French Revolution will be used to explore the concept and functioning of the sacred in a particular context. It will become apparent how useful the concept of the sacred is in understanding the Revolution, but this understanding will not serve as a springboard to universal generalizations about human nature. Rather the Revolution will serve to illuminate the particularities and limits of the concept of the sacred.

Steven Lukes discerns several different explanatory hypotheses in Durkheim's work on the sociology of religion: (1) religious belief and practice are socially determined; (2) religious thought is a cognitive enterprise; (3) religious thought and ritual express and dramatize social relationships; (4) religion functions in a manner conducive to social solidarity.[8] Each of these will be seen as useful in analyzing certain aspects of the French revolutionary experience. Yet, it should be noted from the start that all these explanatory strategies are derived from already fully formed systems of religion, however primitive. Only on rare occasions did Durkheim address the question of the origin of the sacred or try to account for dramatic changes in its functioning. As the opening quote of this chapter makes clear, no object was inherently sacred; only society could make it so. But how did this happen? Epochs or episodes of "effervescence" like the French Revolution attracted Durkheim's attention because they brought the process of investment of sacrality into high relief. "There are periods in history when, under the influence of some great collective shock, social interactions have become much more frequent and active. Men look for each other and assemble together more than ever. That general effervescence results which is characteristic of revolutionary or creative epochs." In the individual, this is described as "an abnormal over-supply of force which overflows and tries to burst out from him" (*The Elementary Forms*, p. 241).

The sacred therefore has its origins in a surplus of energy created by an extraordinarily high level of social interaction. The energy tapped by this intense social exchange is then invested in some object which is taken to represent collective ideals. As Durkheim explained in "Value Judgments and Judgments of Reality," "Collective ideals can only be manifested and become aware of themselves by being concretely realized in material objects that can be seen by all, understood by all, and represented to all minds. . . . All sorts of contingent circumstances determine the manner of its embodiment, and the object once chosen, however commonplace, becomes unique" (p. 94). The material representations of the sacred are in a sense accidents – historically contingent – and only the manner of their operation follows universal patterns.

The contingency of material representations is evident in the experience of the French in 1789. No one could have predicted the emergence of tricolor cockades, liberty trees, red liberty caps, patriotic altars, or goddesses of liberty. They were all created, some from popular sources and others more self-consciously by the leaders, in the heat of excitement in the months that followed the fall of the Bastille. Despite the efforts of historians, who have sometimes followed in the footsteps of the revolutionary leaders themselves, it is impossible to trace the genealogy of these symbols. The liberty tree is a good example. By May 1792, 60,000 of them had been planted all over France.[9] In 1794, one of the deputies in the Convention most interested in the problem of symbolic legitimation, Grégoire, wrote a "Historical and Patriotic Essay on the Trees of Liberty." He tried to trace the invention of the liberty tree to a parish priest in rural Poitou, who planted such a tree in May 1790. Historians have shown, however, that the first trees were in fact maypoles planted by the peasants of the Périgord region during their insurrection against local lords in the winter of 1790. The insurrectionary poles looked like gibbets and frequently were hung with menacing slogans. Officials sent to inquire considered them to be "symbols of revolt" and "monuments of insurrection."[10] Before long, nonetheless, the liberty tree became a general symbol of adherence to the Revolution, and throughout the decade the trees were among the favored sites of public ceremonies. The trees marked hallowed ground, and because they were so central to revolutionary identity they were also the chief focus of rebellion against the Revolution; local records are filled with thousands of accounts of mutilated or torn-up trees that were incessantly replaced by local governments. In the Oise department, for example, two men were executed in February 1794 for sawing down a liberty tree.[11]

The first self-consciously Durkheimian study of revolutionary symbolism was published in 1904 by Albert Mathiez. He concluded that the new symbolic system was formed "almost by chance, without preconceived ideas, and without an overall plan." In his opinion, it was the common product of the bourgeoisie and the people.[12] Mathiez argued that this new symbolic system constituted a revolutionary religion, taking religion in the sense defined by Durkheim in his article, "De la définition des phénomènes religieux," in the *Année sociologique* of 1899. The festivals and federations that were convoked to celebrate important revolutionary events were the rituals of the new religion. At the center of the festivals and federations was the revolutionary oath. Echoing the language of Durkheim, Mathiez asserted that "This social origin of the civic oath succeeded in imprinting on the revolutionary faith the character of religious faith."[13]

Mathiez was not the first to notice the religious character of revolutionary politics. Alexis de Tocqueville made this one of his primary arguments in *The Old Regime and the French Revolution*: "Thus the French Revolution, though ostensibly political in origin, functioned on the lines, and assumed many of the aspects, of a religious revolution."[14] Tocqueville had a rather special definition of religion in mind, however. He was most struck by the messianic quality of revolutionary religion, that is, by the revolutionary will to bring the good news to men everywhere. The Revolution was similar to Christianity in its emphasis on abstract, universalistic ideals, and in its resort to propaganda in favor of a new gospel. Tocqueville largely overlooked the ways in which this new religion created social solidarity at home, and he was little impressed with the cognitive and expressive functions of revolutionary religion.

The Durkheimian parallel between the Revolution and religion has been developed in the greatest detail by Mona Ozouf, in her influential book, *La Fête révolutionnaire, 1789–1799*. Although she does not discuss Durkheim's work at any length, the affiliation is unmistakable. In her view, the revolutionary festival was designed to accomplish "a transference of sacrality." And the social dimension of this translation is evident: "A society which is in the process of instituting itself must sacralize the fact itself of the institution." And, "The sacrality of the oath, for the men of the Revolution, came from the fact that it made visible the act of contracting together; this act was conceived as the fundamental trait of sociability."[15] The festivals functioned as the new ritual basis of the revolutionary community. They revealed an "identical collective need," and they worked to "homogenize" the new society.

By treating the festivals as expressions of an "identical conceptualization" rather than as a hopelessly diverse and often bizarre excretion of the revolutionary mentality, Ozouf demonstrated the fruitfulness of Durkheim's various explanatory hypotheses. The festivals are shown to be a "cognitive enterprise," in Lukes' terms, for they transformed French ceremonial notions of space and time. The revolutionaries sought to repress all spatial reminders of the Catholic past. Festival itineraries either avoided the religious processional routes of the past or showed off new symbolic representations that purposely over-shadowed those reminders. On occasion, the festivals included the ceremonial burning of royalist and Catholic symbols. In their design of the festivals, the revolutionaries usually favored large open spaces. Open spaces had no memories associated with them and thus were well-suited for the expression of new values. Horizontality seemed essential to egalitarianism; verticality was associated with hierarchy and especially with the domination of church towers over the urban landscape.[16]

The designers of the festivals were even more preoccupied with time. Catholic feast days were abolished, new ones instituted, and eventually the entire calendar was redrawn. "Decades" of ten days replaced the weeks, and the new names of months and days were meant to recall nature and reason. Germinal and Floréal, for instance, evoked the buds and flowers of springtime (late April to late June), while primidi, duodi, and so on replaced the saints' names usually associated with the days of the Christian calendar.[17] The revolutionary festivals were essential to this new sense of time, because they both gave shape to the yearly cycle and established the history of the Revolution itself. With every change of regime, the festival calendar had to be rearranged. New festivals were created to celebrate the change, and objectionable reminders of the regime preceding were eliminated.[18]

The concern with space and time followed from the revolutionary desire to form a new community. A new comunity required a new cognitive basis, new categories of definition. In addition to a new sense of space and time, the festivals also helped instill new social values. Old regime corporations were abolished, and processions based on rank and precedence gave way to processions grouped by function and age. For the most part, however, the festivals emphasized consensus and oneness rather than distinctions within the community. In this way, the festivals served as the ritual means of creating social solidarity. A new calendar, new images, and new kinds of processions worked to create a new man by laying a new social foundation for his existence. That "abnormal over-supply of force" which characterized the revolutionary experience was channeled into celebrations of the new Nation.

Linking all of the Durkheimian accounts of revolutionary "religion" is an all-consuming emphasis on social consensus. Missing in them, or at least underemphasized, is a sense of how revolutionary religion was also an object of struggle that was constantly caught up in a process of change. For Durkheim himself, the focus on consensus was virtually inevitable because he started with the problem of moral *obligation*. As he put it in "Individual and Collective Representations,"

While one might perhaps contest the statement that all social facts without exception impose themselves from without upon the individual, the doubt does not seem possible as regards religious beliefs and practices, the rules of morality and the innumerable precepts of law – that is to say, all the most characteristic manifestations of collective life. All are expressly obligatory, and this obligation is the proof that these ways of acting and thinking are not the work of the individual but come from a moral power above him, that which the mystic calls God or which can be more scientifically conceived.[19]

The socialness of religion, as it were, was precisely what made it binding upon the individual. Since Durkheim devoted his efforts to understanding the ways in which the social operated on the individual, he largely neglected conflicts and changes in the nature of obligation. In *Primitive Classification*, Durkheim and Mauss claimed that though "things are above all sacred or profane, pure or impure, friends or enemies, favour-

able or unfavourable . . . the differences and resemblances which determine the fashion in which they are grouped are more affective than
intellectual." Unfortunately, they concluded, "emotion is naturally
refractory to analysis."[20] The analysis of differences between or within
societies was thus eschewed.

In the French Revolution, the question of obligation was of life and
death importance. When they attacked the legitimacy of traditional conceptions of obligation, the revolutionaries opened the door to the
questioning of any kind of obligation. As the opening quote of this chapter demonstrates, the most radical revolutionaries wondered if anything
need be sacred, that is, beyond the realm of reason. If there was to be no
king, should there be any other sacred center? Did a free people need idols
or icons? And if they had none, what was to be the basis of the social
order? Mathiez recognized the significance of these questions. He held to
the Durkheimian view that to be a religion, common beliefs had to be obligatory. In his opinion, the truths formulated in the Declaration of the
Rights of Man and Citizen in 1789 and the oath required by the Constitution of 1791 filled the bill perfectly. Revolutionary religion was not
sacred because it rested on revelation, mystery or totems, but because it
derived from the "political institution" itself. If the forms of this political
institution changed over time, the faith nevertheless "remained fundamentally identical."[21]

In fact, however, the struggles over the defense and even the definition
of revolutionary faith were intense and divisive. There was no stable repertory of revolutionary festivals, no one lasting revolutionary cult. Festivals of Federation were succeeded by particular celebrations of events; the
content of the revolutionary oath was altered by each succeeding regime;
Altars of the Fatherland gave way to the Cult of Reason, which in turn
was replaced by the Cult of the Supreme Being, which in turn was
replaced by Theophilanthropy, which in turn gave way to a revived
Catholicism. The succession of constitutions made manifest the same in-
ability to fix the articles of revolutionary faith. In large measure, conflict
continued unabated because revolutionary religion was based on the political institution "itself"; revolutionary religion was closely tied to the
state, but the state itself was often in the process of modification and even
transformation. The definition of power as well as of the sacred was in
question. The difficulty of the problem involved was captured, perhaps
somewhat too whimsically, by the French Durkheimian sociologist
Roger Caillois: "This virtue that compels obedience to its injunctions is
the same that gives the wind its capacity to blow . . . It is that which is
designated, in its diverse forms, by the Melanesian word *mana* . . .
Power, like the sacred, resembles an exterior grace."[22]

The most thoroughgoing revolutionaries cast doubt precisely on this exteriority of "grace." For them, the sacred center was the people; in speeches and publications of all sorts this was their constant point of reference, their new political touch-stone. There was no one sacred document, no one constitution, no revolutionary Bible. It was, in fact, very difficult to institutionalize or concretize "the people."[23] During the Revolution, even the legitimacy of elected representatives was constantly in doubt, precisely because there had been so many changes in their organization: there were four differently named legislatures in the space of six years, 1789–95. Surely, the sacred and the social were linked in all this turbulence, but how are we to thematize their relationship? Revolutionary society may have been "setting itself up as a god," but it was not finding the task a simple one.

One way to get at the workings of the sacred in the French Revolution is to look at the once most sacred person of the king, Louis XVI, and in particular at his execution. Under the Old Regime the king had been the sacred center of French society. To attack his body was sacrilege and attempted assassinations were punished as such. Michel Foucault opened his *Discipline and Punishment* with a gruesome account of the execution of the would-be assassin Damiens in 1757. Damiens had been legally tortured for weeks beforehand. On the fateful day, he was made to watch his own flesh torn away bit by bit with red-hot pincers, to watch as his hand was burnt with sulphur, and watch as the executioners poured molten lead, boiling oil, burning resin, wax and sulphur on his wounds before being drawn and quartered. He did not die until his limbs were severed by the executioners.[24]

At the end of 1792, after the "second" revolution of 10 August of that year overthrowing the monarchy, the National Convention decided to put Louis XVI on trial. The story of the trial itself is now quite well-known.[25] The Jacobins argued for a military-style execution, but lost and were forced to participate in a trial organized and presided over by the deputies of the National Convention themselves. Most of the debates concerned procedure (should the king be tried, by whom, how should the sentence be determined?) rather than the king's guilt. Virtually all of the deputies agreed that he had betrayed the nation. They disagreed primarily about the consequences to be drawn: should he be killed or banished or imprisoned? Once the vote had been taken, however, there was remarkably little commentary on it or on the king's subsequent death – at least within France itself.

On the day of the execution, one of the regicide deputies spoke on the occasion in the Jacobin Club. He said simply, "Louis Capet has paid his debt; let us speak of it no longer." Then he and the rest of the club members went on to discuss the assassination of deputy Le Peletier by a royalist.[26] In the Convention, in the clubs and in the press, attention shifted almost immediately to the commemoration of the martyrdom of Le Peletier. It was somehow more palatable to celebrate a republican martyr than to relive the death of the tyrant.[27] The press could not ignore the execution, of course, but in Paris and the provinces the reports on it were very much the same. Most papers contented themselves with the reproduction of official proclamations and reports. The papers simply presented the information under the usual rubric of "news from Paris," "city of Paris" and the like. Even the infamous Marat, who editorialized freely on everything, gave a rather solemn account: "The head of the tyrant has just fallen under the blade of the law; the same blow turned over the foundations of monarchy among us; I believe finally in the republic."[28]

Marat compared the execution to a "religious festival" which celebrated the people's deliverance from the weight of oppression. The "final punishment" (*supplice*) of Louis XVI was in his view a world-historical event which would change the course of European history. It would energize the French and terrorize the Revolution's enemies both within and outside of France. Marat was not afraid to admit the parallel with the frightening September massacres of 1792, during which hundreds of prisoners had been murdered after kangaroo-court hearings. In Marat's view, the massacres were the result of a "general insurrection" provoked by the people's rightful desire for justice and protection.[29] Violence was necessary to break with the past, defend the present, and assure hopes for a republican future.

The execution of the king was most comprehensively covered in the radical newspaper *Révolutions de Paris*. Here the parallel with ritual sacrifice is explicit:

We owe to the earth, since we have in a manner of speaking consecrated slavery by our example, we owe a great lesson in the person of the 66th king, more criminal than all his predecessors taken together. The blood of Louis Capet, shed by the blade of the law on 21 January 1793, cleanses us of a stigma of 1300 years. It is only since Monday the 21st that we are republicans, and that we have acquired the right to cite ourselves as models for neighboring nations.

The striking act of justice ... ought perhaps to have taken place on the same altar of federation that was polluted two times by the oaths of the perjuring monarch. The vast expanse of the field would have permitted a much greater number of witnesses to be present at this memorable event, which could not have too many witnesses.

[And finally, the editor concluded that] Liberty resembles that divinity of the Ancients which one cannot make auspicious and favorable except by offering to it in sacrifice the life of a great culprit.[30]

Most striking in this account is the recognition, implicit in others but explicit here, that Louis had to pay not only for his own crimes and those of all French monarchs before him, but also for the guilt of the revolutionaries themselves. The French had consecrated slavery by their own example in the past; a republican future was only possible if the pollution or stigma of their own past could be washed away. Killing the king was essential to the regeneration – the resacralization – of the French nation. The religious or ritual aspects of the killing were also recognized by some of the observers at the scaffold. Many newspapers told how people ran up to the scene to dip their pikes and handkerchiefs in the blood of the king. One zealot sprinkled blood on the crowd and shouted, "Brothers, they tell us that the blood of Louis Capet will fall again on our heads; well, so be it, let it fall . . . Republicans, the blood of a king brings happiness."[31]

For the radical newspapers, an exemplary act of violence was essential to the founding of a new nation in republican form. In contrast, most political leaders, even among the Jacobins, hoped to reduce the execution to a simple criminal and constitutional issue. As the Jacobin *Journal des hommes libres* declared:

Today was resolved that great truth which the prejudices of so many centuries had stifled: today we have just convinced ourselves that a king is only a man, and that no man is above the laws.[32]

In other words, the execution simply showed that France had a new constitution in which the king was only a citizen subject to the law. In this pro-regicide account, there is also nagging uncertainty about the future. As the editor exhorts, "Celebrated day! Day forever memorable! May you [the subjunctive in French: *puisses-tu*] arrive pure for posterity!"[33] – as if the act might be misinterpreted; as if what was involved kept threatening to explode the confines of simple legal issues.

The apprehension, the displacements of responsibility, and the silences in accounts of the execution all bespoke its fundamental, unthinkable or unspeakable nature. The execution was more than a necessary constitutional or juridical act.[34] It brought to a head the semiological crisis which had been implicit in the Revolution for many months. In a recent book, Marc Eli Blanchard argued that the trial of the king authorized the "murder of the signifier," the putting to death by words of the semiological center of Old Regime political discourse.[35] Although this formulation is no doubt exaggerated – the king had long since lost his charismatic authority – it does point to the enormous significance that the killing of the king had for contemporaries. The French did more than "destroy this word 'king'" (the deputies recognized the need for that already in Sept-

ember 1792 when they abolished royalty).[36] The king himself had been
submitted to the laws and outlawed at the same time. By killing the king
in public, revolutionaries had touched the most sensitive, though largely
unconscious, social nerves. They had violated what Freud called one of
the basic laws of totemism, that which forbade the killing of the totem
animal.[37]

In Freud's analysis, "the basis of taboo is a forbidden action for which
there exists a strong inclination in the unconscious" (p. 44). The sons
want to kill the father in order to take over his special, mystical powers;
the taboo against doing so is erected in order to contain the desire for ag-
gression and the feelings of hostility. The would-be assassin of Louis XVI
was subjected to such a horrible death precisely because he had violated
this taboo. Once the brothers have killed the father, they are bound to feel
guilt and remorse. In Freud's interpretation, the sense of guilt "can only
be allayed through the solidarity of all the participants" (p. 189). This
mechanism is exemplified in the *Révolutions de Paris* editorial: the act
ought to have taken place in a larger public space, for then "the vast
expanse of the field would have permitted a much greater number of witnesses to be present at this memorable event, which could not have too
many witnesses." Everyone had to share in the guilt, if no one was to be
guilty.

The French Revolution startled the world, not just because it showed
the potential for popular mobilization and political violence, but also
because it cut to the heart of patriarchal society. The French actually killed
the father, declared him guilty, and announced the gospel of social and
political liberation to the world. The traditional framework of authority
was thus de-centered and decapitated. With the king's head, it was hoped,
went the legitimacy of Old Regime social, political and cultural authority. The new world was to be sacred without a king's presence, without
a figure of patriarchal authority. Needless to say, contemporaries in 1793
did not consciously recognize the pattern which Freud details, though the
Révolutions de Paris editorial comes very close. Yet the rhetoric and icono-
graphy of revolution offer considerable evidence to support some version
of the Freudian view, which supplements in critical ways the Durkheimian analysis of the sacred.

Politicians did not attack patriarchy by name – that would have been
too destructive of social authority. But the emphasis on the family run by
brothers was everywhere. "Fraternity" as a slogan and as an abstract idea
appeared frequently in revolutionary rhetoric. In the *Révolutions de Paris*
editorial, for instance, the man who sprinkled the crowd with the king's
blood called them "brothers," not citizens or fellow republicans. Revolutionaries never called themselves, as in America, "Sons of Liberty"; the

revolution seemed to have no parentage. The ultimate radical symbol, moreover, was Hercules, who stood officially for the "French people." Hercules was not a patriarchal figure; he always looked young, muscular, and often came with his *little* sisters, Liberty and Equality. The use of Hercules was another form of patricide, this time metaphorical. Hercules had been known first in France as the emblem of monarchy, the *Hercule gaulois*. In this figuration, Hercules was king. The radicals made him instead into the emblem of the people's, and especially the brothers', power.[38] They replaced Hercules the king with Hercules the militant revolutionary brother and thereby appropriated and subverted the figure of monarchy itself.

More striking even than the radicals' identification with Hercules was the pervasiveness of the figure of Liberty in revolutionary symbology. In September 1792, before the execution of the king, Liberty was chosen as the symbol of the Republic (its seal); she became the stamp of the Republic's legitimacy.[39] Since Liberty was to be the semiological center of the new society, she consequently presided in some fashion over the ritual sacrifice. As the editor of the *Révolutions de Paris* put it, "Liberty resembles that divinity of the Ancients which one cannot make auspicious and favorable except by offering to it in sacrifice the life of a great culprit." Interestingly, however, Liberty was not in fact present at the scaffold on 21 January. The pedestal, which Liberty occupied after April 1792, and again apparently shortly after the execution of Louis (representations of later executions all show her present), was empty on the fateful day. There is a plausible explanation for this. The pedestal had originally held a statue of Louis XV. Liberty could not occupy it satisfactorily, that is, could not fully replace monarchy, until monarchy itself was removed, until not only the statues and insignia of royalty were destroyed, but also the head of the living king himself. Only then could Liberty become the new "tribal deity."

Liberty was one of the most telling indicators of the revolutionary attack on patriarchal power. Liberty appeared sometimes with children, but most often as a young woman, fragile and in need of the protection of her brothers. She never had a husband or a father present. And is it accidental that the vestal virgins of the new order were those bachelors, Robespierre and St Just, men unencumbered by the ties of family? (Certainly, republicans did not think so, since the new Constitution of 1795 explicitly required that deputies be either married or widowers.) Here the revolutionaries cast some doubt on Freud's own obsessively patriarchal analysis, which is that "psychoanalytic investigation of the individual teaches with especial emphasis that god is in every case modelled after the father ... that god at bottom is nothing but an exalted father" (p. 190). In

Freud's view, there is no escape from the father; there is no escape from the Oedipal complex. French revolutionaries attempted just such an escape; they aimed, however unconsciously, to suppress the father entirely. The new totem was not a simple replacement for the old, but rather a radical departure from it.[40]

Perhaps the most compelling evidence for the mythic, dreamlike, unconsciously primordial nature of the revolutionary moment is the various forms of displacement and (in Freudian terms) repression which accompanied it. As René Girard claims in his work on *Violence and the Sacred*, the sacrificial process requires a certain degree of misunderstanding: "The celebrants do not and must not comprehend the true role of the sacrificial act" (p. 7). Mention of the act did not become exactly taboo, that is, totally forbidden, but it did become a source of anxiety and ambivalence. That anxiety stemmed in part from the difference between ritual sacrifice in 1793 and such sacrifices in tribal societies. Girard maintains that sacrifice is "primarily an act of violence without risk of vengeance" (p. 13). A sheep will not return to kill its murderer. Yet the regicides in France had every reason to fear reprisal at the hands of Louis' relatives abroad and his supporters at home. Accounts of the last days of the trial are filled with complaints from the deputies about receiving threatening letters and messages.[41]

Whether their fears were real or imagined, officials did not want to dwell upon the execution. During 1793 and 1794, no commemorative medals of the execution were struck in France, though this was a very common way to memorialize important events in the Revolution.[42] Most representations of the event came from outside of France and were meant to serve the cause of counter-revolution. Only two engravers in Paris seized upon the event at the time: Villeneuve, who published his work in Robespierre's paper, and the anonymous engraver for the *Révolutions de Paris*.[43] The two engravings in the *Révolutions de Paris* were soberly titled "The Death of Louis XVI, 21 January 1793." Only Villeneuve's print was less than respectful; it was called "Something to Think About for the Crowned Jugglers. Louis XVI's Cut-off Head."[44]

Revolutionaries could not ignore the event altogether, and they memorialized the execution officially in a yearly festival held on the same date. Yet, even the festival illuminates the working of revolutionary ambivalence and the recurring tension between official aims and more radical and popular desires. No plans for a festival had been made until the meeting of the Jacobin Club in Paris on 20 January 1794. One member proposed a typical solution: a public reading of the Declaration of the Rights of Man and a memorial reading of the story of Le Peletier's assassination. A more zealous member asked for a parade of the effigies of all the kings currently at war with France followed by their symbolic beheading. Finally, the Club voted to present itself *en masse* the next day to the Convention to congratulate the deputies on the energy they showed in the trial of the king.[45] On the day of the anniversary itself the Convention voted to hold a festival and left as a group for the Place de la Révolution. There, as part of the commemoration, they found themselves – uncomfortably for many – witnessing the day's executions.[46]

In other parts of France, impromptu, carnivalesque festivals were held with giant manikins and symbolic beheadings. In Grenoble, the victims were figures of Louis, the pope, and the nobility. They were smashed by figures dressed as Hercules.[47] In Lyons, a carnival king sat on a throne, with the nobility represented by a wolf, and the clergy by a fox. There a dragon set the scene on fire.[48] Officials in Paris were happy with neither parodies of violence nor the real thing.[49] It was in order to contain the menace of violence and its re-presentations that they invented official ceremonies of commemoration such as the festival called the Anniversary of the Death of the Last King of the French, held every year on 2 Pluviôse (the date in the revolutionary calendar corresponding to 21 January).

The official festivals showed the aims of the organizers. No manikins, no parodies, only decent behavior designed to reinforce pure republican sentiments. The ceremony of January 1799 is typical in important respects. At 10 a.m. an artillery salute. At 11:30 a.m. the deputies gathered in their legislative costumes and marched into their meeting hall with palm leaves in hand accompanied by trumpets. The tribune was covered with velours on which sat the book of the law ornamented with civic laurels. The law now replaced the king-father as the emblem of authority. Central to the ceremony were the speeches and common oaths to hate both royalty and anarchy. The room was open to the public until 8 p.m., though guards insisted that visitors keep moving and not cause any confusion.[50] The speech by the president was characteristically didactic. We are not here, he asserted, to show joy at the memory of a scaffold and punishment, but to engrave in all souls the immortal truths that have issued from that eternally memorable day.[51] Most of the speech consisted of a capsule history of the Revolution up to Louis' death and a review of the evidence against him. Thus, throughout the revolutionary decade, officials kept trying to displace, contain and dissipate violence even as they recognized the need to remember the violence which inaugurated revolutionary history.

As Girard recognized, violence and the sacred are intertwined. Revolutionary violence was played out in a series of overlapping scenarios, and participants were not always sure of the roles and stages they had chosen for themselves. Many revolutionary leaders hoped that the killing of the king would serve, as Girard's analysis suggests it often does, to protect the entire community from its own violence; the purpose of sacrifice, according to Girard, was to restore harmony to the community.[52] In the same *Révolutions de Paris* editorial, the author concluded: "The fall of a royal head seemed to relieve [the people] of a heavy burden; it was time to release it and to prevent a supplement to the [September massacres]."[53]

Instead, of course, the killing of the king made the crisis more acute than ever; the new basis of moral and political authority was uncertain; the sacred had seemed to evaporate. The struggle for power which ensued took place simultaneously on all levels: social, political, and cultural. During the Terror of 1793–4, as many as 40,000 people were killed in France, 17,000 of them by the guillotine.[54] It is, then, perhaps not surprising that Durkheim felt ambivalent about the Revolution. The "principles of 1789" had "profoundly moved the masses" and had "given birth to great things," but they also seemed to have a "pathological side." The principles of 1789 did not command universal assent. Obligation under the Revolution had to be enforced, ultimately by terror, because the new society had not succeeded in setting itself up as a god for everyone. As the sacred became more difficult to locate – and revolutionary festivals for all their grandiosity never succeeded in replacing the Old Regime's sacred institutions – violence and constraint became more pervasive.

The history of the French Revolution shows that the sacred did indeed have a critical social dimension. The new society tried to set itself up "as a god" through new rituals (federations, festivals), a new relationship between the individual and the community (embodied in the various oaths), and new symbolic representations (liberty trees, Liberty, Hercules, among many others). A Durkheimian perspective has proved essential to understanding the sacralizing project underlying these diverse and sometimes peculiar phenomena. But Durkheim's own focus on already-functioning religions has tended to draw attention to the functional aspects of religion – the way in which it promotes social solidarity through moral obligation – rather than to the sacred as a potential arena for conflict, change, and violence. In all fairness, however, it should be noted that the French Revolution is a very special case (albeit one that was of great interest to Durkheim himself). During the 1790s, the boundaries between the political and the religious were blurred. The new revolutionary faith was based on "the political institution" as Mathiez put it, but many French people continued to practice Catholicism and to reject the efforts of revolutionaries to displace the sacred center of the community from church/king to state/people.[55] Thus, though it can be argued that a fuller account of the sacred requires attention to cultural and perhaps even psychoanalytic sources of motivation, a more fundamental problem still remains: what are the boundaries of the sacred (and can they be theoretically delineated)? How are power, violence, and the sacred separated from each other (and can there be a theoretical answer to this question)?

Notes

1 For example, see his review entitled "The Principles of 1789 and Sociology," in Robert Bellah, ed., *Emile Durkheim: On Morality and Society* (Chicago: University of Chicago Press, 1973).

2 Emile Durkheim, *Montsequieu and Rousseau, Forerunners of Sociology* (Ann Arbor: University of Michigan Press, 1960).

3 *The Elementary Forms of the Religious Life*. Trans. Joseph Ward Swain (New York: Macmillan, 1915 [1912]), p. 241; and "Value Judgments and Judgments of Reality," pp. 91–2.

4 "The Principles of 1789," p. 41.

5 Ibid., p. 35.

6 On Durkheim's politics and his relationship to socialism under the Third Republic, see Steven Lukes, *Emile Durkheim: His Life and Work* (New York: Harper and Row, 1972), especially pp. 320–60.

7 The best review is in ibid., pp. 1–33 and 450–84. See also the Introduction to Emile Durkheim and Marcel Mauss, *Primitive Classification*, trans. Rodney Needham (Chicago: University of Chicago Press, 1963). On Durkheim's later writings, see also Jeffrey C. Alexander, *The Antinomies of Classical Thought: Marx and Durkheim* (Berkeley: University of California Press, 1982), especially pp. 233–66.

8 Ibid., pp. 482–4.

9 On the liberty tree and revolutionary symbolism more generally, see Maurice Dommanget, "Le Symbolisme et le prosélytisme révolutionnaire à Beauvais et dans l'Oise," *Annales historiques de la Révolution française* 2 (1925): 131–50; 3 (1926): 47–58 and 345–62; 4 (1927): 127–34; 5 (1928): 46–57 and 442–56; 6 (1929): 372–91; 7 (1930): 41–53 and 411–42.

10 Mona Ozouf, *La Fête révolutionnaire, 1789–1799* (Paris: Gallimard, 1976), pp. 280–90. See also Albert Mathiez, *Les Origines des cultes révolutionnaires (1789–1792)* (Paris: G. Bellais, 1904), p. 32. All translations from the French, unless otherwise noted, are mine.

11 Dommanget, "Le Symbolisme," 3 (1926): 345–62.

12 *Les Origines des cultes révolutionnaires*, p. 29.

13 Ibid., p. 26.

14 Trans. Stuart Gilbert (New York: Doubleday, 1955), p. 11.

15 *La Fête révolutionnaire*, pp. 333 and 337.

16 Ibid., pp. 149–87.

17 For a brief discussion of the new calendar, see Serge Bianchi, *La Révolution culturelle de l'an II: Élites et peuple (1789–1799)* (Paris: Aubier, 1982), pp. 198–203.

18 Ozouf, *La Fête révolutionnaire*, pp. 188–234.

19 Durkheim, *Sociology and Philosophy*, p. 25.

20 Trans. Rodney Needham (Chicago: University of Chicago Press, 1963), pp. 86 and 88.

21 Mathiez, *Les Origines des cultes révolutionnaires*, pp. 26–7.

22 *L'Homme et le sacré*, 2nd edn (Paris: Gallimard, 1950), p. 116.

23 On the function of "the people" in revolutionary discourse, see François Furet, *Interpreting the French Revolution*, trans. Elborg Forster (Cambridge: Cambridge University Press, 1981), especially pp. 46–79.

24 *Discipline and Punishment: The Birth of the Prison*, trans. Alan Sheridan (New York: Pantheon Books, 1977), pp. 3–31.

25 The trial is described in detail in David P. Jordan, *The King's Trial: The French Revolution vs. Louis XVI* (Berkeley: University of California Press, 1979). For the constitutional issues, see Michael Walzer, *Regicide and Revolution* (Cambridge: Cambridge University Press, 1974).

26 See, for example, the account in *Premier journal de la Convention Nationale, ou le Point du Jour*, no. 22, 22 January 1793.

27 On the rhetorical functions of martyrdom, see Hans Ulrich Gumbrecht, *Funktionen parlamentarischer Rhetorik in der Französischen Revolution* (Munich: W. Fink, 1978), especially "Die Sicherung institutionalisierter Einmütigkeit: Epideiktische Reden zum Tode Marats," pp. 93–125.

28 *Journal de la République Française, par Marat, l'Ami du Peuple* no. 105, 23 January 1793. I do not mean to imply that there were no political differences in reporting of the death of the king. Anti-Jacobin papers tended to give more laconic accounts, to emphasize the "lugubrious silence" which reigned in the streets, and to detail more lovingly the last moments of the monarch. On the atmosphere in Paris, see, for example, the *Courier français*, no. 22, 22 January 1793. For a detailed account of Louis' demeanor, see the *Journal du département de l'Oise*, no. 11, 26 January 1793. The most extensive editorials appeared in the radical newspapers. While the Girondin papers, such as Condorcet's *Journal de Paris*, simply registered the fact of the execution and editorialized only on the need to avoid further violence (see the description of the execution in no. 22, 22 January 1793, and the editorial by Roederer in no. 24, under the rubric "Convention National" – Roederer warned against "cette marche précipitée d'un grand Peuple vers l'extrême liberté"), the most outspokenly radical newspapers probed more deeply into the meaning of the execution.

29 *Journal de la République Française, par Marat, L'Ami du Peuple*, no. 105, 23 January 1793. "Le supplice de Louis XVI, loin de troubler la paix de l'état, ne servira qu'à l'affermir, non-seulement en contenant par la terreur les ennemis du dedans, mais les ennemis du dehors."

30 No. 185, 19–26 January 1793, by Prudhomme, under the title "Mort de Louis XVI, dernier roi de France."

31 Ibid.

32 *Journal des hommes libres de tous les pays*, no. 82, 22 January 1793.

33 Ibid.

34 Walzer's account of the constitutional issues (*Regicide and Revolution*, especially pp. 69–89) is telling, but it overlooks the ways in which the execution necessarily spilled over the bounds of constitutional and legal issues.

35 *Saint-Just & Cie: La Révolution et les mots* (Paris: A. -G. Nizet, 1980), p. 35. It should be added that the actual putting to death of the king's body in France was much more heavy with meaning than the execution of Charles I in England. English political and legal theory had a much more developed doctrine of the king's two bodies, so that when Charles I died, kingship continued. In France, in contrast, the distinction between the natural body of the king and his supernatural and mystical body was more blurred. Killing the king in France – the act itself of murder – therefore threatened the institution of kingship itself. Ernst H. Kantorowicz, *The King's Two Bodies: A Study in Mediaeval Political Theology* (Princeton: Princeton University Press, 1957).

36 See the account in *Archives Parlementaires*, 1st series, vol. 52: 81.

37 Sigmund Freud, *Totem and Taboo: Resemblances between the Psychic Lives of Savages and Neurotics*, trans. A. A. Brill (New York: Moffat, Yard, 1946, [1918]). Page numbers cited in text refer to the 1946 edition. On modern criticisms of Freud's analysis, see René Girard, *Violence and the Sacred*, trans. Patrick Gregory (Baltimore: Johns Hopkins University Press, 1977), pp. 193–222.

38 More on Hercules can be found in my book *Politics, Culture, and Class in the French Revolution* (Berkeley and Los Angeles, University of California Press, 1984), pp. 87–119.

39 Maurice Agulhon, *Marianne au combat: L'Imagerie et la symbolique républicaine de 1789 à 1880* (Paris: Flammarion, 1979).

40 By way of an aside, I should hasten to add that the erection of Liberty as the new totem did not make the French Revolution feminist! Radicals were eager to put forward the claims of the brothers to power, not the sisters. Liberty and Equality and the Republic were feminine deities in need of fraternal protection. Yet, in the course of challenging patriarchal models of power, the revolutionaries did open up willy-nilly the question of women's rights. Their answer was a resounding no, but the significance of their actions in confronting traditional models was hard to deny. Thus, it is no coincidence that women's clubs grew rapidly in numbers after the killing of the king.

41 See, for example, the *Courier français*, no. 22, 22 January 1793.

42 Michel Hennin, *Histoire numismatique de la Révolution française*, 2 vols. (Paris: J. C. Merlin, 1826), vol. I, p. 315.

43 See the list of engravings in *Collection de Vinck*, vol. III.

44 No. 5206 in ibid.

45 F. -A. Aulard, ed., *La Société des Jacobins* (Paris: Librairie Jouaust, 1895), vol. V, pp. 615–66 (Séance du 1er pluviôse an II (20 janvier 1794)).

46 Various reactions to the ceremonies are described in Pierre Caron, ed., *Paris pendant la Terreur: Rapports des agents sécrets du ministre de l'intérieur*, vol. III (28 nivôse an II–20 pluviôse an II (17 janvier 1794–8 fevrier 1794) (Paris: H. Champion, 1943), pp. 67–83.

47 Auguste Prudhomme, *Histoire de Grenoble* (Grenoble: A. Gratier, 1888), pp. 640–1.

The sacred and the French Revolution

48 As described in Joseph Mathieu, *Célébration du 21 janvier depuis 1793 jusqu'à nos jours* (Marseilles: M. Lebon, 1865), pp. 54–5.

49 Mona Ozouf, *La Fête révolutionnaire*, especially p. 122.

50 Corps Legislatif. Conseil des Anciens. Commission des inspecteurs de la salle. *Programme de la fête qui aura lieu le 2 pluviôse de l'an 7, dans l'intérieur du Palais des Anciens, à raison de l'anniversaire de la juste punition du dernier tyran des Français.*

51 Corps Legislatif. Conseil des Anciens. *Discours prononcé par Garat, Président du Conseil des Anciens, le 2 pluviôse an 7, anniversaire du 21 janvier 1792 (sic), et du serment de haine à la royauté et à l'anarchie.*

52 *Violence and the Sacred.*

53 No. 185, du 19 au 26 janvier 1793.

54 There are no definitive statistics. The most detailed study remains that of Donald Greer, *The Incidence of the Terror during the French Revolution* (Cambridge: Harvard University Press, 1935). He gives figures of 500,000 suspects, 17,000 executions, and 35–40,000 total non-war related deaths (including, however, campaigns against counter-revolutionaries within France) during the Terror.

55 On the blurring of the religions and the political, see Suzanne Desan, "The Revival of Religion during the French Revolution, 1794–1799." Ph.D. Dissertation, University of California, Berkeley, 1985.

2 From Durkheim to Managua: revolutions as religious revivals

Edward A. Tiryakian

I

Although an infrequent class of social phenomena, revolutions have been of great interest to students of political modernity and social change. The general breakdown of a social regime and the attempted establishment in its wake of a new social order, all this taking place within a compact time frame, continue to be an intriguing topic of historical and sociological research (Goldstone 1980, 1982; Taylor 1984; Zimmermann 1983).

The low incidence but high interest in revolutions at the macro level bears resemblance to the low incidence but high sociological interest in suicides at the micro level. Needless to say, it is Durkheim who very boldly placed suicide (more correctly, suicide rates) in the sociological consciousness not only by demonstrating that it can be analyzed as a social phenomenon but also that some aspects of it are an ingress to core features of modernity. If this seemingly irrational act can be shown to have socially conditioned patterns, then is it not less plausible to seek a sociological accounting of a collective act – revolution – an accounting that would bring to light underlying patterns operative in historical revolutions? While various paths and models have been used to "make sense" of revolutions (particularly drawing from Marx and Weber), one source that has not been common currency is Durkheim, perhaps because of his image as a founder of "functionalism," with its conservative connotation.[1]

I would like in approaching contemporary revolutions to give his due to the author of *The Elementary Forms of the Religious Life*; this is of course recognized as a sociological classic that continues as a leaven (Jones 1977; Tiryakian 1981), but it has not been thought of in the context of political sociology. As the title of the present chapter suggests, it will be the purpose here to treat one manifestation of revolutions that has remained outside the gaze of sociological scrutiny: namely, revolutions as religious revivals.[2] Although Durkheim himself does not offer a theory of revolutions, *The Elementary Forms* not only contains elements of a cyclic theory of societal renewal but also clearly makes use of the historical instance of a major social revolution, the French, to suggest the possibility of modern societal renovation.

Drawing from his analysis, this chapter will examine social revolutions as carrying out at various levels what may be viewed as aspects of the process of *dedifferentiation*, the obverse of the more familiar master process of *differentiation* (Luhmann 1982). If Durkheim in *The Elementary Forms* places "the religious life" – which he also saw as "the serious" side of the human condition – as the hub of society, so shall we view the religious sector as intrinsically involved in revolutionary movements. The process of dedifferentiation (Tiryakian 1985) at the societal level involves a transformation of consciousness, one in which the relatively distinct individual consciousness of everyday life becomes sentient with others in a common situation and in a common enterprise; this transformation is characterized by a high level of energy, for the individual and for the aggregate. It is a process in which the profane becomes transformed into a sacred context (the "transvaluation" of mundane values) – quite the obverse of the secularization process that has preoccupied so much of the sociology of religion and its image of "modernization."

It may be that the above remarks will evoke the impression that rather than "revolution" we are presenting a jaded if not dated discussion of the "counterculture" and "altered states of consciousness" associated with the drug culture. Assuredly not, although the transformation of social consciousness does link theoretically the "counterculture" and "revolutions"; the empirical referents for this chapter postdate the counterculture movement of the 1960s and early 1970s.

The end of the 1970s and the beginning of the present decade witnessed major global shock waves: the oil crisis of 1979, double-digit inflation in industrial countries, a severe debt crisis in Third World countries, and, of still growing significance, the rise of East Asia (and particularly Japan) as a new economic center of industrial productivity successfully challenging the established Western center (Tsurumi 1984). Politically, a major global trend of the past ten years seemed to be a conservative swing in Western democracies, with a few exceptions where social democratic parties prevailed (e.g. France, Spain, Greece).

On the whole, the recent sharp economic constriction seemed to entail or go with greater political prudence, unlike the 1930s, or, for that matter, unlike the 1960s when the cornucopia of economic abundance and unlimited growth seemed to foster political radicalization. There is a set of anomalies to this conservative swing, the set which constitutes the empirical basis for our theoretical reflection. The set is comprised of three nation-states which underwent social revolutions between 1979 and 1981, and in which the religious factor has been central – not in mystifying the revolution, as a Marxist perspective might have it, but in catalyzing the revolutionary movement. The three are Iran, Nicaragua, and Poland. Each revolution is, of course, the fruit of a specific socio-historical trajectory and each revolution has features distinct to its particular context.[3] Yet it is their world-significant import and their common denominators which are sociologically intriguing.

The Iranian Revolution, which toppled the imperial regime early in 1979, sought not only to transform a Westernizing bourgeois yet authoritarian regime into a theocratic "Islamic Republic," but also to export this project throughout the Islamic world, thereby sending shock waves throughout the Middle East (Ramazani 1986). The Polish Revolution, uneasily contained since December 1981, was revolutionary at two levels at least during its peak 1980-1 period. Internally, this was the first instance within a communist country of state-recognized institutions whose existence and autonomy were outside the monolithic power structure of the state and its party. This had been the basis of the socialist revolution laid down by Lenin; the workers' challenge of state authority in the Solidarity movement was thus a "revolution" within the socialist revolution. Externally, just as Iran threatened a domino effect for the Middle East (at least, for Sunni and/or conservative regimes), so did Poland and its Solidarity movement threaten a crack in Russian hegemony throughout Eastern Europe: Solidarity's appeal to the workers in other satellite countries and the appeal of nationalism constituted a potential spark in a tinder box. As to Nicaragua, the Sandinista Revolution was a demonstration that urban and rural populations could unite into an effective opposition movement that could neutralize a militarily superior regime – in this respect, a situation very similiar to that of Iran. But, equally significant, the Sandinista Revolution contained a model of socio-economic transformation and development that clearly challenged the typical "dependency" relation of Central America's export economies *vis-à-vis* the United States. Just as the Soviet Union applied every pressure, including military shows of strength on the Polish border, so has the Reagan administration done nearly everything to destabilize economically and otherwise the Sandinista government, so as to prevent a domino effect in the region.

The future of these contemporary revolutions is hard to discern, particularly because of their respective external environments. Polish nationalism and the democratization of the regime are severely constrained by Russia looking askance upon any threat to its security system (especially with Polish windows to the West, including a Polish pope who has entered into cordial diplomatic ties with the United States).

Nicaraguan nationalism, seeking internal social reforms and external autonomy from American hegemony, has become the bête noire par excellence of the Reagan administration, the latter extending rather than innovating a traditional American interventionist policy in Central America. Iran has been deadlocked in a war with Iraq, but if that should cease tomorrow, Khomeini's Iran would remain as much of a sore spot in the Gulf region as was Mossadeq's Iran in the 1950s.

Exogenous forces are operating to untrack the projects of these three revolutions, and it is perhaps more likely than not that before the end of the century the respective revolutionary movements will remain only in collective memories rather than having become institutionalized in new, long-term social arrangements and societal reorganization. After all, if we look at the totality of historical revolutions, and not just at our three contemporary instances, weight must be given to Orwell's sober observation, "All revolutions are failure, but they are not all the same failure" (quoted in Ash 1984:275).

Perhaps revolutionary movements are failures in the same sense as charismatic movements fail in carrying out the total transformation of the world contained in the promise of charisma.[4] Yet, revolutionary movements are also successes, for their inception and early phases punctuate the historical process with new beginnings, with the possibility of new bases of societal organization and restructuration.[5] Again, let me invoke Durkheim, the seeming conservative sociologist, who in the Conclusion of *The Elementary Forms* anticipates for modern society "hours of creative effervescence, in the course of which new ideas and new formulae are found which serve for a while as a guide to humanity" (p. 475). And where does he look in retrospect for this inspiration? At the French Revolution and the civil religion which it promulgated but could not successfully institutionalize:

the French Revolution established a whole cycle of holidays to keep the principles with which it was inspired in a state of perpetual youth. If this institution quickly fell away, it was because the revolutionary faith lasted but a moment ... But though the work may have miscarried, it enables us to imagine what might have happened in other conditions; and everything leads us to believe that it will be taken up again sooner or later. (p. 476)

The societal transformations sought in the initial projects of the revolutionary movements in Iran, Poland and Nicaragua, those that received popular enthusiasm, may well falter and abort from internal and external factors. But that they were launched and that the religious factor played a central role in the launching have become irrevocably part of the contemporary scene and cannot be expunged from the world historical setting or dropped in an Orwellian "memory hole." If one takes into account that each occurred in a highly repressive regime that was either eventually toppled (Nicaragua and Iran) or forced to make previously unheard of concessions (Poland), then the actualization of the movements must also qualify as important historical moments that merit empirical and theoretical attention. In the context in which they have taken place, each represents a project of modernity, a radical alternative to being doomed to peripheral status as a client state of alien powers. Should the respective project not succeed, for whatever reasons, we can still affirm for the contemporary revolutions Durkheim's observation about the French Revolution: "But this experiment, though short-lived, keeps all its sociological interest" (p. 245).

II

To draw upon *The Elementary Forms* as the theoretical mainspring for interpreting contemporary revolutionary movements may seem like a far-fetched excursus into the sociological classics. After all, this is a work which is not only a fountainhead of modern functionalism but also a secondary analysis of ethnographic data pertaining to structures of primitive society. Yet, as already mentioned, the work contains several pregnant references to the French Revolution. Durkheim explicitly uses that historical happening, not only to illustrate the applicability of his theory of the genesis of the sacred as being at the heart of social renewal[6] but also to anticipate as one scenario of the future of modernity a religious effervescence that would provide a new set of guiding principles for the society of tomorrow.[7] To see its bearing for an understanding of contemporary revolutions and to see what validation these may offer Durkheim's analysis will be the purpose of the following reconsideration of aspects of *The Elementary Forms*.

Abstracting from the abundance of ethnographic materials crafted together by Durkheim into a unified sociological collage, the starting point of his analysis of the social order is his well-known dualism of things sacred and things profane: sacred and profane objects, sacred and profane activities, and, more generally, the sacred and profane worlds. In the "normal" setting of the social world, each has its own delimited sphere: it is in their confrontation, so to speak, that the drama of the social world – societal regeneration – takes place. Most sociologists of religion have implicitly considered the drama to be the intrusion of the profane in the sphere of the sacred: the enlargement of the sphere of the profane at the expense of the sacred is one major meaning of "secularization."[8] Durkheim's analysis, however, provides us with a complementary aspect: the enlargement, in extraordinary settings, of the sacred sphere, what may be termed the "sacralization" of aspects of the profane.

In his doctoral dissertation, *The Division of Labor in Society*, Durkheim had placed the world of work and its occupational structure as the key node of society. The socio-economic sphere in *The Elementary Forms* is that of the profane world *par excellence* (p. 346), but its image in this later work is considerably downgraded. The economic sphere fractionates individuals from each other into a social life which is "uniform, languishing, and dull" (p. 246), and "too great slavishness of daily work" (p. 426) leads to mental fatigue which requires recreation from other sources. What also needs renewal from sources outside the everyday world is the renewal of non-kin social solidarity.

Recall that the sphere of the sacred for Durkheim is the one in which the religious life takes place: it is generated – and regenerated – by great collective gatherings which provide actors with the direct consciousness of belonging to and participating in something greater than individual lives.[9]

Let me draw attention to a related point Durkheim makes which is appropriate for an understanding of the onset of revolutionary movements. In book II, chapter 7, Durkheim talks about the increased energy and the increase in force which individuals feel when they assemble together. He makes clear (pp. 240ff.) that this effervescence leading to "this exceptional increase of force" (p. 241) is not limited to primitive society; it is also "characteristic of revolutionary or creative epochs" (p. 241). And much later in his analysis, Durkheim, in discussing the genesis of the philosophical notion of causality, will reiterate the importance of the group assembling in giving rise to the consciousness of *power*, which stems from the moral forces of the collectivity (pp. 408ff.). Durkheim's sociological analysis echoes the French adage, "l'union fait la force": the act of coming together, of uniting in collective assemblies, generates societal consciousness for the actor and in doing so provides him with exultation and a feeling of force or energy which, on an aggregate basis, conveys a sense of power. The power to do things, and, in certain circumstances, to transform (or re-form) the social order.

How does this relate to an understanding of revolutions? A revolutionary movement entails the sustained interaction of large numbers of persons; it entails the coming together and welding of various social fractions into a larger whole having consciousness of itself in a collective purpose. The social space and social time of the everyday world is transformed into an extraordinary setting which will become the *axis mundi*, to borrow from Eliade (1959), of the renovated social order. It is important to bear in mind that revolutionary movements unite actors *against an ongoing social order*; the power or collective force which the actors feel in uniting is essential if there is any chance that collective behavior may succeed in over-coming an established social order that commands important economic and military resources. The power that a revolutionary movement generates is, ultimately, an enthusiastic conviction that the overthrow of the established social order is morally right and just. Since Durkheim's analysis is in the context of rituals, it takes us only part of the way in look-ing at contemporary revolutions, which intend to alter drastically rather than reaffirm and renovate, the present order.[10]

Just what is revived? For Charles Grandison Finney, the great exponent, theoretician and practician of religious revivals in the Age of Jackson, a re-vival, which requires the excitement of protracted meetings, seeks ulti-mately to rekindle the desire of self to be united with God.

The state of the world is still such, and probably will be till the millennium is fully come, that religion must be mainly promoted by these excitements. How long and how often has the experiment been tried, to bring the church to act steadily for God, without these periodical excitements. (Finney 1960:10)

A revival . . . brings them to such vantage ground that they get a fresh impulse towards heaven. They have a new foretaste of heaven, and new desires after union to God; and the charm of the world is broken. (Ibid.:16)

Durkheim's analysis provides a sociologistic translation of the above. Instead of solidarity with God needing renewal, it is solidarity with society which has to be periodically revived, and this consciousness or sentiment comes about in assemblies (Durkheim, p. 391), just as for Finney. For Durkheim, in fact, all organized groups ("political, econ-omic or confessional") need to have periodical reunions (p. 240) lest com-mitment to the group fall into desuetude.

Where Durkheim uses "society," I would propose that technically it is better to follow Talcott Parsons and use "societal community" or, as he notes in the case of modern society, "nation," to designate

the collective structure in which members are united, or, in some sense, associ-ated. Its most important property is the kind and level of solidarity which charac-terizes the relations between its members. (Parsons 1968:461)

Sociological analysis of "nation" has been underdeveloped despite im-portant early conceptualizations by Weber and Mauss, respectively (Tiry-akian and Nevitte 1985), with the tendency until recently to accept uncritically the coupling of "nation" with the juridical and organizational "state."[11] The nation should be seen as a political and cultural "total social phenomenon" (in Mauss' expression), having intersubjective and objec-tive features which taken together provide a matrix for social identity (one's nationality) and for differentiated social institutions that are in turn constituted by differentiated role-sets.

In the everyday, profane world, consciousness of belonging to the "nation" is subordinated to belonging to and participating in more differentiated structures. Actors occupy different positions in social space, with important differentials of power and resources that characterize the social stratification system. It is in extraordinary settings – typically, settings of crisis (such as wars, the holding overseas of hostages, and so on) – that these differentials are suspended if not eliminated and that consciousness of common membership in a single "nation" emerges to the fore as the basic structure underlying public intersubjectivity. It is particularly in the modern period of the past two centuries that "nation" has become salient as the societal community, and revolutionary movements as well as nationalistic movements have used it tacitly or explicitly for the purpose of social mobilization. "Nation" is more than secular grouping; it has tended to become a surrogate for the deity, with "In the name of the nation," or "In the name of national unity" replacing "In the name of God" as a call for collective action and sacrifice.

To extend the Parsonian conceptualization, revolutions and revivals may be viewed as representing "cycles of affective activity" in contradistinction to cycles of "instrumental-adaptive" activity.[12] The latter entails processes of differentiation, the former of dedifferentiation (Parsons, Bales and Shils 1953:167). The religious revival which concerned Finney so much is also central in Perry Miller's brilliant analysis of the formation of the American national character: Miller saw in the evangelical fervor (of the 1830s) "the primary force in maintaining 'the grand unity of national strength'" (Miller 1965:95). Miller emphasizes the significance of the "great awakening" in reviving consciousness of belonging to the same American polity, of having common values and a shared purpose.

This is pertinent to the notion of dedifferentiation because the setting for the revival (typically in the American case, the campsite or outdoor tent meeting) placed participants on the same social plane, emphasizing the social equality between actors.[13] A religious revival and a genuine social revolution tend to devalue if not abolish social rankings, and this typically occurs in settings of high affectivity of "enthusiasm." With the dissolution of the structures and strictures of the everyday, profane world (its destructuration), there emerges the discovery of the societal community as the fountainhead of the social body.

In terms of the Parsonian A–G–I–L four-function schema of action systems, dedifferentiation would suggest a phase movement of action from differentiated, institutional structures to the more primitive "L" cell of the religious–expressive sphere. The process of dedifferentiation seems in general to be attended by a high level of energy release,[14] and once underway, it tends to accelerate.

This combination can often take pathological forms which may paralyze the living system involved: cancer in biological systems, antinomianism in (some) movements of religious enthusiasm, anarchism or "mob rule" in some collective uprisings. Religious systems seem to be aware of consequences of the profane coming into contact with the sacred (which is, to be sure, the ultimate goal of religious activity) by setting up careful, institutionalized procedures (rituals) which regulate the nature of the interaction. Political systems also seek differentiated means (such as the divisions of government) to regulate or control the access to political power. Revolutionary movements, however, sweep aside the rituals or institutional procedures (which may have been swept aside by the prevailing regime) and this may be attended by great violence – against others in the case of social revolutions, or against the self in some religious movements of enthusiasm. While this aspect of dedifferentiation may well appear noxious, it is also necessary to bear in mind that historical collective beginnings – of religious as well as political collectivities – more frequently than not are marked by violence.

It is now time to take up a discussion of the revolutions in our contemporary setting which represent attempted new beginnings for three nations, new endeavors at social mobilization to include actors who were excluded by the respective regime from active participation. One may say that in the cases of Iran, Poland and Nicaragua, "state" had become phenomenologically differentiated from, and in fact pitted against, "nation"; the religious factor was important in launching the process of dedifferentiation as a process of societal renewal.

III

The previous discussion has developed the twofold argument that modern religious revivals and revolutionary movements in their inception are processes of dedifferentiation and that their political significance lies in delegitimating the present social order and uniting against it socially heterogeneous and scattered actors. The essential dynamics of this transformation of the everyday social world into the realm of the sacred is contained in *The Elementary Forms*.

Extending the argument, the nexus between religion and polity, including between religious and political movements, can be viewed as intrinsic – not only to previous historical periods but also to the setting of modern society (Merkl and Smart 1983). The etymology of religion (*religare*, to bind back or bind together) suggests that societal bonds are grounded in the realm of the sacred. "Nation" as the modern societal community partakes of the sacred in providing the basic political bonds of societal actors. Restoring or redeeming the nation from bondage (from what is perceived as alien rule), restoring or providing the nation with autonomy, are primary endeavors of the revolutionary movement. To the extent that revolutionary movements take place in conjunction with an ongoing "church" or religious institution which has historical linkage with the nation as its common religion, that is, the religion of the great majority of the people, then that religious institution may well play an important catalytic role in the national "awakening" and consequent political mobilization. This seems strikingly illustrated by the contemporary revolutions in Iran, Nicaragua and Poland.

It is not part of my argument that if revolutions have occurred in these three countries it is because of religious causes that were not present in earlier historical social revolutions. Fischer's observation on the Iranian Revolution here seems appropriate for all three countries:

The causes of the revolution, and its timing, were economic and political; the form of the revolution, and its pacing, owed much to the tradition of religious protest. (Fischer 1980:190)

In each instance, the years preceding the revolution were marked by sharply deteriorating economic conditions for the masses, and by the ruling elites using widespread cultural and physical repression – ranging from media censorship to the brutal use of the National Guard by Somoza and SAVAK by the Shah. In each case, the regime faced growing opposition from the religious sector, which underwent radicalization and which became in the 1970s the one area having a certain degree of autonomy from the centralizing and totalitarian tendencies of the regime.

In Iran the secularizing, Westernizing orientation of the Shah as much as his pro-American policies (for example, violating the Arab oil embargo in the wake of the Yom Kippur War) generated increasing opposition from the country's Shi'ite religious leaders, such as the ayatallahs Shari'at-Madari, Mahmud Taleqani and Ruhallah Khomeini, the latter having been forced into exile in 1964 until his dramatic return in 1979. In between, various clandestine movements had sprung up, including secular leftist factions, but the ones with greatest popular appeal were those which interpreted the situation in terms of widely understood Islamic symbolism and tradition. Effective opposition to the Pahlavi regime was provided by the writings of such intellectuals as Jalal Al-i Ahmad and Ali Shari'ati, who redefined an autonomous Iranian cultural identity liberated from the disease of "Westoxication." Along with this, the writings of Khomeini (particularly *Islamic Government*) were widely distributed, read and heard on smuggled cassettes by a growing number of religious students. Shi'ism and its Holy City of Qom thus became important levers against official society. As Harney points out in his review of Bakhash,

Khomeini had never been a forgotten exile in Iraq. Religious leaders within Iran had kept in touch with him over the years and in this way a network had been created which in effect amounted to a parallel society and authority within Iran. (Harney 1985:65)

In Nicaragua, the combination of Vatican II, the rise of liberation theology, and the Latin American Bishops' Conference at Medellin (Colombia) in 1968 set the stage for a dramatic reorientation in the 1970s of the Catholic Church, a traditional basis of regime support in Latin America. This entailed withdrawal of regime support by the primate of the Church (Archbishop Obando), particularly following the earthquake of 1972 in protest at the appropriation by Somoza of international relief. Throughout the 1970s, an increasing number of the clergy – Catholic and Protestant Evangelical – turned socially and politically active in organizing "base communities" for the rural and urban poor, in staging protests in and out of churches, and even became participants in the opposition underground movement that had developed in the 1960s, the FSLN (Sandina National Liberation Front).

By late 1972 church people were involved in the initial stages of the anti-Somoza struggle ... there were significant contacts between the FSLN and some people in the church. The clergy and the hierarchy had been involved in conflictive situations, particularly in protest over human-rights abuses, and the hierarchy had taken some steps ... to move from its traditional posture of legitimation. (Berryman 1984:64)

In many areas, the churches came to be the only source of refuge. By providing refuge, the churches came under attack, and so became a focal point of popular resistance ... So, in the insurrection the weight of the institutional Church was perceived in the popular imagination as anti-regime. Meanwhile, much of the Evangelical leadership within the country openly embraced the FSLN as the legitimate representative of the Nicaraguan people. (Dodson and Montgomery 1982:163)

As to Poland, the Catholic Church was associated with national identity for centuries, and, particularly after Poland's partition, had developed a double sense of mission: not only the strictly religious mission of the keeper of the faith until Christ's return, but also keeper of the national heritage until the return of an autonomous and integral Poland. Even after the communist take-over, the Church had deep roots and profound appeal in the rural areas as well as the newer industrial areas. For this

reason, a certain *modus vivendi* was established in the post-Stalin years between the regime and the Church headed by Cardinal Wyszynski, with
the Church having a de facto recognition, which permitted it to criticize
openly aspects of the regime which the Church saw as abuses of the Polish
people. It was thus an exceptional lever within the communist bloc of
countries:

Even for those [intelligentsia] who were by no means religious, the Church
offered the only opportunity of openly expressing their disapproval of the
Government by attending Sunday mass. The Church pulpit became a unique
source of the uncensored word, of a voice eminently concerned for the material
and non-material well-being of the people of Poland. (Szajkowski 1983:3)

I have used the past tense, but the situation still prevails in Poland today,
since the Solidarity Revolution of 1980-1 ended in defeat (or stalemate?),
leaving the Church today in a situation similar to the pre-1979 setting.

Thus, Adam Michnik, a foremost intellectual dissident liberated from
prison in 1984, commented about the present Polish situation:

I saw churches that served as oases of spiritual independence and provided home
for centers of aid to the victims of repression . . . the Catholic Church is the only
institution in Poland that is simultaneously legal and authentic, independent of
the totalitarian power structure and fully accepted by the people. The pope is for
the Poles the greatest teacher of human values and obligations. (Michnik
1985:44-6)

And just as many clergy in Somoza's Nicaragua used churches and masses
to express cultural opposition, so even today is this the case in Poland, as
exemplified by the weekly "mass for the Fatherland" at the "Christian
University of the Workers," organized near Krakow by Father Jancarz,
continuing for steelworkers and intellectuals a tradition begun by Father
Popieluszko for steelworkers in Warsaw, before his murder in 1984
(Michnik, p. 43; Ash 1985:5).

Let me emphasize that in the respective pre-revolutionary settings of
Nicaragua, Iran, and Poland, the religious sector was not the sole source
of opposition to the regime. A revolutionary movement, as any broad-
based collective current, has different streams. The religious factor is significant in providing the movement with a moral force and symbolic
means to neutralize and delegitimate the established regime and to affirm
the legitimacy of the opposition. By so doing, it provides members with
the courage and motivation that is needed to band together in active opposition and to risk their lives, if necessary, in seeking to topple the regime.
This is particularly true in the case of the Catholic Church (and the Evangelical missions in Nicaragua) and Shi'ism, respectively, because of their

emphasis upon the acceptance of suffering and martyrdom in emulation of their founders – Christ for the former, Ali and his son Husayn, for the latter.[15]

Durkheim's analysis of the societal setting in which collective regeneration takes place is rather bare, and it is not clear just what incites or leads the Australians to come together; nor does Durkheim discuss the preconditions for the collective effervescence of revolutionary epochs. But the revolutionary settings of Iran, Nicaragua and Poland suggest that the "dullness of life" of the everyday, secular world, which Durkheim noted, was a function of decreased standards of living for the majority of the population *and* increased political and cultural repression by the regime. Grievances against the respective regimes had accumulated over the years, with episodic outbreaks, riots, and so on.

In all three countries religious leaders made common front with secular ones in denouncing the immorality of the regime. The opposition movement that grew in each country in the 1970s had a comingling of clergy, laity and secularists. The presence of recognized religious leaders in the midst of the opposition is highly significant in uniting and encouraging individual actors to engage in opposition to the regime. Durkheim talks about the phase of the profane social world and the "dispersed condition in which the society finds itself" (Durkheim, p. 246). It is not just economic differentiation which disperses (stratifies, fractionalizes) the societal community: it is also in the nature of repressive and totalitarian regimes to disperse actors and to seek to prevent them from coming together. On the other hand, the religious leaders in the three societal settings we have been talking about played a crucial role in the welding of the opposition into a cohesive, committed social body. Note the passage in *The Elementary Forms*:

> To strengthen those sentiments which, if left to themselves, would soon weaken; it is sufficient to bring those who hold them together and to put them into closer and more active relations with one another. (pp. 240-1)

And Durkheim, without using the term "charismatic leader" goes on to talk about the role of the man able to enter into communion with the crowd; dominated "by a moral force which is greater than he and of which he is only the interpreter," he is able to generate an "exceptional increase of force" and "passionate energies" (p. 241). Durkheim might well have in mind as examples for this analysis Desmoulins or Danton during the French Revolution or Jean Jaurès in his own days. But in our contemporary setting, the catalytic agents of the revolutionary movements have been religious figures as much as secular ones.

So, for example, the election of Karol Wojtyla as pope in October 1978 was greeted in Poland as a miracle and "triggered off an unprecedented demonstration of national and civic awareness" (Szajkowski 1983:60). Even the Polish Communist Party (PUWP) sent to John Paul II a congratulatory message with a nationalistic ring. The collective effervescence, which rose to a peak in 1981 in such manifestations as the Solidarity Congress, the ceremonies of the 1956 uprising in Poznan, and the March general strike,[16] may be said to have been triggered off in June 1979 by the return home of John Paul II:

This papal visit to Poland was a psychological earthquake, an opportunity for mass political catharsis. The Pope expressed in public what had been hidden for decades, the people's private hopes and sorrows, their longing for uncensored truth, for dignity and courage in defense of their civil and human rights. (Szajkowski 1983:72)

... his return visit ... brought millions of Poles, particularly the young, together in massive demonstrations of national unity and religious fervour. (Sanford 1985:8)

In Iran, the exiled Khomeini (in nearby Iraq until the authorities, becoming worried about Shi'ite radicalism, forced him to leave for Paris in October 1978) became the national rallying point for various sectors of society, including secular intellectuals, particularly after the death in 1977 of Ali Shari'ati. Collective effervescence grew in intensity in 1978 with marches, processions and strikes against the Pahlavi regime; banners in these demonstrations always included a picture of Khomeini.

In Tehran on 2 December 1978, the first day of Muharram (a month of special significance for Shi'ism since Husayn's martyrdom took place then) was placed under curfew. Returning home from mosques, people began shouting anti-Shah slogans and from their roofs began chanting "Kill the Shah!," "God is Great!" and "Bring Back Khomeini!"

The cry was picked up as others in the same and adjacent neighborhoods took up the clamor. Spreading from quarter to quarter throughout the city, in Tehran at least, the entire populace seemed to be ignoring the curfew ... The chants were hypnotic, and as hysteria seemed to grow, people almost lost control. (Green 1982:127)

The Iranian situation (but also the Polish one since John Paul II is a very effective national symbol of Polish unity even away in the Vatican, witness the respective visits of both Polish authorities and Lech Walesa there) indicates that the physical presence of religious figures is not necessary in galvanizing the cohesion of the revolutionary movement. It is important that different groups unite *feeling his presence*, which acts as a symbol of national unification.

Collective effervescence in Iran may have reached a zenith the day in February 1979 when Khomeini returned, greeted by two million people, and it may have reached a climax in Nicaragua on 20 July 1979 when the FSLN definitively took over Managua after the collapse of the Somoza dynasty. However, the effervescence of a revolutionary movement is part of an accelerating process, which this chapter has discussed in terms of dedifferentiation. The Iranian Revolution and the Sandinista Revolution became successes in 1979, as did the Polish Revolution in 1980-1 (in terms of the legal recognition of unions and other major regime concessions to groups outside the party). Collective effervescence as part of the renewal of the societal community, in opposition to official society, is a dramatic surfacing of interactions between groups and individual actors that take place well before a peak is reached or success achieved in overcoming the regime. What is involved is a twofold process of "demoralization" of the existent regime and welding together strands of the opposition into a single moral community, which is defined by the leaders of the movement as "the authentic nation." The task of the revolution, of course, is not achieved by the peak of the collective effervescence. The process of unification, of defining the new moral community which will renew the nation previously submerged in an alien regime, has to be complemented by a new phase of differentiation involved in institutionalizing the revolutionary movement, that is, in restructuring the societal institutions in accord with the principles of the movement.

The latter phase of contemporary revolutions lies beyond the scope and intention of this chapter. As mentioned in the introductory section, the eventual outcome of the respective revolutionary situations is hard to prognosticate, to a large extent because of exogenous factors, albeit the latter are paradoxically of some importance in maintaining the cohesion of national solidarity. The virulent opposition of Washington to Sandinista Managua, of Moscow to Solidarity, and of Sunni Islam to Khomeini's Iran, functions – as in earlier revolutions faced by invasion from counter-revolutionary forces – to provide the new regime with popular support, which might otherwise dissipate. In the case of both Nicaragua and Poland an exogenous variable is the relation of the indigenous Catholic Church to the Vatican, with John Paul II showing increased opposition to liberation theology and to the political involvement of the faithful in social movements. These and various other particular aspects of the empirical cases call for a different line of analysis than that attempted in these pages.

In conclusion, I have tried to frame an important cluster of large-scale social phenomena in our own immediate period within a conceptual frame that derives from a sociological masterpiece. Durkheim's *Elementary Forms* is a magnificent sociological testament of the significance of the religious factor in the organization (and dynamics) of human society. Yet Durkheim himself was very ambivalent towards the surviving organized religions of his day, particularly the Catholic Church. How would he view the contemporary situations that we have interpreted in this chapter? I would like to think he would find very apt the following attitude of Adam Michnik (intellectual and adviser to Solidarity), described by Alain Touraine:

If he had been a Frenchman at the beginning of the twentieth century, he told us, he would have taken part in the fight against clericalism and would have been in favour of the separation of Church and state. But, he added, it is impossible to compare a democratic situation with a totalitarian one. In the latter, the Church is a force resisting absolute power; it protects civil society against the state, and therefore plays a fundamentally democratic role, even when it continues to adopt culturally conservative positions which reinforce its hold over the population. (Touraine *et al.* 1983:46)

Postscript: the Philippines Revolution of 1986

Subsequent to the preparation of the above chapter, the Philippines underwent in February 1986 a dramatic series of political events that makes this a striking fourth contemporary instance of the role of religion in revolutionary situations. To recall the salient features of the Philippine Revolution, the twenty-year-old regime of Ferdinand Marcos had become increasingly incapable of dealing with economic deterioration and massive popular discontent. Under pressure from the United States to demonstrate popular support, Marcos called for a "snap" election on 7 February, and the National Assembly which his KBL party controlled declared him the winner on 14 February. However, in the days that followed, a unified Roman Catholic Church, the "institutional Church" of the country since the Spanish colonial period, took an unprecedented active role which led to the ultimate delegitimation and deposition of the Marcos regime and to the subsequent legitimation of Corazon Aquino as the rightful new president.

Prior to the elections, in many rural areas not controlled by the guerrilla forces of the Communist National Democratic Front, the Church had virtually become the only vocal government opposition; several priests, ministers, and lay leaders had been killed, with the evidence pointing to the military (Peerman 1986:228). The electoral campaign itself contributed to the collective effervescence, as the Aquino campaign was forced to utilize "unconventional means of generating public awareness and indignation" (Chanco and Milano 1986:31). The color yellow became the symbol of the "people power," with shredded pages of the yellow pages of phone books thrown from tall buildings during rallies, and a popular jukebox hit, "Tie a Yellow Ribbon," as one of the battle hymns. The radio network of the Catholic Church, Radio Veritas, provided live coverage for the opposition campaign during the entire four-day revolution, unlike other official media such as television networks supportive of Marcos (Chanco and Milano 1986:2) More important in the delegitimation of the *ancien régime* were major pastoral letters by the bishops, beginning with Jaime Cardinal Sin, the chief prelate, whose letter, read in all churches on 18 January 1986, virtually accused the party in power of attempted fraud and intimidation. Even while the national assembly was declaring Marcos the official winner, Ricardo Cardinal Vidal and Bishop Claver, speaking for the Catholic Bishops' Conference, declared that "a government that assumes or retains power through fraudulent means has no moral basis ... the church will not recognize President Marcos even if he is proclaimed winner" (Buruma 1986:11).

The bishops' forceful Valentine Day's declaration proclaiming the moral obligation of the people to right the fraudulence of the regime and its call for "active resistance of evil by peaceful means" was a momentous occasion. As Peerman has observed, "never before had the bishops of any nation condemned a government as unworthy of allegiance and championed a revolution – albeit a nonviolent one – against it" (Peerman 1987:4). Indeed, the "institutional Church" was a crucial factor in the promotion of the February revolution, including the remarkable overthrowing of a repressive regime with non-violent means of delegitimation. The state of collective effervescence that characterized the cases of Poland, Iran, and Nicaragua is also indicated for the Philippines in the following statement: "that revolution did come, in four tense but exhilarating days in late February. Despite its potential for tragedy, the virtually bloodless uprising took on the aspect of a religious festival, with colorful banners flying, nuns saying the rosary, and people extending food and flowers to the enemy" (Peerman 1987:4).

Notes

1 For relevant discussions, see Moore 1978; Lacroix 1981; Coenen-Huther 1984; and Fenton 1984.

2 There is one recent study of revolutions, Billington's *Fire in the Minds of Men*

(1980), which highlights the religious factor in European revolutions, from the French to the Russian.

3 There is an abundant literature on each revolution. Among works that I have found particularly informative on Iran see Bakhash 1982, 1984; Fischer 1980; Keddie 1981. For Nicaragua: Booth 1982; LaFeber 1983; Walker 1982. For Poland: Ash 1984; Ruane 1982; Szajkowski 1983; Touraine et al. 1983.

4 Indeed, one can consider revolutionary movements as a sub-set of charismatic movements, with charisma residing in the movement itself, rather than specific individuals. This assertion, which complements rather than contradicts the Weberian perspective on charisma, is based on the following suggestive passage in *The Elementary Forms* that parallels Weber's conceptualization:

We say that an object, whether individual *or collective*, inspires respect when the representation expressing it in the mind is gifted with such force that it automatically causes or inhibits action, without regard for any consideration relative to their useful or injurious effects . . . This is why commands generally take a short, peremptory form leaving no place for hesitation; it is because . . . it excludes all idea of deliberation or calculation; it gets its efficacy from the intensity of the mental state in which it is placed. It is this intensity which creates what is called a moral ascendancy. (1961:237-8, emphasis mine)

5 Note, for example, the following pertaining to the Sandinistas' launching of the Literacy Crusade in Year I of the Revolution:

Implicit in this process of transformation was the vision of a new society and of an educational model that would help bring about its realization. According to revolutionary thinking, that vision rested principally on the intelligent, creative involvement of a new kind of citizen in new participatory forms of social organization. Essentially, it called for the formation of the "new man" and the "new woman," a revolutionary citizen inspired by the goals of community service rather than individual gain . . . The new social order meant creating a different set of institutions which would respond to the interests and needs of the majority. (Miller 1982:247-8)

6 Elsewhere (Tiryakian 1978) I have suggested that Durkheim might well have drawn upon other and closer collective experiences of the Third Republic – such as the trans-Paris funeral procession of the remains of Victor Hugo and the tumultuous pro- and anti-Dreyfus demonstrations – as occasions where great assemblies give rise to collective enthusiasm and sentiments of participating in a world that transcends the everyday, mundane sphere.

7 *Obiter dictum*, this is a striking parallel to Weber's own foreseeing as one alternative to the mechanized, bureaucratized petrification of capitalistic society the possibility of a new charismatic renewal.

8 Luckmann's perspective (1967) as to the growing centrality of the "privatization" of the religious in individual autonomy is the reciprocal of Durkheim's noting (1961[1912]:347) the rudimentary aspect of the individual cult.

9 "Society is able to revivify the sentiment it has of itself only by assembling" (*The Elementary Forms*, p. 391).

10 Of course, revolutions often develop elaborate rituals: for interesting materials on the French Revolution in this vein, see Ehrard and Viallaneix 1977 and Hunt 1984.

11 For recent discussions that bring back the centrality of "nation" as a social category, see Nielsson 1985, Tiryakian and Nevitte 1985, Armstrong 1982, and the review essay by Waldron 1985.

12 The periodicity which Durkheim noted in *The Elementary Forms* as characterizing oscillations between sacred and profane activity receives an important corroboration in Bales' research and analysis of phase movements in small groups (Bales 1953:123).

13 Recall that de Tocqueville's voyage to America, in which he noted both the vitality of religion and the importance of equality in the new republic, took place in the midst of the great revival.

14 Very broadly, we may think of processes of differentiation as evolving from L→I→G→A, and dedifferentiation as a reverse movement. The high intensity of "I-L" interchanges, we suggest, would be in Parsonian action terms the equivalent of Durkheim's notion of "collective effervescence."

15 Note, for example, these passages in Fischer's discussion of the Iranian Revolution: "The theme of martyrdom was of course central to the revolution" (Fischer, p. 214), and "Muharram [December 1978] began with an explosion. For three consecutive nights, men in white shrouds signifying their willingness to be martyred went into the streets in defiance of the curfew" (p. 204).

In the Central American situation, the murders of fellow Maryknoll and other priests and nuns in Guatemala and El Salvador, climaxed by the assassination of Archbishop Romero, have made the theme of martyrdom in the service of the oppressed and the poor particularly salient to the clergy participating in the Sandinista Revolution.

Note, for example, the interweaving of Nicaraguan realities and the Christian passion in Ernesto Cardenal's remarkable *The Gospel in Solentiname*, as pointed out by Berryman:

Jesus before the Sanhedrin is like Tomas Borge, the Sandinista leader, who had been put on trial; the Roman soldiers are like Somoza's National Guard or like Green Berets ... There is an extensive comparison between the death of Jesus and that of Sandino ... (Berryman 1984:10)

In the case of Poland, the theme of martyrdom and sacrifice have many important symbols drawn from the historical experience and suffering of that country. A very important figure is Stanislaw Szczepanowski, patron saint of Poland; this eleventh-century bishop of Krakow was slain, while saying mass, by a tyrannical ruler whose immoral rule he had defied. Szajkowski notes about the bishop, "For Poles he remained for centuries a symbol of civil courage and religious zeal, as well as of national identity" (p. 62). Upon his accession to the papacy, John Paul II, whose see had been Krakow, sought to visit Poland in May 1979 to take part in the ceremonies for the 900th anniversary of Stanislaw's martyrdom. The regime, all too aware of the symbolism, had the visit put off until the following month.

16 "At eight o'clock on Friday 27 March the factory sirens sounded from Gdansk to Jastrzebie and Poland stopped work. For the next four hours Polish society demonstrated its unity and self-discipline in the largest strike in the history of the Soviet bloc" (Ash 1983:157). A departmental colleague who happened to be in

Poland in early September 1981 reported that during the week he was there the Polish sociologists, no less than the general population, were having "a collective experience of a high."

References

Armstrong, John A. 1982. *Nations Before Nationalism*. Chapel Hill, NC: University of North Carolina Press.

Ash, Timothy Gorton. 1984. *The Polish Revolution: Solidarity*. New York: Charles Scribner's Sons.

1985. "Poland: The Uses of Adversity." *New York Review of Books* 32 (June 27):5-10.

Bakhash, Shaul. 1982. "The Revolution Against Itself." *New York Review of Books* 30 (November 18):19-20, 22-6.

1984. *The Reign of the Ayatollahs: Iran and the Islamic Revolution*. New York: Basic Books.

Bales, Robert F. 1953. "The Equilibrium Problem in Small Groups." In Talcott Parsons, R. F. Bales and Edward A. Shils, *Working Papers in the Theory of Action* pp. 111-61. New York: Free Press.

Berryman, Phillip. 1984. *The Religious Roots of Rebellion. Christians in Central American Revolutions*. Maryknoll, NY: Orbis.

Billington, James H. 1980. *Fire in the Minds of Men. Origins of the Revolutionary Faith*. New York: Basic Books.

Booth, John A. 1982. *The End and the Beginning. The Nicaraguan Revolution*. Boulder, CO: Westview.

Buruma, Ian. 1986. "Bishops in Open Defiance," *Far Eastern Economic Review* (Hong Kong) 131 (27 February):11-13.

Chanco, Pedro A. and Benjamin H. Milano. 1986. "A Different Kind of Revolution." *Communication World* 3 (September):31-3.

Coenen-Huther, Jacques. 1984. *Le Fonctionalisme en sociologie: et après?* Brussels: Éditions de l'Université de Bruxelles.

Dodson, Michael and T. S. Montgomery. 1982. "The Churches in the Nicaraguan Revolution." In Thomas W. Walker, ed., *Nicaragua in Revolution*, pp. 161-80. New York: Praeger.

Durkheim, Emile. 1961 [1912]. *The Elementary Forms of the Religious Life*. Trans. Joseph Ward Swain. New York: Collier.

Ehrard, Jean and Paul Viallaneix, eds. 1977. *Les Fêtes de la Révolution*. Paris: Société des Études Robespierristes.

Eliade, Mircea. 1959. *The Sacred and the Profane. The Nature of Religion*. New York: Harcourt, Brace.

Fenton, Steve. 1984. *Durkheim and Modern Sociology*. Cambridge: Cambridge University Press.

Finney, Charles Grandison. 1960 [1835]. *Lectures on Revivals of Religion*, edited by

    William G. McLoughlin. Cambridge, MA: Belknap/Harvard University Press.

Fischer, Michael M. J. 1980. *Iran. From Religious Dispute to Revolution.* Cambridge, MA: Harvard University Press.

Goldstone, Jack. 1980. "Theories of Revolution: The Third Generation." *World Politics* 32 (April):425-53.

    1982. "The Comparative and Historical Study of Revolutions." *Annual Review of Sociology* 8:187-207.

Green, Jerrold D. 1982. *Revolution in Iran. The Politics of Countermobilization.* New York: Praeger.

Harney, Desmond. 1985. "Iran's Triumphant Islam." *The World Today* 41 (March):65-6.

Hunt, Lynn. 1984. *Politics, Culture, and Class in the French Revolution.* Berkeley, Los Angeles and London: University of California Press.

Jones, Robert A. 1977. "On Understanding a Sociological Classic," *American Journal of Sociology* 83 (September):279-319.

Keddie, Nikki R. 1981. *Roots of Revolution. An Interpretive History of Modern Iran.* New Haven: Yale University Press.

Lacroix, Bernard. 1981. *Durkheim et le politique.* Paris: Presses de la Fondation Nationale des Sciences Politiques, and Montreal: Presses de l'Université de Montréal.

LaFeber, Walter. 1983. *Inevitable Revolutions. The United States in Central America.* New York: W. W. Norton.

Luckmann, Thomas. 1967. *The Invisible Religion: The Problem of Religion in Modern Society.* New York: Macmillan.

Luhmann, Niklas. 1982. *The Differentiation of Society.* New York: Columbia University Press.

Merkl, Peter H. and Ninian Smart, eds. 1983. *Religion and Politics in the Modern World.* New York: New York University Press.

Michnik, Adam. 1985. "Letter from the Gdansk Prison." *New York Review of Books* 32 (July 18):42-8.

Miller, Perry. 1965. *The Life of the Mind in America. From the Revolution to the Civil War.* New York: Harcourt, Brace and World.

Miller, Valerie. 1982. "The Nicaraguan Literacy Crusade." In Thomas W. Walker, ed., *Nicaragua in Revolution,* pp. 241-58. New York: Praeger.

Moore, Wilbert E. 1978. "Functionalism." In Tom Bottomore and Robert Nisbet, eds., *A History of Sociological Analysis,* pp. 321-61. New York: Basic Books.

Nielsson, Gunnar P. 1985. "States and Nation-Groups." In E.A. Tiryakian and Ronald Rogowski, eds., *New Nationalisms of the Developed West.* London and Boston: Allen and Unwin.

Parsons, Talcott. 1968. "Social Systems." In David L. Sills, ed., *International Encyclopedia of the Social Sciences,* vol. 15, pp. 458-73. New York: Macmillan and Free Press.

Parsons, Talcott, R. F. Bales and Edward A. Shils. 1953. *Working Papers in the Theory of Action.* New York: Free Press.

Peerman, Dean. 1986. "'People Power' in the Philippines." *The Christian Century* 103, no. 8 (5 March):228-9.

1987. "Corino Aquino: Religious Newsmaker No.1." *The Christian Century* 104, no.1 (7-14 Jan.):3-4.

Ramazani, R. K. 1986. *Revolutionary Iran: Challenge and Response in the Middle East*. Baltimore and London: Johns Hopkins University Press.

Ruane, Kevin. 1982. *The Polish Challenge*. London: British Broadcasting Corporation.

Sanford, George. 1985. "Poland's Recurring Crises: An Interpretation." *The World Today* 41 (January):8-11.

Szajkowski, Bogdan. 1983. *Next to God . . . Poland. Politics and Religion in Contemporary Poland*. New York: St Martin's Press.

Taylor, Stan. 1984. *Social Science and Revolutions*. New York: St Martin's Press.

Tiryakian, Edward A. 1978. "Emile Durkheim." In Tom Bottomore and Robert Nisbet, eds., *A History of Sociological Analysis*, pp. 187-236. New York: Basic Books.

1981. "*The Elementary Forms* as 'Revelation.'" In Buford Rhea, ed., *The Future of the Sociological Classics*, pp. 114-35. London: Allen and Unwin.

1985. "On the Significance of Dedifferentiation." In S. N. Eisenstadt, ed., *Perspectives on Macro-Sociological Theory*, pp. 118-34. London and Beverly Hills, CA: Sage.

Tiryakian, Edward A. and Neil Nevitte. 1985. "Nationalism and Modernity." In E. A. Tiryakian and Ronald Rogowski, eds., *New Nationalisms of the Developed West*. London and Boston: Allen and Unwin.

Touraine, Alain, François Dubet, Michel Wieviorka and Jan Strzelecki. 1983. *Solidarity. The Analysis of a Social Movement: Poland 1980-1981*. Cambridge: Cambridge University Press, and Paris: Éditions de la Maison des Sciences de l'Homme.

Tsurumi, Yoshi. 1984. "The Challenges of the Pacific Age." *World Policy Journal* II (Fall):63-86.

Waldron, Arthur N. 1985. "Theories of Nationalism and Historical Explanation." *World Politics* 37 (April):416-33.

Walker, Thomas W. ed., 1982. *Nicaragua in Revolution*. New York: Praeger.

Zimmermann, Ekkart. 1983. *Political Violence, Crises, and Revolutions: Theories and Research*. Cambridge, MA: Schenkman.

3 The Liminal fight: mass strikes as ritual and interpretation[1]

Eric W. Rothenbuhler

Durkheim's legacy is a rich one. It is a tribute to the power of his legacy that it manifests itself in the style and logic of scholars who feel little need for explicit citation of his work. Edward Shils, Mary Douglas, Clifford Geertz, and Victor Turner obviously work under Durkheim's influence without need for either reference or discussion. For these writers and their readers, Durkheimian logic is completely unproblematic. It can be taken for granted.

But taken-for-granted knowledge is always partial knowledge; some re-problematization of Durkheim's legacy is past due. Durkheimian logic cannot be taken for granted in contemporary analyses of economics, power, conflict, or practical affairs. There are exceptions, of course. One thinks here, especially, of Mary Douglas' work on risk and commodities and of Marshall Sahlins' work on "practical reason" (Douglas and Isherwood [1979]; Douglas and Wildavsky 1982; Sahlins 1976). The present chapters continue these theoretical openings. I will bring Durkheimian logic to bear on a key episode of social conflict, and I hope I will do so in distinctive ways.

First, in the course of this chapter I will explicate and extend Turner's concept of "liminality." In so doing I pull Turner more explicitly back into the Durkheimian tradition, correct certain shortcomings in the concept, and extend its empirical scope. Turner's (1977 [1969]) use of liminality and the structure/anti-structure pair, I suggest, echoes Durkheim's (1965 [1912]) insistence that there must be periodic celebrations of social solidarity and the division between sacred and profane. Neither is Turner's (1977 [1969]) definition of liminality as a ritual "time out," a subjunctive time and place in which quotidian roles and statuses do not apply, entirely new. It is anticipated, once again, by the most fundamental precepts of Durkhemian sociology: "The religious life and the profane life cannot coexist in the same unit of time. It is necessary to assign determined days or periods to the first, from which all profane occupations are

66

excluded" (Durkheim 1965 [1912]:342). Similarly, Durkheim's treatment of the "individual cult" anticipates Turner's (1982) later concept, "liminoid." My dialogue with Durkheim, then, is through Turner, and one subtext of the chapter is that Durkheim is more relevant to a reading of Turner than is usually thought.

My second departure from conventional Durkheimianism presents itself as a dialogue with contemporary cultural studies. Important strains in this movement share the "idealist" limitations mentioned above in reference to the Durkheimians. They have tended to focus on political ritual of social centers, on official or traditionally sanctioned culture, on religious orders, the symbolics of social control, the trivial, or the spectacular (e.g. Barthes 1977; the Bowling Green school of popular culture; Gusfield 1981; Gusfield and Michalowicz 1984; Hebdige 1979; Shils 1975; Turner 1977 [1969]; Williams 1983; Willis 1978). I want to stress, by contrast, that there is also a class of meaningful situations that are political and which may appear to be ecstatic, trivial and spectacular, but which intend to do violence to the official culture and its central structures. These cultural situations often develop into overt social conflict and they are usually promulgated by the initially unwilling residents of society's bottoms, margins or cracks. In such cases, the forces of the structural center will be preoccupied with denying the meaningfulness of the situation while containing whatever physical manifestations the conflict may entail. Thus we have a fight, within a fight, about the meaning of the fight.

We begin with political ritual. Lukes (1975:301) recommends that

Political ritual should be seen as reinforcing, recreating and organizing [collective representations] . . . that the symbolism of political ritual represents, *inter alia*, particular models or political paradigms of society and how it functions. In this sense, such ritual plays, as Durkheim argued, a cognitive role, rendering intelligible society and social relationships, serving to organize people's knowledge of the past and present and their capacity to imagine the future.

Here, then, it can be seen that political ritual is as important to the powers of the periphery as to the powers of the center, and that it is important for the center that the rituals of the periphery do not become widely practiced. For it is by the practicing of a ritual that a people gives meaning to its collective life. The center cannot afford a meaning other than its own to be widely held.

In the pages which follow I analyze an extreme case of this phenomenon. My subject is a ritualizing group so liminal to the dominant social structure that it cannot be made sense of within that structure. For this reason, its rituals are not seen as alternative interpretations of a given social order but as the actions of an alternative social order itself. The threatened dominant order must, in turn, prevent these actions from being interpreted as performatives signifying the viability of that alternative structuration. My concern in this chapter is directed to the fight between the two groups over the sign-value of their social conflict. I extend the concept "liminality" to situations of social conflict in which social structural occupants actively reject the signification assigned them by the system.

I

As a theoretical category, liminality derives from analysis of socially sanctioned rites of passage (Turner 1977 adapted his usage from van Gennep 1909). As a formal category, however, it need not refer back to that from which it derived. I take "liminality" as referring to that which falls in the cracks of social structure, that is, in between socially sanctioned roles. In Turner's analysis of rites of passage, the liminal residence of individuals was not only designed to be temporary but was actually socially sanctioned and meaningfully legitimate within the system: the chief-to-be could not become so without ritually passing through a period of liminality. The temporary lack of structuration found in the liminal zone was, in other words, necessary for the maintenance of social order.

When, however, some members of a society reside in a liminal zone that is not a part of that society's legitimate ritual code, their behavior cannot be meaningfully explained by the governing myths. If their actions are assigned meaning outside the mythology of the dominant social structure, then their liminal existence constitutes a threat to the social order. Efforts will be made to prevent this significance. Their actions must either be interpreted within the social structure or be denied meaningfulness.

In terms of their relation to the sacred, the socially sanctioned cases of liminality that Turner analyzed are equivalent to the festivals and ceremonies analyzed by Durkheim (1965 [1912]). Unsanctioned liminal activities also touch the sacred, but negatively. Whereas festivals and ceremonies clearly uphold the sacred and allow the actor access to it, liminal action cannot be seen as simply both. It follows from the double nature of the sacred which Durkheim discusses in *The Elementary Forms* that factional liminality is, far from being merely profane, the dangerous opposite of the sacred (see also Douglas 1978 [1966]).

Factional liminality may be recognized by the following attributes. (1) The members of a normal social structural position, call it A, suddenly become not-A; and (2) the members of not-A and the society at large engage in a fight about the meaning of not-A and the actions of its members.

These conditions delimit the area of concern. Specifically excluded are those types of social deviance for which society already has a name. Anticipating my later case study the quotation that follows illustrates what my definition means to include. I draw from a newspaper editorial about the 1912 textile strike in Lawrence, Massachusetts.

> On all sides people are asking: Is this a new thing in the industrial world? . . . Are we to see another serious, perhaps successful, attempt to organize labor by whole industrial groups instead of by trades? Are we to expect that instead of playing the game respectfully, or else breaking out into lawless riot which we know well enough how to deal with, the laborers are to listen to a subtle anarchistic philosophy which challenges the fundamental idea of law and order, inculcating such strange doctrines as those of "direct action," "sabotage," "syndicalism," "the general strike," and "violence?" . . . (Quoted in Brissenden 1919:293)

This is the frame of factional liminality. The workers have become non-workers and they are doing so in a manner for which the larger society has no good name. They are neither respectful of the social order nor lawless. Notice that the writer does not call them anarchists, but fears they may be under the sway of an "anarchistic philosophy." It is something anarchist-like; the rough equivalent of not society-like. Notice also that the writer is so unsure of what he is dealing with that violence becomes a "strange doctrine."

There are four possible outcomes of a period of factional liminality. First, society may rid itself of the liminal group, as American authorities did, for example, in quashing the rebellion of the Weather Underground. Second, society may give the liminal group a name and assign it a place in the social order such that its activities can be understood as accepted forms either of innovation (e.g. the occupational title "artist") or of deviance (e.g. the Hell's Angels). Third, liminal individuals or groups may achieve a recognized personal or social value in the period of factional liminality and in so doing voluntarily give up their liminal activities and return to society refreshed, re-created, inspired, or in some other sense "bettered." In this case, factional liminality is functional for the society as a whole (for examples of this and the previous form see Turner 1975, 1982). The fourth is a logical possibility although a rare empirical case: the dominant society may be defeated by the liminal faction. This requires that the establishment give up its sense-making rules and adopt those of the liminal group. In this case, the liminal group is genuinely revolutionary. In order to be so, they must propose a new order, sanctioned by new myths and performed by new rituals. This, of course, requires the routinization of charisma, the rationalization of experience, the crystalization of expression into structure. To refuse to do so is to engage in theatre, carnival, and acting out rather than in revolution – a situation that has been analyzed by Turkle (1975).

II

In this section I will develop a more coherent definition of terms.

My motivating idea in this chapter is that there are times when only a fraction of society moves into a state of liminality and that at such times the meaning of the actions of these liminal social members is fundamentally ambiguous.

The term "social structure" is used here to refer to something more primordial than the patterns of behavior, roles, and relationships found in most sociological definitions (e.g. House 1981:525; Merton 1968:422; Parsons 1954:230) and something less formal, more closely associated with the on-going performance of social life than the unconscious systems of cognitive categories referred to by Lévi-Strauss (e.g. 1963:277–80). Turner (1975:236–7; original emphasis) rejects the latter and opts for the former:

What I intend to convey by social structure here – and what is implicitly regarded as the frame of social order in most societies – is not a system of unconscious categories, but quite simply, in Robert Mertonian terms, "the patterned arrangements of role-sets, status-sets, and status-sequences" *consciously* recognized and regularly operative in a given society.

But if social structure is nothing more primordial than a system of consciously chosen roles, then we cannot explain the sense of violation that accompanies innovations to the system (Douglas 1978 [1966]; Rothenbuhler 1985a). Social structure is the pattern of behaviors and relationships, but these are built up from a logical system of classifications that models the society in which it occurs (Durkheim and Mauss 1963; Lévi-Strauss 1963). Together these constitute an elaborate system of names and rules of which social actors are partially aware and by which they render the patterns of behaviors and relationships in their lives meaningful.

Liminality, following Turner's (1977:125, 128) usage, is found in the "interstices" of social structure: "liminal entities are neither here nor there; they are betwixt and between the positions assigned and arrayed by law, custom, convention, and ceremonial" (p. 95). Due to Turner's (1977) inductive style, "liminality" takes on the empirical attributes of the example at hand, usually one chosen in order to illuminate solidaristic "communitas." I have chosen, rather, a formal definition of liminality based on a strict interpretation of its logical requirements. Seen in this way, liminality is an empty state; it is defined by *where* it is – that is, in the cracks – not by *what* it is. What we find there may differ radically from what Turner found. The most important implication of this definition is that the liminal person is between meaningful units.

As I have suggested, Turner's (1975, 1977) primary concern is to identify liminality as a time and place for producing "communitas," "society as an unstructured or rudimentarily structured and relatively undifferentiated *comitatus*, community, or even communion of equal individuals" (1977:96). My concern here is different, although it, too, can be seen as Turner's central concept.

> From the perspectival viewpoint of those concerned with the maintenance of "structure," all sustained manifestations of communitas [or, I claim, any other activity of factional liminality] must appear as dangerous and anarchical, and have to be hedged around with prescriptions, prohibitions, and conditions. And as Mary Douglas [1978] has recently argued, that which can not be clearly classified in terms of traditional criteria of classification, or falls between classificatory boundaries, is almost everywhere regarded as "polluting" and "dangerous." (Turner 1977:109)

Just as Lukes (1975) noted that not all social rituals were integrative in function, I suggest that not all manifestations of communitas are derived from brotherly love; some are, in fact, overtly combative. Conflict at a given social level may produce communitas at a level subordinate to it, within the conflicting groups. This communitas derives from two phenomena. First, as Simmel (1955) pointed out, conflict itself is superordinate to the particular interests of the members of either of the conflicting camps and produces an integration among them. Secondly, beyond the internally coalescing forces of conflict, ritual itself produces a social integration. The members of a group struggling together against another are all the more a group to the extent that they do so ritually as well as materially. As Lukes (1975) points out, the same rituals which are conflictual on the national level are integrative on the subgroup level.

I place great stock in the connotations of the words structure and interstice, especially when juxtaposed with the word communitas. I do not think these words made their way into our theoretical lexicon haphazardly. Social structure is something that binds us. But that binding has cracks in it – the interstices – and occasionally we pour through these cracks into the liminal zone. This zone is as likely as not to produce communitas, a community of genuine relations in which status, role distinctions and social prescriptions lose their governing force. This leads to descriptions of the liminal with such words as relief, escape and liberation.

Thus we find a liminality of relief at the weekend, stopping for a drink on the way home from work, in the mid-afternoon nap, in amateur sports, or in any of a variety of leisure activities. These are times and places that fall between prescribed roles, in which the latitude of permissible activities is wider and the force of prescription and proscription less, in which social relations are conducted between relative status equals, in which instrumental roles account for less and expressive activities account for more. This is a functional liminality in which individuals, in answer to their own needs, opt out now and then only to return, "recreated," to the social structure. The maintenance of the structure dialectically requires occasional relief from the structure.

This is a phenomenon principally of industrial societies and it is a weaker form than the dialectic between liminality and structure in preindustrial societies. It is more voluntary, tends to be conducted on an individual rather than collective basis, is more diffuse through time, place, and population, and has wider latitude for idiosyncratic variations on ritual and symbol. Turner (1982) described this liminality of industrial relief as "liminoid" (see also Rothenbuhler 1985b).

Because they are explicable within the dominant mythic structure, these liminoid phenomena are not the concern of this chapter. Industrial social structures have made allowances for them and they are, therefore, comprehensible from within that social structure. My concern here is with the more completely liminal situations in which social actors and their observers sense the crossing of a genuine and dangerous threshold. This is the threshold that delimits meaningful social categories. The concern of this chapter is with those times and places when some subgroup of a society's members resides and acts between meaningful social categories, when their activities become, literally, not meaningful.

III

I regard the labor strike as a performative, the signification of which can be found either within or without the dominant social structure. The forces of the order will try at all times to interpret the actions of the workers within the social structure: workers will at times behave according to the myths of that structure and at times they will not. When they do not, the forces of the social order will attempt either to deny them a felicitous performance or, failing that, to limit the communicative potential of their performance.

A strike is always rudimentarily liminal; it is a period in which workers become non-workers. But this is a surface manifestation only. As long as the strike is motivated and resolvable by elements of the mythic structure of industrial society, the workers have not achieved the true escape from the social structure of a genuine liminality. As long as workers strike about wages, they accept the myth of the labor market which gives meaning to their behavior within the industrial social structure.

As soon as strikers behave as if not motivated by wages, their behavior cannot be made meaningful within the social structure and it becomes a threat to that structure. Here they have accomplished two things. First, they have escaped everyday structuration and achieved a genuine liminality. Second, because they have not taken all of society's members into liminality together, their liminality is at the expense of those who, still residing in the industrial social structure, cannot make sense of their liminal anti-structure behavior.

The differences that lead to strikes which are only superficially liminal as compared with those which are genuinely liminal can be illumined by reference to Lévi-Strauss' discussion of Shamanistic cures. The laboring mother-to-be in "The Effectiveness of Symbols" (1963:186–205) is experiencing "incoherent and arbitrary pains, which are an alien element in her system." The shaman who successfully intervenes in this birthing

> provides the sick woman with a *language*, by means of which unexpressed, and otherwise inexpressible, psychic states can be immediately expressed. And it is the transition to this verbal expression – at the same time making it possible to undergo in an ordered and intelligible form a real experience that would otherwise be chaotic and inexpressible – which induces the [cure]. (pp. 197–8)

Lévi-Strauss suggests that the language with the power to bring about these results is myth.

In the case of organized industrial conflict, workers are experiencing incoherent and arbitrary pains: unannounced speed-ups, schedule changes, pay-cuts and so on. They call for the intervention of their union, and some action follows. It is here that the industrial situation faces a fork. The union may follow the example of Lévi-Strauss' shaman and call upon myth to achieve a cure, or it may take a truly political action the result of which cannot be predicted. Should the union choose the shaman's cure, the myths available in our society tell the worker that the capitalists have a property right and that the workers have sold their labor power in a free market. They are just as free to withdraw from the market as the factory-owner is to control his or her property. Within that myth, if there is a violation of the contract the union will look into it. The "shaman" will enter arbitration and institute grievance procedures, for this is how labor pains are made meaningful. By contrast, the political or revolutionary union does not cure labor pains with myth, for myth preserves rather than changes structure (Barthes 1972 [1957]). The revolutionary action is to return one's labor pains from whence they came – back to the owners and managers. For the workers to turn their labor pains into the labor pains of the owners requires their escape from the social structure, for this is something the structure does not allow. Thus the revolutionary workers' action is to (a) refuse to be workers, and (b) refuse to be wage-motivated strikers. This puts them beyond the explanatory power of the myths of industrial culture. It makes them factionally liminal – liminal at the expense of the social structure.

This sort of rejection of structural motivation could be expected to arise most often in spontaneous actions by those without structural status distinctions. An example would be the resolution unanimously adopted by striking miners in one district of Illinois, suggesting that their governor "go to hell," (Brecher 1972:101). Another would be the teamster rank and file singing "We'll hang Michael Casey from a sour apple tree" while Casey, their local president, argued that a strike at that time was "ill-advised" (Brecher 1972:154). Rejections of structural motivations should not be expected of an organization or its leaders, for an organization is inherently structured and with status distinctions comes respect for the structure that yields them.

The Industrial Workers of the World, however, formed one organization that for a time – primarily 1909 to 1917 – consistently led workers into liminal battles.[2] They were qualified for this role on two accounts. First, analogous to Turner's (1977) religious orders, they were liminal to this world, viewing it as merely a transitional stage to a better one. Secondly, and most importantly, they were an organization built on the communitas of the fight.

IV

The Industrial Workers of the World – the IWW or Wobblies – was a labor organization exhibiting all of the crucial antecedents of Turner's communitas. Its strength was among the lowest and most marginal elements of society: the immigrant, unskilled, and migratory laborers. This was something of which they were proud and they eschewed status distinctions. At their second annual convention in 1906 they ousted the skilled laborers from leadership positions and abolished the office of president. By their fourth convention they had outsted founding member Daniel DeLeon and the members of his Socialist Labor Party for being too intellectual and political (that is, too parliamentarian as opposed to syndicalist). At this fourth convention the hall in Chicago was packed by men calling themselves the overall brigade, who had ridden the rails from the lumber camps of the Pacific coast. They interrupted DeLeon's speeches by singing "Halleluja, I'm a Bum." He referred to them, not affectionately, as the Bummery, and claimed they slept in the lake-front parks during the convention.[3]

This is the stuff of the Wobbly legend and it is reported thoroughly enough elsewhere. The point here is that it was an organization of the most marginal elements of the society and that they were united in and proud of that marginality. Further, it was a rank-and-file organization. Their slogan was "we are all leaders" (DeCaux 1978:14). Their most famous labor activities were situations when they came in to assist in spontaneous strikes by either unorganized workers or workers acting in defiance of their unions.

The Wobblies were a liminal group in that they existed for a society not yet in existence and they refused to enter into arrangements with elements of this society. One of their organizers, Joe Ettor, called it "revolutionary in methods as well as final purpose" (quoted in Foner 1965:472).

They simply refused to behave as a labor organization "should." Their dues were too low to build a budget and they had no system to see that dues were even paid regularly. They built no strike funds and offered no unemployment, sickness, death or retirement compensation. There was no picket pay. They rotated local officials, preventing the development of local loyalties and hierarchies. In their view, the class warrior needed none of these motivators (see especially Foner 1965:462–72). During their famous free-speech fights, they moved unemployed, or as they preferred "footloose," members *into* struck towns and had their members intentionally jailed to paralyze the legal structure. But, most revealing of all, they shunned signing labor contracts – the very thing for which most unions existed and fought. Brecher (1972) concludes they were "more of a social movement than a normal union" (p. 102).

The Wobblies were also great communicators. The organization survived on oration, sloganeering, and propagandizing. Their every move was symbolic and they left behind a wealth of artifacts and stories for analysis. Their first fame derived from the free-speech fights. They would flood towns where they had been denied the right to speak with union members intending to speak and be arrested. This developed what they called the "four word speech." Members would climb aboard a soapbox, announce "fellow workers and friends," and look around for the sheriff's deputies (see Brissenden 1919:260–4; DeCaux 1978:48–56; Foner 1965:173–213; Kornbluh 1964:94–126; Thompson and Murfin 1976:48–50). The nationally distributed call for one free-speech fight read simply, "Wanted – Men to fill the jails of Spokane" (DeCaux 1978:52; Kornbluh 1964:95). Small western towns were literally filled to the breaking point with outlawed speakers. Once in jail they sang, banged on the bars, and gave speeches from the windows. This form of non-violent civil disobedience was unique at the time. The San Francisco newspaper *Call* commented:

It is one of those strange situations that crop up suddenly and are hard to understand. Some thousands of men, whose business it is to work with their hands, tramping and stealing rides, suffering hardships and facing dangers – to get into jail. And to get into one particular jail in a town of which they had never heard before, in which they have no direct interest. (Quoted in Kornbluh 1964:96)

Why a labor organization would be so interested in free speech – interested enough to persevere in the face of the violence and death which was often the result of the fights – and why its members so anxiously volunteered to defend it is not explicable in instrumental terms. Although there were clear strategic dimensions to the defense of free speech – they needed the right to speak in order to recruit – the extent of their defense went far beyond rational strategy.

In addition to being great stuntsmen, the Wobblies published newspapers and pamphlets in a number of languages and are most remembered to this day for their song books. They were also, by all accounts, led by men and women capable of communicating a vision to uneducated masses in a powerful and real way. Witness this comment by a contemporary journalist:

This man ... steeped in the literature of revolutionary socialism and anarchism, swayed the undisciplined mob as completely as any general ever controlled the disciplined troops [and was able] to organize these thousands of heterogeneous, heretofore unsympathetic and jealous nationalities, into a militant body of class-conscious workers. His followers firmly believed, as they were told, that success meant that they were about to enter a new era of brotherhood, in which there would be no more union of trades and no more departmental distinctions, but all workers would become the real bosses in the mills. (Quoted in Brissenden 1919: 289)

The Wobblies were fighters of the liminal zone. They searched for cracks in the social order – that liminal zone where workers became non-workers – and through those cracks they poured their signifiers. Because they were experts in stunts – performing a strike more than holding one – they simply could not be ignored. Their tactics were guided by an ethic that could not be made sensible in a system based on property, exchange value, and the sale of labor power. Their signifying performance rubbed their liminal status in the face of a social structure that could only understand economic motives.

It was by their refusal to enter into normal relations with society that the Wobblies were revolutionary. They weren't revolutionary because they led labor strikes, but because they refused to sign labor contracts when the strikes were won. They weren't revolutionary because they broke the laws, but because they intentionally filled jails to the breaking point. They weren't revolutionary because they prepared for revolution, but because they didn't. They weren't revolutionary because they advocated revolution, but because they acted it out.

The Wobblies danced their new society right on the head of the old one and it was often such a bizarre sight that it crumbled the naming abilities of those they fought. By acting in ways to which the myth had no recourse they cracked the social structure. The Wobblies were precisely nothing that was comprehendable in that structure. Given that, they were correctly apprehended as a danger to the contemporary social order.

The 1912 Lawrence textile strike

Lawrence made the I.W.W. famous, especially in the East. It stirred the country with alarming slogans of a new kind of revolution. Socialism was respectable – even reactionary – by comparison. The "Wobblies" frankly abjured the rules under which, as they would express it, the capitalist game is played ... Lawrence was not an ordinary strike. It was a social revolution *in parvo*. (Brissenden 1919: 291)

The I.W.W. abjures current ethics and morality as bourgeois, and therefore inimical to the exploited proletarian for whom a new and approved system of proletarian morality is set forth. In this proletarian code the sanctions of conduct are founded on the (material) interests of the proletarian, *as such*. The criterion is expediency ... This means that staid old New England was confronted with an organization which derided all her fond moralities. (Brissenden 1919:291–2)

The town of Lawrence in 1912 possessed the surface elements that contribute to the break-in of communitas. It had inferiority: the major employers were the textile mills which ran largely on unskilled labor. Surveys of the period found the workers of Lawrence more poorly paid, the housing scarcer, more crowded and more expensive, and the cost of living higher than other compared cities (Brissenden 1919; Foner 1965). It had marginality: "within a one-mile radius of the mill district, there lived 25 different nationalities, speaking a half hundred different languages" (Foner 1965:308). Most of the mill workers had immigrated since 1890, 15,000 between 1905 and 1910, and the companies advertised for workers in Southern and Eastern Europe to keep the flow coming (Foner 1965).

But the most important thing in Lawrence in 1912 was a strike that was big enough to involve 60 per cent of the residents. That strike was organized, though neither instigated nor led, by the IWW. As just discussed, the IWW was an organization that lived for the liminal fight and the 1912

77

strike of Lawrence quickly became just that. The strike was a crack in the social order in which status and meaning became ambiguous.

The textile strike at Lawrence was an essentially spontaneous affair; while both the American Federation of Labor and the Industrial Workers of the World had small locals in Lawrence, neither organization played a role in the start of the strike. The AFL had organized some of the skilled trades working in the mills, by far the minority of the workers, while the IWW had recently led a losing strike by unskilled workers in one of the mills. The IWW local, however, anticipated the possibility of an uprising and was in communication with its national organization (Brissenden 1919; Foner 1965; Kornbluh 1964).

On 1 January 1912, legislation went into effect reducing work hours for women and children to 54 per week. The mills' response was to cut the hours of all workers. This resulted in lost income that the workers measured in loaves of bread (4 to 10 of them, depending on the author). The companies did not announce the pay-cut, but the workers anticipated it, for their efforts to confer with the mill agents on the issue were ignored. January 12 was to be pay day and on January 10 the Italians voted to strike if their pay was short. (Lawrence was both formally and informally organized by ethnic groups – something most labor organizations saw as disadvantageous but which the Wobblies turned to a strength.) Pay envelopes were distributed at mid-morning on Friday, January 12:

Just like any other Friday, the paymaster, with the usual armed guard, wheeled a truck containing hundreds of pay envelopes to the head of a long line of anxiously waiting people. There was much chattering in different languages, and much gesticulation. I stood with Gyp halfway along the line. When the great moment came, the first ones nervously opened their envelopes and found that the company had deducted two hours' pay. They looked silly, embarrassed and uncertain what to do. Milling around, they waited for someone to start something. They didn't have long to wait, for one lively young Italian had his mind thoroughly made up and swung into action without even looking into his pay envelope.

"Strike! Strike!" he yelled. To lend strength to his words, he threw his hands in the air like a cheer-leader.

"Strike! Strike! Strike!"

He yelled these words as he ran, past our line, then down the room between spinning frames. The shop was alive with cries of "Strike" after the paymaster left. A few French-Canadian spinners went back to work. A tall Syrian worker pulled a switch and the powerful speed belts that gave life to the bobbins slackened to a stop.

There were cries: "All Out!"

And then hell broke loose in the spinning room. The silent, mute frames became an object of intense hatred, something against which to vent our stored-up feelings. Gears were smashed and belts cut. The Italians had long sharp knives and with one zip the belts dangled helplessly on the pulleys. Lefty Louie and I went from frame to frame, breaking "ends," while Tony smashed windows. Queenie barricaded herself behind trucks and let loose a barrage of bobbins on Gyp, who seemed determined to get hold of her tongue. It was a madhouse, a thrilling one, nevertheless. (Fred E. Beal, "Strike!" from *Proletarian Journey*, 1937, in Kornbluh 1964:178)

After closing their own mills the workers ran to those that were still operating.

In the mass assaults on the five mills, the strikers had destroyed and damaged machinery and other equipment. Some workers had been slightly injured and six Italians arrested for inciting to riot.

By Saturday night, January 13, the strikers estimated that 20,000 textile workers had left their machines. By Monday night, January 15, Lawrence was an armed camp; police and militia guarded the mills through the night. (Foner 1965: 317)

At a mass meeting on Friday afternoon, the first day of the strike, the strikers voted to send for the IWW's Joseph (Smilin' Joe) Ettor to organize the strike. He and Arturo Giovannitti, who was not a Wobbly at the time but edited *Il Proletario* and worked with the Italian Socialist Federation, arrived on Saturday. Ettor set up a strike committee of 56, 4 representatives from each of the 14 largest nationality groups elected directly by the workers themselves. Few of the members of the strike committee were IWW members at the beginning of the strike, and all major decisions were made by the workers themselves in mass meetings. Anticipating arrests, each representative on the committee had an alternative with full knowledge of committee work (see Brissenden 1919; Foner 1965).

The strike continued until March 14 and during its period no new material was produced by any of the mills in Lawrence (Foner 1965:321).

In a second action, Lawrence was struck from September 27 to September 30 to mark the beginning of the trials of Ettor and Giovannitti who, charged with murder, were acquitted on November 25. This rank and file strike – over the protestations of Ettor and Giovannitti – involved 12,000 workers and closed five of the mills.

Even though the Lawrence strike began in reaction to wage cuts, and was eventually settled with wage increases, it is the opinion of many observers of the period, and most historians, that that is not what it was genuinely about. When John Golden, president of the United Textile Workers – associated with the AFL, he worked to break the strike – appeared before the House of Representatives he stated: "This is a revolution, not a strike" (in Foner 1965:339). The appearance of wage motivation among the strikers is belied by five elements. First, the destruction during the first unorganized days of the strike was out of proportion to the wage cuts. Secondly, the scale of the strike, its length and the spectacular tactics of the strikers discussed below, was not at the time considered a normal or legitimate response to a small pay-cut. Thirdly, the mill owners offered to reinstate previous pay levels very early in the strike; this offer was rejected. Fourthly, the strikers' willingness to risk a second strike in honor of their jailed leaders indicates a consciousness beyond the pay check. Finally the unusually thorough control measures enacted by the legal forces of Lawrence – not only was Lawrence unofficially under martial law, but simply to call a person a scab was a misdemeanor (Foner 1965:329–30) – indicate that the authorities saw themselves faced by a different animal from the usual wage-strike.

These points will become clearer in the pages that follow, where a number of the specific activities of the strikers and authorities are examined.

Pickets, parades and performatives
The Lawrence strike provides several examples of the fight over signification between the community of strikers and the social order they stood against.

The strikers were granted permission to picket, but when they gathered in front of the mill gates the police attempted to disperse them. Finding that they could not mass at the mill entrance, as was the picketing custom of the time, they devised a new technique; they formed chains that snaked through the mill district. The entrance was blocked, but not by more than a few people at a time and no one loitered; the police could not say "move along now." These chains were at times 20,000 strong, they included women and children, they sang as they marched, and they did not cease 24 hours a day until a few days before the end of the strike.[4]

In addition to single-file marches, the strikers held parades. "Every few days a parade would be held, with from 3,000 to 10,000 people marching to the music of bands and drum corps, singing 'The Internationale,' 'The Marseillaise,' 'Solidarity Forever,' and other radical and wobbly songs," (Foner 1965:322).

It is the first strike I ever saw that sang. I shall not soon forget the curious lift, the strange sudden fire of the mingled nationalities at the strike meetings when they broke into the universal language of song. And not only at the meetings did they sing, but in the soup houses and in the streets. I saw one group of women strikers who were peeling potatoes at a relief station suddenly break into the swing of the "Internationale." They have a whole book of songs fitted to familiar tunes – "The Eight Hour Song," "The Banner of Labor," "Workers, Shall the Masters Rule

Us?" But the favorite of all was the "Internationale." (Ray Stannard Baker, *The American Magazine*, 1912, in Kornbluh 1964:158)

When the militia forbad all parades and mass meetings, the strikers began sidewalk parades. "Groups of 20, 30, or 50 would lock arms on the sidewalk, take up its entire width, and walk along, sweeping everyone off the sidewalks or against the walls of buildings" (Foner 1965:322). When the police broke up these sidewalk parades, the strikers would walk in, through, and out of stores. They didn't buy anything, they just walked through, in large numbers.

Here are a number of signification battles centered on the form of picketing and parading. These battles indicate a negotiation, as it were, between two conflicting social units over the form of the rituals in which they act out their conflict.

The picket is the public presence of the strike. It is the manner in which the strikers enforce their strike, not only on their employer, but on their society. As an event, it is a performative; as a meaning unit, it is a sign function (following Austin 1962; and Barthes 1968).

The strikers have opted out of the social order, they are in a liminal phase; the strike is a crack in the social order in which there are no workers. The function of the picket is to prevent scabbing, to intimidate would-be strike breakers. As a sign, its signifier is the number of people present, the signs they carry, the clothes they wear, and their behavior. To the strikers, its signified is strength and its connotation is unity. If it is successful, or as Austin (1962) would prefer, felicitous, the picket becomes a performative and the whole of the social order is implicated. By our striking, you are struck. For the defenders of the status quo, those who do not accept this cracking of the social order, the connotation of the picket is threat. The role of the enforcers of the social order, then, is first to prevent the felicitousness of the picket, and failing that to limit the range of its communicability. The logic is simple: if one cannot prevent the social order from cracking occasionally, then surely one can prevent the cracks being meaningful.

The strikers first tried to picket as they normally would, by massing at the factory gates. The police refused them the status of picket and responded as to an unruly crowd; a potential riot must be dispersed. The strikers, insisting that they meant "picket" and not "riot," restated themselves as one would in conversation. Choosing words which could not, even in the language of the police, be understood as "riot," they reinstated the pickets within the law.

With the moving chain picket, the function of picketing was achieved, while its sign value was perhaps increased. The police failed in preventing either the felicitousness of the picket or its communicative spread. By refusing to allow the strikers to mass, the police succeeded in spreading them around the city.

More damaging to the besieged social order, the interstitial nature of this behavior was clear while it could not be explained away as criminal. If society were functioning normally, thousands of people would not be walking around as human chains, singing, 24 hours a day. Neither would they be doing so if society were under attack by criminal, anarchistic hordes. In allowing the police to refuse them definition as a mass, the strikers forced the police to accept their definition as organized – to wit: an alternative social order.

As to the parades, they were surely a show of force, but they had a celebratory connotation that was not missed by observers. This celebratory aspect of the Wobblies' actions is largely what their legend is based on (see, for example, Conlin 1969; DeCaux 1978; Kornbluh 1964; Renshaw 1967). Parades with bands and singing do not occur every three days in a mill town, not when society is in working order. But parades do not occur when society is falling apart either. They occur in those cases of interstice and liminality in which Turner (1977) was first interested. They mark or memorialize changes, signify rites of passage. As long as the strikers paraded celebratorily, they could not easily be defined as extra-societal elements – that is, attacking armies – for they were operating with the very signs of societal integration. The tools of national holidays were being used to mark workers as, for now, non-workers. Just as on the Fourth of July, when the banker is not a banker but an American, in the parade the loom-tender is not a loom-tender but a striker, and equally proud of it.

If the forces of the social order could deny the striker the parade, they would deny a powerful weapon indeed. But in pushing the strikers from the street to the sidewalks and on into the stores, the society only festered its own wound. By striking the workers had opened a small cut in the social order and the parade celebrated it. By denying the parade, the police and militia had bandaged the cut, hidden it from view, but without cleaning it; when they looked again, the dirt had worked in deeper.

With the strikers' assault on the stores, the juxtaposition of their liminality and the town's attempt to live the social order as usual was pushed to its most ludicrous. The absurdity of crowds of people walking into stores, up and down the aisles, and back out again, without buying anything was too much. The chief of police testified before Congress that the store owners were terrified (Foner 1965:323). Shops are for shopping. The shopkeepers could not conceive of them any other way. But one does not shop while on holiday, and when the holiday one is celebrating is called a strike, one parades, endlessly. In a struck town everywhere the mass of strikers go, everything they do is a parade. To be a parader is to make a parade; by our parading, your store is a parade ground.

In this way the striker performs a struck society. The myths of the shopkeeper are defenseless against a parader; paraders are neither shoppers nor shoplifters. They are a phenomenon which renders the shopkeepers' social structure incoherent. The police cannot enter with a shamanistic cure, for nothing in the myth allows for the removal of paraders from shops. The world is incomprehensible, or it is the strikers'.

Perhaps the single event that attracted the most outside attention to the strike was the exodus of the children. In February the strike committee decided to send the children of the strikers to live with sympathetic families in non-struck cities. It was a common tactic in European strikes but had never before been seen in America (Foner 1965). And this was its significance, that it be seen, rather than simply used.

Suitable host homes were found in New York and other cities, the children were organized into groups, identification papers were filled out, signed by parents and pinned to their jackets, and under the chaperone of strike leaders they set off by train for New York. On arrival they marched down Fifth Avenue carrying signs denouncing their exodus and supporting the strike (see the photographs in Kornbluh 1964). This dramatic move, of course, received much media attention.

After several contingents of children had left Lawrence, the authorities announced that no more would be allowed to leave. Another group was scheduled to go the next day. On arrival at the station they found the trains barricaded by police and militia. When they tried to board, children and mothers were forcibly separated, the mothers arrested for neglect and the children made wards of the courts (Brissenden 1919; Foner 1965; Kornbluh 1964; and others).

The important element here is the contrast between the definitions of the situation acted upon by the striking families and the authorities of Lawrence. According to the myths – that is, the sense-making tools – of the industrial social structure, workers are those who sell their labor power in an open market. The strike, thereby, is an attempt on the part of the workers to alter the balance of supply and demand in that market, and so achieve more favorable conditions of sale. This is not only the view of those at the pinnacle of the social structure, but of all of those who accept and operate within its perceptual schemes. The AFL for instance denounced the Lawrence strike because it was not about wages.

The exodus of the children was a central battle between the economic and class war-sign systems. It had a function: the children were malnourished and by a month into the strike food was scarce in Lawrence. The striking parents simply wished to send their children where they could be better cared for. But if it had had no sign value, it could have been done quietly. This function had a clear sign value, and it was a value that irreparably damaged the economic definition of the situation: exodus signifies war.

One does not send one's children away from the scene of an economic negotiation, but from a battlefield. In removing their children the strikers made them refugees; in being refugees the children made the strike a civil war.

The city officials responded to the exodus on two levels. Pragmatically they saw the move, correctly, as one with tremendous propaganda value. From the beginning its sign value was perceived. As a machine that runs on property tax, the city's function in a strike (economically defined via the myths of industrial structure) is to limit the strikers' impact on the labor market. A major portion of achieving this function is in limiting the range of the strike, not only in time but in place. They had to deny the strike communicability. Therefore the attempt to stop the children from leaving was literally to prevent the strike from escaping their boundaries.

But the way in which they prevented the children from leaving indicates a much deeper level of response. The exodus of the children attempted to signify Lawrence not as the scene of an economic dispute but as a battleground. And the city fathers did not fail to notice this, yet they had no means by which to assimilate it in their mythic structure. In our society the workers do not all send their children out of town, neither, however, is there a law forbidding it. An action that is neither proscribed nor prohibited by the social structure, and yet carries a clear sign value is a threat to the relevance and continuity of that social structure.

The city officials saw the exodus just as all significant actions falling beyond the range of conventional meaningful category systems: as pollution, as a danger, as something to be put right (Douglas 1978). The exodus of the children spread the pollution, spread the strike. The children were its carriers, its communicants. Their refugee march in New York performed the strike as a civil war.

In arresting the mothers of the refugee children for neglect, the city officials attempted to deny the function of the exodus, to portray it as only a sign. If it were only a communication strategy its sign value could be prohibited without threat to the children. Further, since the mothers were acting as mothers do not act in this society, they must be neglectful mothers. But the published reports of the health of the children testified that neglect was precisely what the mothers were trying to avoid. Here the strikers denied the sign value of the move; by articulating it as function only, they signified the move of the police as inhumane. Their success is indicated by the large amounts of press attention and the Congressional investigation which were the results of the move (Brissenden 1919; Foner 1965).

Summary

Throughout the Lawrence strike we see the actions of the strikers as performative signs, the value of which is not assimilable by the meaning structure of industrial culture. The actions of the strikers are incoherent and arbitrary and appeals to the shamans of the society – the legal system – cannot cure the pains, for the strikers are literally without the system. The myth system of industrial society cannot make meaningful the actions of strikers uninterested in economic motives, for workers unmotivated by wages are literally non-workers and as such they exist in the interstices of industrial society. In this liminal space the meaning systems of the social order are as irrelevant to their actions as their actions are incoherent to it. Within this general frame we find that specific actions serving specific functions can be tactically defined as with or without sign value, with or without function.

V

We see, then, that liminal situations arise not only in socially sanctioned rites of passage but in a variety of social situations. These include the liminoid patterns of structural re-creation and the factional liminality analyzed here. This latter denotes times and places such as the Lawrence strike in which some subgroup of society opts out of the social structure – performs roles not defined in the dominant social order, pursues goals not established by the society's myths, performs rituals not meaningful in the everyday social system. The actions of these factionally liminal groups are seen as dangers to the social order; they threaten its comprehensiveness if not its absolute viability. This can be seen in the attempts of the authorities of Lawrence to suppress the strikers, to prevent their performances.

The actors of the social order must deny any threat to their meaning system at these times; they must insist on interpreting the actions of the factionally liminal group within the categories of the dominant social structure. To fail to do so is to admit either (a) there is a range of performable social action that one's social order does not anticipate, cannot name or evaluate, or (b) that the social order performed by the factionally liminal group is a viable alternative to one's own. Neither, of course, is an acceptable alternative. And so we found the authorities of Lawrence, as well as the media, leaders of non-striking labor associations and other observers, persistently straining to understand the strikers as wage-motivated strikers, as criminals, as foreign hordes, or as revolutionaries.

These strained understandings of the factionally liminal group by the social order are rough fits at best. The on-going activities of the liminal individuals provide continued challenges to the order. A liminal perform-ance engenders in response an attempted understanding within the social order, which in turn yields another challenging performance and requires another attempt to understand. And so we see the negotiation pattern of the strikers and authorities over the form and meaning of pickets and parades.

The final point is that factional liminality requires some end. The nego-tiated pattern of performance and interpretation may result in some sort of agreement on the name and rules of a new form of deviance, or the energy of liminality can disperse and its actors return to the social struc-ture, or as in Lawrence some formal end to the activities can be met. In any case, liminality can never be an on-going concern. It can sustain beyond spontaneous enactment only through routinization, which inevi-tably results in crystallization into structure.

In demonstrating that Turner's concept "liminality" applies to conflict as well as consensus situations, that it appears in challenges to the social order as well as in the rites of passage that re-create the social order, we have done the same for Durkheim's religious sociology. In threatening the sense-making capabilities of the social order, the striking workers' ac-tivities threatened the sacred beliefs and values on which that order was founded. The ritual, violence and arationality on both sides of the conflict point beyond strategic motivations to contentions over the facticity of sacred facts, the sacredness of authorities, the meaning of ritual practices, and the sharedness of collective representations. That which the social order placed beyond interdiction was being questioned, and that required defense.

Further, in pointing out that liminality must come to an end we rein Turner back in a little closer to Durkheim. Clearly the periodic social gatherings for celebrating social solidarity that Durkheim discusses in *The Elementary Forms* are liminal periods of close contact with the sacred. But their importance is in their function for the on-going society, not in their own nature. By focusing on the extent to which they are a rupture of the routine activities of that society – their anti-structure elements – Turner misses this point. Liminal periods can also be a celebration of structure, as in Shils' and Young's (in Shils 1975) famous analysis of the coronation of Queen Elizabeth II, Katz's and Dayan's work on media events (for example, in this volume), and my work on the Olympics (Rothenbuhler, 1985b). Conversely, as in the case analyzed here, liminal periods can contain challenges to a given social order – challenges precisely because they are not anti-structural. These factionally liminal activities are, rather, other-structural and so are challenges to the facticity of the dominant structure's social facts. As such they not only touch but violently poke at the sacred foundation of society.

Notes

1 My thanks go especially to Daniel Dayan, in whose seminar this paper was first conceived. I also want to thank Elihu Katz, John Peters, Dan Schiller and Jeff Alexander, each of whom made helpful comments on an earlier draft. Jeff Alexander's editing also improved a somewhat unwieldy manuscript.

2 The group was founded in 1905 and, by the testimony of a few members, still exists, although it has not been much more than an office in Chicago and some letterheads for many years; see Conlin 1969; Renshaw 1967; Thompson and Murfin, 1976.

3 Here and below, my information on the Wobblies and their strikes comes from a number of highly similar texts; see Brissenden 1919; Conlin 1969; DeCaux 1978; Foner 1965; Kornbluh 1964; Renshaw 1967; Taft 1983; Taft and Ross 1969; and Thompson and Murfin 1976. Brissenden and Foner are the most detailed and most thoroughly documented works; Kornbluh provides a valuable collection of original Wobbly material including articles, pamphlets, songs, cartoons, and photographs.

4 Accounts are available in most Wobbly histories, but Foner (1965) provides the most detail and the most thorough documentation.

References

Austin, J. L. 1962. *How to Do Things with Words* (2nd edn). Cambridge, MA: Harvard University Press.

Barthes, R. 1968 [1964]. *Elements of Semiology*. Selec. and trans. A. Lavers and C. Smith. New York: Hill and Wang.

1972 [1957]. *Mythologies*. Selec. & trans. A. Lavers. New York: Hill and Wang.

1977. *Image, Music, Text*. Selec. and trans. S. Heath. New York: Hill and Wang.

Brecher, J. 1972. *Strike*. Boston: South End Press.

Brissenden, P. F. 1919. *The I.W.W.: A Study in American Syndicalism*. No. 193 of *Studies in History, Economics and Public Law*. New York: Columbia University.

Conlin, J. R. 1969. *Bread and Roses Too: Studies of the Wobblies*. Westport, Connecticut: Greenwood Publishing.

DeCaux, L. 1978. *The Living Spirit of the Wobblies*. New York: International Publishers.

Douglas, M. 1978 [1966]. *Purity and Danger: An Analysis of the Concepts of Pollution and Taboo*. London: Routledge and Kegan Paul.

Douglas, M. and B. Isherwood. 1982 [1979]. *The World of Goods: Towards an Anthropology of Consumption*. New York: Norton.

Douglas, M. and A. Wildavsky. 1982. *Risk and Culture: An Essay on the Selection of Technical and Environmental Dangers*. Berkeley and Los Angeles: University of California Press.

Durkheim, E. 1965 [1912]. *The Elementary Forms of the Religious Life*. New York: Free Press.

Durkheim, E. and M. Mauss. 1963. *Primitive Classification*. Trans. and ed. R. Needham. Chicago: University of Chicago Press.

Foner, P. S. 1965. *The Industrial Workers of the World: 1905–1917*. Vol. 4 of *History of the Labor Movement in the United States*. New York: International Publishers.

Gennep, A. van. 1909. *The Rites of Passage*. Trans. M. B. Vizedom and G. L. Caffee. London: Routledge and Kegan Paul.

Gusfield, J. R. 1981. *The Culture of Public Problems: Drinking-Driving and the Symbolic Order*. Chicago: University of Chicago Press.

Gusfield, J. R. and J. Michalowicz. 1984. "Secular Symbolism: Studies of Ritual, Ceremony, and the Symbolic Order in Modern Life." *Annual Review of Sociology* 10: 417–35.

Hebdige, D. 1979. *Subculture: The Meaning of Style*, London: Methuen.

House, J. S. 1981. "Social Structure and Personality." In M. Rosenberg and R. H. Turner, eds., *Social Psychology: Sociological Perspectives*. New York: Basic Books.

Kornbluh, J. L. 1964. ed. *Rebel Voices: An I.W.W. Anthology*. Ann Arbor: University of Michigan Press.

Lévi-Strauss, C. 1963. *Structural Anthropology*. Trans. C. Jacobson and B. G. Schoeff. New York: Basic Books.

Lukes, S. 1975. "Political Ritual and Social Integration." *Sociology* 9: 289–308.

Merton, R. K. 1968. *Social Theory and Social Structure*. New York: Free Press.

Parsons, T. 1954. "The Present Position and Prospects of Systematic Theory in Sociology." In *Essays in Sociological Theory* (rev. edn). New York: Free Press.

Renshaw, P. 1967. *The Wobblies: The Story of Syndicalism in the United States*. New York: Doubleday.

Rothenbuhler, E. W. 1985a. "Cracks in the Structure and Process of Society: Status Inconsistency as a Problem of Interpretation." In H. Strasser and R W. Hodge, eds., *Status Inconsistency in Modern Societies*. Duisburg, FRG: Sozialwissenschaftliche Kooperative.

1985b. "Media Events, Civil Religion, and Social Solidarity: The Living

Room Celebration of the Olympic Games." Unpublished Ph.D. Dissertation, Annenberg School of Communications, University of Southern California.

Sahlins, M. 1976. *Culture and Practical Reason*. Chicago: University of Chicago Press.

Shils, E. 1975. *Center and Periphery: Essays in Macrosociology*. Chicago: University of Chicago Press.

Simmel, G. 1955. *Conflict and the Web of Group-Affiliations*. Trans. K. H. Wolff and R. Bendix. New York: Free Press.

Taft, P. 1983. "Workers of a New Century." In R. B. Morris, ed., *A History of the American Worker*. Princeton: Princeton University Press.

Taft, P. and P. Ross. 1969. "American Labor Violence: Its Causes, Characters, and Outcome." In H. D. Graham and T. R. Gurr, eds., *The History of Violence in America: Historical and Comparative Perspectives*. New York: Praeger.

Thompson, F. and P. Murfin. 1976. *The I.W.W.: Its First Seventy Years (1905–1975)*. Chicago: Industrial Workers of the World.

Turkle, S. R. 1975. "Symbol and Festival in the French Student Uprising (May–June 1968)." In S. F. Moore and B. G. Myerhoff, eds. *Symbol and Politics in Communal Ideology: Cases and Questions*. Ithaca, NY: Cornell University Press.

Turner, V. 1975 [1974]. *Dramas, Fields, and Metaphors: Symbolic Action in Human Society*. Ithaca, NY: Cornell University Press.

1977 [1969]. *The Ritual Process: Structure and Anti-structure*. Ithaca, NY: Cornell University Press.

1982. *From Ritual to Theatre: The Human Seriousness of Play*. New York: Performing Arts Journals Publications.

Williams, R. 1983 [1958]. *Culture and Society: 1780–1950*. New York: Columbia University Press.

Willis, P. E. 1978. *Profane Culture*. London: Routledge and Kegan Paul.

Micro and macro in symbolic context

4 Religious elements in friendship: Durkheimian theory in an empirical context[1]

Ruth A. Wallace and Shirley F. Hartley

Introduction

Emile Durkheim's work on religion is well known, but his work on friendship is not, perhaps because much of it exists in an as yet untranslated necrology that he wrote for his close friend, Victor Hommay.[2] Although Durkheim wrote it early in his professional career, well before shifting his interests to the study of religion, this necrology contains some of the religious concepts elaborated later in *The Elementary Forms of the Religious Life*.

Durkheim briefly discusses friendship in *The Division of Labor in Society* (1964 [1893]:54–6), and alludes to it in *Moral Education* (1961 [1925]:240). Moreover, only a few social theorists have seriously analyzed the phenomenon of friendship as an important unit of social solidarity (Toennies 1957:42; Simmel 1950:326; Sorokin 1943:167, 1947:100; Collins 1975:124). Many more theorists have alluded to it only peripherally or implicitly in their writings (Parsons 1951:62,189,418; Blau 1964:36; Mullin 1979:35; Goffman 1983:8), and most have simply ignored it.[3] Very few social theorists have compiled either quantitative or qualitative data on this phenomenon. In this chapter, we explore Durkheim's ideas on friendship. Arguing on the basis of interpretation as well as empirical data, we suggest that Durkheim viewed friendship as a functional alternative to religion for individuals in modern society.

Durkheim's preoccupation with social integration

Social solidarity – group cohesion based on shared values – is a theme that runs throughout Emile Durkheim's work. In his evolutionary model, *The Division of Labor*, Durkheim argued that the absence of social integration and the integrative sentiments that accompany it was one of the chief characteristics of modern societies. In *Suicide* (1951 [1897]) he hypo-thesized that the lack of both integration and regulation (egoism and anomie) accounted for higher suicide rates.

This preoccupation and his view that modern individuals lack a sense of meaning led Durkheim to propose a possible solution. He saw occu-pational groups as supplying the *Gemeinschaft* element that was missing in a predominantly *Gesellschaft* society.[4] In the Preface to the 2nd edition of *Division of Labor* written after the completion of *Suicide*, Durkheim elabo-rated on the individual's need for such groupings:

A nation can be maintained only if, between the State and the individual, there is intercalated a whole series of secondary groups near enough to the individuals to attract them strongly in their sphere of action and drag them, in this way, into the general torrent of social life. (p. 28)

This integrative function cannot be limited to occupational groups alone, as Durkheim's use of the phrase "series of secondary groups" sug-gests. For instance, in his extensive writings on education, Durkheim strongly emphasized the integrative function of the school. He saw the creation of patriotic citizens as the primary aim of the public schools in France. A striking example is his statement concerning the bravery of the French troops during the First World War (1919:188):

All peoples ... render homage to the virtues she [France] has shown, the heroism of her troops, to the grave and calm endurance with which the country has borne the frightful calamities of a war unparalleled in history. What does this mean if not that our educational methods have produced the best effects that could be ex-pected of them; that our public school has made men of the children confided to it?

Another secondary group mentioned by Durkheim which arouses a sentiment of solidarity is the family. Alexander (1982:268) presents Durk-heim's argument that the family's subjective interaction produces a kind of religious cohesion. He concludes that what Durkheim had in mind was a private domestic religion, a "new religion of the hearth."

In this chapter we argue that friendship can be seen as another func-tional alternative to religion in modern society because it provides the type of integrative element Durkheim proposed in his discussion of secondary groups. We view friendship as a quintessential sociological phenomenon. It necessarily involves an orientation to another individual, for friendship is an intimate relationship between two human beings which results in a social bonding. In addition we assume that close friend-ships, like religion, can offer a solution to the problem of meaning for the individuals involved.

In his final great work, *The Elementary Forms of the Religious Life*, Durkheim examined the integrative force of religion in primitive societies. Religion, as defined by Durkheim (p. 62), "is a unified system of beliefs and practices relative to sacred things, that is to say, things set apart and forbidden – beliefs and practices which unite into one single moral community called a Church, all those who adhere to them."

We will show in the next section that Durkheim's work on friendship does, in fact, include some of the religious concepts he presented later in *The Elementary Forms*.[5] Moreover, when we analyzed data we have been gathering over the past several years, we discovered many of Durkheim's transcendental and integrative references in respondents' characterizations of their friendships. In both depth interviews and extensive written responses to questionnaires, respondents described friendship in terms that included both manifest and latent religious concepts.

We begin by examining the link between friendship and religion implicit in some of the lesser known writings of Durkheim. We then discuss our research and use examples from it to illuminate the ways in which people characterize friendship in religious terms. Rather than looking at the entire continuum of the phenomenon of friendship, we will concentrate on closest or best friends. It is in these intimate relationships that religious transcendence – that is, a sense of extending beyond oneself and feeling a sense of unity with others – is most evident.

Durkheim on religion in friendship

Initially it may seem strange to look to Durkheim for insights on a micro-level phenomenon like friendship.[6] However, there is a rich source for Durkheim's subjective interpretation of friendship in the necrology written by him on the premature death of his close friend Victor Hommay, published in *Emile Durkheim Textes: 1. Elements d'une Théorie Sociale* (1975:418–24). Hommay had been one of Durkheim's closest friends since their student days at the École Normale Supérieure, and he took his own life in 1886.[7] Of his friendship with Hommay, Durkheim wrote the following (1975:419):

I do not remember how we came to be linked. One can only suppose that it happened by itself, little by little, for I cannot recall any particular circumstance giving birth to a friendship which soon became for me the sweetest intimacy.

Later Durkheim drew on his own experience as a student when he wrote in *Moral Education* that what is taught to students is not as important as "how to make them acquire a liking for the collective life." He explains that, as a result of such experience, "The child feels himself stronger, more confident, when he feels that he is not alone. There is something in all common activities that warms the heart and fortifies the will." Durkheim continues:

There is a pleasure in saying "we" rather than "I," because anyone in a position to say "we" feels behind him a support, a force on which he can count, a force that is much more intense than that upon which isolated individuals can rely. (1961 [1925]:240)

That Durkheim saw the school performing an integrative function is well known (Coser 1971; Bellah 1973; Wallace 1973; Wallwork 1972). But a religious element is also contained in Durkheim's very choice of words. We juxtapose the above quote with an excerpt from his *Elementary Forms* to elaborate this sacred element of friendship:

The believer who has communicated with his god is not merely a man who sees new truths of which the unbeliever is ignorant; he is a man who is *stronger*. He feels within him more force, either to endure the trials of existence, or to conquer them. (p. 464)

It would seem that the school performs a religious function, since it encourages its students in the formation of friendships and in common activities in order to, as Durkheim puts it (1961 [1925]:240), "give the child a taste for this pleasure and to instill in him the need for it." In Durkheim's eyes, the immediate environment of the school can (and should) facilitate a liking for the collective life among students. Though he does not explicitly mention friendships here, Durkheim's own experiences of friendship during his student days suggest to us that he includes them implicitly.

The depth of the relationship with Hommay is clearly indicated in Durkheim's statements in the necrology. Moreover, the direct link between friendship and religion emerges when Durkheim says of Hommay (1975:424), "He had the passion of self-sacrifice and the religion of friendship." The way Durkheim describes his friendship with Hommay, and his own words, "the religion of friendship," suggest a religious quality in the relationship. We now turn to these religious concepts, and in doing so we also draw on Durkheim's major work on religion, *The Elementary Forms of the Religious Life*.

Religious elements in friendship

Four of the central religious concepts in *The Elementary Forms* may be related to Durkheim's statements regarding friendship: (1) common actions or rituals; (2) the experience of a transformation or rebirth; (3) the experience of a moral force or support; and (4) self-sacrifice. After describing each of them in turn, we present an analysis of our data on friendship, utilizing these religious concepts.[8]

Common actions or rituals

In *The Elementary Forms* Durkheim describes (p. 52) the religious rite as involving "words, expressions, formulas which can be pronounced only by the mouth of the consecrated person; these are gestures and movements which everybody cannot perform." Moreover, Durkheim (pp. 431–2) emphasizes the importance of the believers coming together and sharing when he says.

The essential thing is that men are assembled, that sentiments are felt in common and expressed in common acts ... Men who feel themselves united ... by a community of interest and tradition, assemble and become conscious of their moral unity.

What are the rituals or common actions of a friendship? Durkheim only alludes to them when he uses the term "sweetest intimacy" to describe the quality of his conversations with Hommay. We suggest that what makes these conversations like sacred rituals is that they are necessarily exclusive and they are set apart from the ordinary. Only with a close friend does one discuss the subjects closest to one's heart, subjects which are most sacred to a person. Time spent conversing with a friend is time separated from the mundane or profane. It is time set aside for the experience of the "weness" of the relationship as an end in itself.

The repetition of these meetings is as important in the creation of a friendship as is the repetition of religious rituals to the believer. Recall that Durkheim described the birth of the friendship with Hommay as happening "little by little," through the sharing of countless activities. Friends strive to create time and space for repeated meetings, conversations and joint actions, just as religious believers set aside time for their participation in sacred rituals.

Durkheim describes the time at the École as "three holy years" for Hommay. He continues (1975:419),

But for us, his friends, what perhaps was more striking to us were the lessons we heard from him and above all, his ardent conversations in which, daily, he opened himself to us freely, easily and unreservedly.

Just as the most sacred rituals of a tribal people are not usually discussed or seen by outsiders, so the intimate conversations with a friend are not readily shared with outsiders. We found, for instance, that only in depth interviews were we able to establish a sense of trust and then obtain data on the ritual aspect of our respondents' friendship experiences. One respondent described her intimate conversations with a close friend thus:

Friendship is the most important and vital type of relationship there is, at least it is for me. I find I am able to talk about anything to my best friend, things I feel I can't talk about to anyone else. I have many friends, but I have one best friend who is similar to me and we have the same attitudes about things. This type of relationship is very rare, and I have only felt this way about only this one person. I mainly feel this is what the friendship is about, and this is the only person I can tell all my problems to and trust.

Another respondent, who explicitly refers to the ritual element in friendship, describes it thus:

Friendship means that you have a close relationship with someone that you can either share your thoughts, experiences, troubles or hobbies with. It is something that is very genuine. It entails people who have to be willing to devote or take on the responsibility of giving and sharing the self to somebody or a group of people. To me friendship is something like a ritual; you have to continue to do it, you just can't be someone's friend for two days and then completely give them up.

The intimate nature of the relationship is both celebrated and expressed in the friendship ritual of conversations. Both Durkheim and our respondents attest to the central importance of the experiences they share with close friends, most often in the form of intimate conversations. Collins (1975:24), in fact, defines friendship as "a history of mutually rewarding conversational exchanges." Because frequent conversation is such an important element in friendship, letters and telephone calls are often substituted when face-to-face interaction is impossible. To repeat the words of our respondent quoted above, "Friendship is something like a ritual; you have to continue to do it."

The experience of a transformation or rebirth
In *The Elementary Forms* (p. 54) Durkheim discusses the change of state experienced by a religious participant. Through the religious initiation rites the believer's whole being is transformed. The new believer could be described as experiencing a rebirth because she/he has passed from the profane to the sacred realm. As Durkheim puts it (p. 465), religious sentiments "raise him outside himself." In short, the new believer is a different person.

Durkheim's definition of religion (p. 62) also includes a common belief system; as he puts it, "a unified system of beliefs and practices." The degree of trust involved in a close friendship suggests that strongly held beliefs would tend to be shared, for differences in belief could be divisive, and thus threaten the relationship. We would expect, then, that friends who are religious believers would share the same faith, and this has been documented by social researchers (Heirich 1977; Bainbridge and Stark 1981).[9] Among believers a common religious membership tends to increase the solidarity of a friendship.

In like manner, the conversations and shared activities of two people which culminate in a friendship transform the two separate individuals into a new social entity. What originally was two separate "Is" is now a "we." Note what Durkheim says concerning his own transformation through the friendship with Hommay:

During our three years at the École, we truly lived the same life: we worked in the same room; we pursued the same studies; we even spent almost all of our free days together. In the course of those long conversations, what plans did we not make for each other! I can no longer recall them without sadness and bitterness.

For Durkheim the experiences he shared with Hommay, especially the long conversations, both led to and then maintained the friendship relationship. The necrology suggests that Hommay's friendship transformed the time Durkheim spent at the École.

In his brief analysis of friendship Sorokin also refers to the transformation experience. He explains (1943:167) that when there is a contact between the two persons involved in a friendship relationship, "the individual ego is merged in a sense of 'we.' ... Joys and sorrows are shared in common. The individuals need one another, seek one another, love one another and gladly sacrifice themselves for one another – in brief, they represent a single solidary body." Later Sorokin argues (1947:100) that in a true friendship relationship there is a spontaneous internal unity between the friends, "a complete merging of their selves into a single 'we.'"

When describing their own friendships many respondents talked about their experiences of this transformation of self. One spoke of a real friend as "an extension of myself, as I am of her or him." Another said,

It is something that is within, something between people that is unexplainable with words. It's an inner peace between two people. It's when they KNOW exactly what's going on with you before you tell them. It's a bonding that is so reassuring and comforting. It's wonderful!

A young male (age 21) presented a graphic description of the we-ness of friendship when he said,

To me, friendship is like two notes in harmony. Each separate, unique and beautiful by themselves; yet when together, they blend and strengthen their good points.

Another respondent directly mentioned transformation:

Recently I went through a major transformation. I've always been there for my friends, but I never let them be there for me; I lived in a shell. Not long ago I found myself in a situation that tore me up, and I discovered what true friendship and love is all about. My closest friends were there for me – they let me cry on their shoulders, yell at their ears, and made me laugh when I thought all my laughter had gone out of my life. They gave me back myself and glued us together in a special way that will never let me go back inside my shell.

The transformational element is also alluded to by Mullin (1979:31–5), when he describes the significance of communication between friends thus: "To communicate is not to speak and hear another but to recognize that self and other are interchangeable." Because of the sacredness of the relationship friends tend to refrain from allowing themselves or others to speak ill of their close friends.

The experience of a moral force or support

Earlier we quoted Durkheim on the moral support of a "we" relationship as "a force that is much more intense than that upon which the isolated individual can rely." In the second half of his definition of religion, Durkheim says (1961 [1912]:62) that religious beliefs and practices "unite into one single moral community called a Church, all those who adhere to them." In like manner the mutual trust and the intimate conversations between friends unite them into a single moral community called a friendship.

Durkheim explains (pp. 463–4) that believers who lead the religious life and have a direct sensation of what it really is feel that "the real function of religion is not to make us think, to enrich our knowledge . . . but rather, it is to make us act, to aid us to live." Religion can, then, provide a solution to the problem of meaning in life. What are the consequences when such moral support is lost? For Hommay, the experience of separation from his friends was debilitating. In a letter to Durkheim he said (1975:421):

When I think of those good years in the École . . . especially in this second year, where we lived so much of the real life, the only one worth being attached to, when I think of our dreams of that time, of our concerns, of our works, the present life appears to me as something pale, discolored, monotonous, insipid; and I really wonder whether the nice days are really not over for us, for a long while at least. When my thoughts darken too much, I close myself up in my books which are now my only friends . . .

For Hommay, living without intimate friends was living without meaning. It was not long after writing the words above that he took his own life.[10]

Our respondents likewise spoke with much conviction about the moral support of friendship. A very successful businessman in his late 40s said,

I don't believe in God in human form. But why is it that we love? What force allows us to risk our lives for another? A similar force or power, a magnetic force is involved in friendship. One can't deny that force between two people, the caring, intensity . . . of different strengths with different people, but very real.

Another respondent explained,

Part of friendship is learning to be a source of support for each other. There reaches a point in a relationship when you *know* that person will be there for you when things go bad.

Finally, a mother gives testimony of a friend's support in a crisis situation:

Barbara was crucial to me when I really needed help. I have known her for a long time. When my son had cancer she stood by me the whole time. She made me strong when I felt like collapsing. She built my confidence up when I thought there was just no hope. Even after he passed away she was still there, and I love her for everything she did.

How are the elements of religion related to the friendship process? People who have experienced mutual trust in intimate conversations with a close friend tend to form a close social bond as the two individuals become one in friendship. As a consequence of this process, wherein the element of ritual experience leads to transformation, friends feel the strength of the bond, which in turn gives meaning and power to their lives. In addition to moral support, which can be seen as a reward of the relationship, we now turn to another consequence of the friendship bond, which can be viewed as a responsibility, namely a readiness to devote unlimited amounts of time and energy to a friend's welfare.

Self-sacrifice

As we saw above, for Durkheim self-sacrifice is at the heart of friendship. Earlier we noted that Durkheim described his friend Hommay thus: "He had the passion of self-sacrifice and the religion of friendship." Durkheim also recalls an example of Hommay's self-sacrifice. When on vacation in Paris a year before Hommay's death, Durkheim, feeling ill and fatigued, wrote to Hommay who was in Angers (about 175 miles from Paris), and expressed his anxieties about his illness. Hommay immediately arranged a few free days for himself and rushed to Paris, knowing Durkheim was alone. Within twenty-four hours Hommay was at Durkheim's door. Durkheim explains (1975:424):

He came only to keep me company and comfort me. Then we spent a few good days together which reminded us of the happy time in the École. But we were not to meet again.

In *The Division of Labor in Society* Durkheim (1964 [1893]:412–13) had written, "True love, which consists in self-giving, necessarily implies that I subordinate myself to an end transcending me ... For example, does conjugal society deny that man and wife give themselves mutually and wholly to one another?"

For the individuals involved in a close relationship, the rituals of friendship create and recreate the basic norm of friendship, which is the readiness to sacrifice oneself for one's friend. Just as a believer is willing to sacrifice all for her/his faith, so is a friend ready to give all for the friendship, but the "faith" of friendship is faith in a friend, rather than faith in a deity or another abstract moral force.

The following statements from our respondents illustrate the importance of this concept, and the different forms self-sacrifice can take. One respondent sums up the voluntary commitment to sacrifice for a friend thus:

Friendship is a feeling you have for a person, that is you want to help this person or they want to help you in making you laugh or helping you through a rough time. It entails a willingness to give of yourself and a willingness to receive openly of others without being judgmental.

A male respondent said,

I feel very strongly about self-sacrifice in friendship. I feel that it is a very necessary and vital part of a friendship. We judge our worth as a friend by how much we are willing to give to that friend.

We give, not because we expect anything in return; we give because we love and value the friendship. We judge not in the amount of giving, but in the meaning behind it. We give because we love. And we love because we give.

Likewise a middle-aged male said,

Friendship entails being aware of the other person's needs and feelings. It means being there when the other person needs you. It means accepting support when you need it. A true friendship will last over time and space.

What is it that inspires a friend's self-sacrifice? Blau (1964:36) argues that close friendships are of intrinsic importance to individuals. Friends are willing to make great sacrifices in order to continue the association, which is in itself extremely valuable to them. Blau continues,

Under these conditions of intrinsic attachment, selfless devotion to another's welfare can be observed ... Contributions to the welfare of a loved one are not intended to elicit specific returns in the form of proper extrinsic benefits for each favor done. Instead, they serve as expressive symbols of the individual's firm commitment to the relationship and as inducements for the other to make a corresponding commitment and continue the association.

As suggested above, the basic structure emerging from our analysis of the religious elements in friendship is the following: participation in the rituals of friendship leads to a transformation experience, and with the formation of a friendship a new social entity emerges. The two remaining elements, moral support and self-sacrifice, are consequences of the friendship bond. We view friendship as a continuing process, similar to the process whereby religion is maintained. As long as the rituals of friendship are practiced on a frequent basis, that is, as long as the friends continue to engage in intimate conversations with each other (communications which are characterized by Simmel (1950:326) as "reciprocal revelations"), the friendship bond will not only be recreated and maintained but it will also be strengthened. Durkheim (1961 [1912]:22) explains that religious rituals "excite, maintain or recreate certain mental states." In like manner reciprocal revelations between friends recreate the friendship bond and the concomitant feelings of support and meaning in life which, in turn, inspire self-sacrifice.

Conclusion

In this chapter we have suggested that the work of the "later Durkheim" may not constitute a radical change from his previous thinking. His life-long interest in social integration led him to devote much of his professional career to an analysis of functional alternatives to religion in modern society, such as family, friendships, occupational groups, education and patriotism.[11]

Because they share some characteristics, solidarity, friendship and religion are overlapping concepts. Although Durkheim typically uses solidarity with reference to large groups or total societies, friendship, which implies cohesion between two human beings, can be viewed as a micro-level form of solidarity. Religion and friendship are also similar in that both concepts include a coming together and sharing, as well as a solution for the individual to the problem of meaning in life.

In searching for the religious elements in friendship, our chief sources of data were twofold. First we examined a eulogy Durkheim wrote for his best friend in 1887, during his early professional period, which illustrated Durkheim's preoccupation with the issue of social solidarity. Durkheim's analysis of his friendship with Hommay included some elements of religion which he later elaborated in *The Elementary Forms of the Religious Life*, namely ritual, transformation or rebirth, moral force and self-sacrifice. We have found Durkheim's ideas useful for the analysis of our on-going study of friendship, and we want to emphasize the need for further research which will incorporate these Durkheimian insights.

Notes

1 We want to thank Charles Camic, Kathryn Meadow-Orlans, Whitney Pope, David Sciulli, Jacqueline Wiseman, and Ernest Wallwork for their helpful comments on earlier drafts.

2 A necrology, similar to an obituary, is a eulogy for a deceased person. We would like to thank John Frey and Pierre Henri Barbe for their help in the translation.

3 Although one might be tempted to speculate on the reasons for such a generally off-handed treatment of a uniquely sociological phenomenon on the part of social theorists, we feel that it is beyond the scope of this chapter.

4 See Luhmann (1985) for a more recent analysis of the diminishing importance of religion for pattern maintenance in modern society.

5 We agree with Bellah (1973:xlvi) that Durkheim's shift of interest to religion should not be overdramatized, for he recognized the importance of religion in his earliest writings; see also Wallwork (1985). Hommay's necrology is an indication of this early interest.

6 See Hammond (1983) on Durkheim's contribution to the sociology of emotions.

7 Hommay's death may have been the motivating force for Durkheim's study of suicide. Durkheim's first article on suicide was published in 1887, one year after Hommay's death.

8 Data on the multiple meanings of friendship have been compiled from both depth interviews and a questionnaire administered to a convenience sample of 233 adults, ranging in age from 18 to 84. This is an on-going exploratory study of friendship as a social phenomenon. Students trained in social-psychological interview methods were asked to search for adults with contrasting friendship patterns, e.g., those with many and those with few friends. One of the authors (Hartley) personally conducted 28 in-depth interviews. We present these quotations as illustrative of the elements of religion in friendship as suggested by Durkheim.

9 In an earlier study, Wallace (1975:350) found a positive relationship between intimate friendships and change of religious affiliation. Subjects describing most

of their intimate friends as Catholic were more likely to join the Catholic Church.

10 Lukes (1972:51) suggests that the impact of his friend's suicide is evident in a number of passages in *Suicide* where Durkheim relates egoistic suicide to isolation. The issue of Hommay's isolation is also raised by Alexander (1982:416), when he points to the central importance of friendship for Hommay. Alexander explains, "It was the closeness and intimacy of Hommay's contacts that mattered, and small groups and individual friendships were more important than large groups and public relationships."

11 One wonders to what degree Durkheim experienced "religious cohesion" in his own life in his friendships (especially after Hommay's death), family, occupational groups (like the staff at *L'Année Sociologique*, faculty and students at the university), and, finally, from his own patriotic efforts during the First World War.

References

Alexander, Jeffrey. 1982. *The Antinomies of Classical Thought: Marx and Durkheim.* vol. 2. *Theoretical Logic in Sociology.* Berkeley: University of California Press.

Bainbridge, William and Rodney Stark. 1981. "Friendship, Religion, and the Occult: A Network Study." *Review of Religious Research* 22: 313–27.

Bellah, Robert N. 1973. *Emile Durkheim on Morality and Society.* Chicago: University of Chicago Press.

Blau, Peter M. 1964. *Exchange and Power in Social Life.* New York: John Wiley.

Collins, Randall. 1975. *Conflict Sociology.* New York: Academic Press.

    1981. 'On the Microfoundations of Macrosociology." *American Journal of Sociology* 86:984–1014.

Coser, Lewis A. 1971. *Masters of Sociological Thought.* New York: Harcourt, Brace, Jovanovich.

Durkheim, Emile. 1964 [1893]. *The Division of Labor in Society.* New York: Free Press.

    1951 [1897]. *Suicide: A Study in Sociology.* Trans. John A. Spaulding and George Simpson. Glencoe, Ill.: Free Press.

    1961 [1912]. *The Elementary Forms of the Religious Life.* Trans. Joseph Ward Swain. New York: Collier.

    1919. "The School of Tomorrow." In Ferdinand Buisson and Frederick E. Farrington, eds., *French Educational Ideals of Today.* New York: World Book Company.

    1961 [1925]. *Moral Education: A Study in the Theory and Application of the Sociology of Education.* New York: Free Press.

    1975. *Textes.* vol. 1. *Elements d'une théorie sociale,* edited by V. Karady. Paris: Éditions de Minuit.

Goffman, Erving. 1983. "The Interaction Order." *American Sociological Review*

48:1–17.

Hammond, Michael. 1983. "The Sociology of Emotions and the History of Social Differentiation." In Randall Collins, ed., *Sociological Theory*, pp. 90–119. San Francisco: Jossey-Bass.

Heirich, Max. 1977. "Change of Heart: A Test of Some Widely Held Theories about Religious Conversion." *American Journal of Sociology* 83:653–77.

Luhmann, Niklas. 1985. "Society, Meaning. Religion ... Based on Self-Reference." *Sociological Analysis* 46:5–20.

Lukes, Steven. 1972. *Emile Durkheim: His Life and Work*. New York: Harper and Row.

Mullin, Jay. 1979. "Phenomenology and Friendship." In Alan Blum and Peter McHugh, eds., *Friends, Enemies and Strangers*, pp. 31–5. Norwood, NJ: Ablex.

Parsons, Talcott. 1951. *The Social System*. New York: Free Press.

    1973. "Durkheim on Religion Revisited: Another Look at the Elementary Forms of the Religious Life." In Charles Y. Glock and Phillip E. Hammond, eds., *Beyond the Classics? Essays in the Scientific Study of Religion*, pp. 156–80. New York: Harper and Row.

Simmel, Georg. 1950. *The Sociology of Georg Simmel*. Trans. and ed. Kurt Wolff. Glencoe: Free Press.

Sorokin, Pitirim. 1943. *The Crisis of Our Age*. New York: E. P. Dutton.

    1947. *Society, Culture and Personality: Their Structure and Dynamics*. New York: Harper and Row.

Toennies, Ferdinand. 1957. *Community and Society*. Trans and ed. Charles P. Loomis. East Lansing: Michigan State University Press.

Wallace, Ruth A. 1973. "The Secular Ethic and the Spirit of Patriotism." *Sociological Analysis* 34:3–11.

    1975. "A Model of Change of Religious Affiliation." *Journal for the Scientific Study of Religion* 14:345–55.

    1985. "Religion, Privatization and Maladaptation: Comment on Niklas Luhmann." *Sociological Analysis* 46:27–31.

Wallwork, Ernest. 1972. *Durkheim: Morality and Milieu*. Cambridge, MA: Harvard University Press.

    1985. "Durkheim's Early Sociology of Religion." *Sociological Analysis* 46:201–17.

5 The Durkheimian tradition in conflict sociology

Randall Collins

Of the great classic figures of sociology, at the present time Durkheim's reputation is the lowest. In recent decades, Marx has been riding at his highest wave of sociological popularity of the entire century since his death in 1883. Weber, too, is probably at his peak influence, especially in the U.S., but also for the first time in German sociology, where he has recently become the subject of massive reinterpretation and appropriation by various theoretical programs. As Marxism falters in its appeal in Germany, Weberianism looks in good position to overtake it. But Emile Durkheim, the most classic of the triumvirate – the only one to actually hold a chair of sociology, the author of sociology's most powerful manifestos, "Mr. Sociology" himself – is probably at his low point in popularity in the seventy years since his death in 1915.

The reason is not hard to find. Durkheim was introduced into sociology largely under the auspices of the functionalists of the English-speaking world: Radcliffe-Brown and his followers in Britain, Merton and Parsons in the U.S. Relatedly, Durkheim was picked up as a founder of multivariate statistics, and hence given a place in the positivist/ quantitative camp of the 1950s and 60s. No wonder then that most of the intellectual factions today have nothing but disdain for Durkheim. He is regarded as a conservative defender of the status quo by the Left, as an arch-functionalist by the anti-functionalists, as a naive unilinear evolutionist by the historicists. The subjectivistic sociologies tend to see in Durkheim, if not always a materialist, at least a social reductionist of a disturbingly deterministic sort. For the humanists, Durkheim is the anti-Christ; for the micro-sociologists, Durkheim is the most reified of the macro. It is small wonder that Durkheim's reputation is at its ebb.

The ill repute is due to a rather one-sided selection of Durkheim's works. His most famous book is no doubt *Suicide* (1966 [1897]): partly for its popularistic topic (and Durkheim's anthologizably unexpected explanation), but also because of its use of multivariate statistics. But neither substantively nor methodically is *Suicide* considered very forefront any more (Pope 1976). It is a "sealed" classic, safely dead and turned over to the intellectual historians. Some of the ideas of *The Division of Labor* (1964 [1893]) are current. Interpretations of Durkheim's main theory (e.g. Turner 1983) have stressed mainly his macro-structural functionalism and evolutionism, the factors explaining the differentiation of society on the largest scale. *The Rules of the Sociological Method* (1982 [1895]) also has a certain amount of notoriety for its outspoken emphasis on *sui generis* social facts (as a sign of the times, repudiated in Anthony Giddens' *New Rules of Sociological Method* (1976)). Durkheim's rather sensationalist interpretation of the functional significance of crime is also known, though few sociologists defend it (three of them: Kai Erikson 1966; Donald Black 1984; and myself, 1981a).

What is left out? Generally speaking, what I would consider the more valuable parts of Durkheim. His most important book, *The Elementary Forms of the Religious Life* (1961 [1912]) seems to be regarded as a special-ized matter for sociologists of religion, though some references (usually very critical) are made to its social reductionist theory of knowledge.[1] I will show below that this book had a powerful effect on Erving Goff-man, a fact which has not dawned on most sociologists, who persist in seeing Goffman as some kind of symbolic interactionist or phenomenolo-gist: a circumstance which casts some light on how unfamiliar the ritual side of Durkheim's theory is today. The best parts of *The Division of Labor*, too, seem to be obscured under its lesser parts. The argument about the non-rational foundations of rationality, the critique of utilitaria-nism as a solution of the problem of order, and the significance of "precontractual solidarity" were stressed by Parsons (1937), no unsophisticated observer, as the foundation-stone of his own general theory of action (and presumably any other general sociology); but the message did not spread. Durkheim's powerful argument that God is a symbol of society, the forerunner of his later theory of social rituals, is surprisingly underused even in our introductory texts (though again Goffman and some other sophisticates have made good use of it); his point that the level of inclusiveness and abstraction of the gods is a corre-late of social differentiation is the foundation of Parsons' religious soci-ology, but otherwise it is generally neglected.[2]

I will argue, however, that there is an underground wing of the Durk-heimian tradition which feeds very nicely into conflict theory. In so doing, it answers most of the objections of Durkheim's modern oppon-ents. Durkheimian theory is quite viable without its functionalism. It does not neglect human situational consciousness, but offers a better handle on micro-reality, I will claim, than phenomenology, symbolic interactionism, or the other subjectivistic sociologies of today. And although one of the most famous aspects of functionalist Durkheimianism has been Davis and Moore's (1945) "Some Principles of Stratification," in fact Durkheim provides an important part of a conflict theory of stratification: the social laws determining class cultures and the moral solidarity within conflict groups. Probably the most notable Durkheimians of recent years (Basil Bernstein, Mary Douglas) have been those who apply the theory to situations of stratification.

To be sure, Durkheimian conflict sociology remains as determinist as Durkheim was himself. Though this offends our humanistic sentiments, nevertheless I think it is an intellectual virtue, not a weakness. Creating validly generalizable explanations is the name of the science game; we may never narrow down the level of real-world predictability beyond a certain limit, but the intellectual challenge is in trying, not preaching against making the effort. Durkheimian sociologists – at least some of them – have not only tried but succeeded. There are a series of principles in Durkheimian theory that hold across a very important part of sociology. It happens (and here my personal theoretical bias is obvious) that the parts of the Durkheimian intellectual tradition that fit this description are safely ensconced inside the camp of conflict theory.

Durkheim in the theory of class cultures

Durkheim himself tended to minimize the significance of social classes and their conflicts. Nevertheless, if we recognize the existence of conflicting interest groups as a major focus for sociology, Durkheim's theory provides a crucial means of showing what determines their internal group solidarity, as well as the nature of the symbols and sentiments that make up their class cultures. In short, Durkheim contributes to what has been considered in the conflict tradition the Marxian issue of class consciousness, or the Weberian notion of status groups.

To grasp this, it is necessary to treat Durkheim's theoretical statements analytically rather than concretely. That is to say, when he speaks of the principles of a "society" and its integration, we should not take this to mean that *empirically* this necessarily refers to a "whole society" as conventionally defined (which in practice usually means a political unit, especially a nation state). Instead, we should take "society" in its generic sense, as any instance of prolonged sociation, whatever its boundaries in space or in time. In this sense, a social class may well be a "society," though it need not always be; in fact, the Durkheimian theory shows us the variable conditions under which its integration and moral solidarity is greatest or weakest.[3]

The ingredients of Durkheim's theory of solidarity are in all his major works, though the formulations in *The Division of Labor* and *The Elementary Forms* are especially central. The important argument of the former, in this connection, is that a society with little internal differentiation has a strong and repressive collective conscience, along with a tendency to outbursts of emotional outrage and severe punishments for comparatively trivial or ceremonial violations of customs (taboos). At the opposite end of what we should take to be a continuum, a society with an elaborate division of labor is more formalistic in its collective consciousness, less given to violent punishment and ceremonial observance, more technical in its application of law. The point may be made in terms of religious beliefs: the tightly integrated, undifferentiated society worships particularistic symbols and distrusts the malevolent forces beyond its own group; the highly differentiated society makes its god abstract as well as universalistic, eventually arriving at the divinity of sheer moral principles. Durkheim states this argument in terms of concrete "societies," thinking of the ancient Hebrew tribes or early Greek city-states for the undifferentiated case, of modern states like France for the latter. And like Parsons (1966), who explicitly formulates the sequence of religious beliefs as historical stages, Durkheim treats his typology as a model of evolution. But it does not need to be identified with this concrete level, nor does its validity hinge on that of evolutionary theory. It does not even have to refer to entire (i.e. politically organized) societies, although it certainly helps validate the general theory that Swanson (1962) has shown comparatively that the degree of abstraction and elevation of a society's gods is correlated with its complexity of social structure, especially the number of levels of political hierarchy. Instead, one can formulate the general principles as applying to the structure of social relationships typically experienced by members of a social class. In this way, we arrive at a conception of modern stratification, in which the entire stratification order is a line-up of different types of "societies," with Durkheimian "tribes" at the bottom, and members of differentiated networks at the top.

Before expressing this in general principles, let us pause to add one more ingredient from Durkheim's corpus. In *The Elementary Forms*, Durkheim focuses on the undifferentiated end of the continuum, on the theory of "mechanical solidarity." The theory of social rituals which he develops, and applies especially to the analysis of religious ideas, is nevertheless capable of analytical abstraction and hence of wider application. For not only are the mechanisms of "mechanical solidarity" still found empirically, at certain points and times within even an overall highly differentiated modern society; the theory of social rituals itself is capable of being expressed in terms of variations. It gives what I think are some of the "basic laws" of sociology: principles of how different degrees and conditions of structural density of interaction result in degrees of "moral density" and hence in different kinds of symbolic and emotional consciousness of the group.

To put these briefly: Durkheim describes the most heightened social consciousness as the result of a highly participatory ritual. Thinking of Spencer and Gillen's description of the Arunta of central Australia, he describes the tribe coming together and becoming excited by each other's presence. (Think of the noise level at a party going up as the festivities get going.) The excitement is heightened and focused by carrying out activities in common: chants, dances, ritual gestures. During the ceremony, certain symbols are invoked, perhaps concretely represented by religious objects. For Durkheim, the social gathering is a kind of machinery for charging such objects with sacredness. They are elevated above the mundane because they now represent membership in the group (which is to say, the recollection of group emotion). Thereafter, they become "batteries" (my expression, of course, not Durkheim's) for carrying over this moral energy into subsequent situations, when individuals are away from the intense sources of moral power. Nevertheless they continue to carry society's moral consciousness with them. They guide the individual in expressions of symbolic loyalty (just as does the flag of a modern nation, as Durkheim points out); and they provide a touchstone for deciding whether other individuals are friends or foes, depending on whether or not they treat these sacred objects with respect. In the latter case, the group's moral consciousness stored up in its members is released, like a bolt of electricity, in the form of moral outrage and hence ritual punishment.[4]

Analytically, one can treat the ingredients of ritual as lying across a broad continuum in time and space. At one end of the continuum we have the highly focused situations about which Durkheim wrote: rituals themselves, where the group is assembled face to face, consciousness is centered and emotions intensified, and so forth. But this is merely the formula for the most intense kind of experience of group solidarity and its concomitants, group pressure for comformity and for moral respect for sacred objects. In general, we may characterize any individual's experiences in terms of the amount of time they spend in the presence of other people, and the extent to which they share a focus of attention and circulate common emotions among themselves; and hence we may predict from Durkheimian principles what kind of symbolic and moral consciousness he or she will have. Similarly, we may characterize a group, of any size, in terms of the typical social and moral density experienced by its members, and thus derive its resulting consciousness.

Notice that this analytical expansion of the ritual model from *The Elementary Forms* gives, as one of its derivations, the applications to entire societies which Durkheim stated in *The Division of Labor*. The sum of the daily experiences of members of undifferentiated tribal societies or small isolated communities is an overall situation of very high moral density, hence resulting in highly reified symbols of group membership and violent punishments for violations (which themselves constitute further high-density rituals). The sum of the experiences of members of a highly differentiated modern nation-state, on the other hand, tend towards the relatively low-density end of the continuum; hence the symbols charged with social significance are abstract, universalistic, and there is generally less cognitive reification (for example, religious superstition and taboos) and less emotionally compelling punishments of violations.

There are various applications of this general logic to modern stratification, of which I will mention only a few. Basil Bernstein (1971–5) shows empirically that the language codes of middle-class and working-class persons differ along precisely the dimensions predicted by the Durkheimian model: the former speak a more abstract and context-independent code, the latter a more concrete and particularistic form of talk, tailored to the consistently taken-for-granted understandings of an always-present and little-changing membership group. Herbert Gans (1962) sums up research on working-class and middle-class cultures by characterizing the former as structurally more localistic, the latter more cosmopolitan; related to the working-class structure is a cultural style which emphasizes conformity and tradition, as well as distrust of outsiders; whereas middle-class culture focuses on more abstract culture, more future orientation, an identification with rather than distrust of community groups and ideals. The middle- (or especially upper-middle) class, inhabits Durkheim's "modern" division of labor and has "organic solidarity" as its class culture; whereas the working class tends to consist of a set of localized enclaves, which Gans goes so far as to refer to as "Urban Villages" in the midst of modern society. Melvin Kohn (1977) has shown the same pattern in the child-rearing values of middle- and working-class families: the former emphasizing more abstract psychological goals for their children, the latter stressing sheer external conformity. Further, Kohn is able to show that the aspect of the typical social class situation that produces these patterns is the degree of complexity and autonomy of the work situation, which are precisely the Durkheimian dimensions of social density and differentiation of social contacts. Neither Gans nor Kohn explicitly formulates their theoretical explanations in Durkheimian terms, but the congruence with the model is striking.

One other important development of the Durkheimian tradition needs to be mentioned here. Erving Goffman's analysis of *Interaction Ritual* (1967) and of *The Presentation of Self in Everyday Life* (1959) follow the inner logic of Durkheim's model of social rituals. Goffman innovates in showing that any aspect of any social encounter, no matter how fleeting, may be taken as elements of ritual in Durkheim's sense. The more obvious of these are the little ceremonies of politeness which create shared moral solidarities, perhaps only temporarily, among interactants. But more generally and analytically, any conversation is a ritual construction of reality, as imposing – during the moments it is the subject of its members' attention – as any religious ritual (and usually as mythical), and as full of significance for their moral consciousness and group membership. As I have argued (1975:90–160), the micro-reality of such concepts as "status group" always comes down to the enactment of little moments of shared solidarity in conversations. Words and ideas, even of the most banal sort, are little sacred objects conveying social solidarity in the stratified groups which make up the larger structure of the social world.

Goffman is especially useful for translating a theory of stratification into a series of Durkheimian rituals which occur in everyday life, thus establishing an ultra-empirical basis for both theories. Goffman implicitly shows there are two different kinds of ritual relationships: those which create solidarity among insiders (sociable politeness, mutually engrossing conversations), and those which separate off dominants from subordinates (Goffman's famous picture of frontstage and backstage relationships). Most of the empirical bases of the latter are drawn from occupational settings: "teams" of workers who control the work-pace but put on a ritual of deference to the boss; "teams" of salesmen cooperating to pressure customers; "teams" of executives and officials who guard their backstage informality in order to present the maximally impressive image of their self when they ritually appear before subordinates. Goffman implicitly demonstrates that rituals are one of the weapons of class domination, as well as of the manufacture of "horizontal" class solidarity.

I have abstractly formulated the general principles of class cultures in my *Conflict Sociology* (1975:73–7), incorporating evidence of the sort cited above. The theory that emerges is couched on a high level of abstraction, in the sense that *there are multiple processes which determine various aspects of class cultures.* We are not stuck with an invariant number of monolithic classes, but have a flexible analytical instrument which can detect as many lines of cultural mixture and variation as may empirically be produced by the distribution of these causal factors across the social landscape. Some individuals or subgroups may be high on one factor of ritual interaction, low or intermediate on another. The lines of stratification are analytical principles underlying the widest possible variety of empirical structures. These principles can also be applied to historical comparisons across various communities and societies, explaining the historical differences in their cultures.[5]

1. Ritualized interaction between order-givers and order-takers. This gives us the power (Dahrendorfian) dimension of society. The Goffmanian model of this stratified interaction ritual shows that it breaks people off into competing teams, meeting on the frontstage while guarding their own informal backstages. Furthermore, we may characterize the different identifications of the classes: the order-giving class identifies with the official values, with the "sacred objects" which are the content of their order-giving discourse. The order-taking class, because it is being dominated by these rituals, tends to be implicitly alienated from them, and hence withdraws into identification with its backstage group. In Goffmanian terms, the order-giving classes have a "frontstage culture," the order-taking classes have a "backstage" culture.

2. A second dimension of class distinctions is the more directly Durkheimian morphology of social interactions. Persons who are usually in highly localized situations, always dealing with the same circle of interactants, develop a "mechanical solidarity" with the group and a corresponding form of symbolism. This is of course more common the lower one goes in the class structure (partly for motivational reasons already given in the previous principle). Persons who encounter larger numbers of persons and interact with populations of shifting composition, develop an "organic soldarity" and its symbolic accompaniments. This is exemplified in the occupational and sociable experience of the higher social classes; these all the more cosmopolitan because organizational power is created by participation in networks, the more far-flung the better.

Analytically, there are really two subprocesses operating here (which in *Conflict Sociology* I label 2.1 and 2.2). (a) There is the sheer *social and moral density per se*, the amount of time an individual spends in the presence of other people. According to the Durkheimian principle, the higher this density, the stronger the pressures to conformity for both self and others, and hence the more vehement the reaction to the violation of traditional symbols representing group membership. This, too, should determine the strength of the group boundary and the degree of distrust of outsiders. (b) The number and variety of persons with whom one comes into contact.[6] Thus individuals in *cosmopolitan networks* show Durkheim's pattern of abstract consciousness, with its correlates: more long-run orientation, less reification, more universalistic moral principles as well as conceptual generalization in thinking. (See the literature on social differences in respect for civil liberties, for instance, which I believe mainly reflects this factor, although it has usually been crudely operationalized as "class" or "education.") Those persons in *localized networks* correspondingly have reified consciousness, moral traditionalism, short-run attitudes towards time, and particularistic cognitions.

Again, we should see these are a continuum of conditions, with individuals possibly exposed to different mixtures even within the confines of any particular "class" we may focus upon. The Durkheim-based conflict theory of stratification is fully multidimensional. It is precisely these variations that determine the degree to which class consciousness, in the traditional Marxian sense, is widespread and militant, or in various degrees fragmented into smaller group loyalties.[7]

Toward a theory of ritual politics

For Durkheim, politics was a rather superficial aspect of society. Nevertheless, one of the most striking applications of Durkheim is to turn him into a theory of political conflict. Again, this means treating Durkheimian theory analytically, as applicable to localized pieces of social interaction instead of an organic metaphor of "a society" as a whole. In this case, we arrive at a theory of politics which distinguishes a surface of ordinary political belief and behavior, from the social mechanisms in the depths which produce them. It becomes a ritual theory of politics.[8]

For the most part such a theory has not been explicitly formulated. Talcott Parsons made an approach to it, in a somewhat ad hoc way, in critiquing C. Wright Mills' (1956) view that U.S. elections deal only with the trivial or "intermediate" levels of power and do not touch the sphere of the power elite. Parsons (1960) commented, among other rejoinders, that elections do not have to be involved in the real transfer of power or in rational decisions of issues for them to be socially effective: elections, instead, are a ritual by which loyalty to the political system itself is mobilized and demonstrated. For Parsons, this was an impersonal, functional activity of the self-equilibrating social system, and he did not see this ritual evocation of solidarity as instrumentally serving the interests of any particular political faction over any other. But the more basic point can be detached from Parsons' functionalism. Election campaigns do operate as a ritual, much like any other: they bring about an increase in the social and moral density, produce social assemblies and focus attention, and intensify common emotional moods by rapid circulation and reverberation. The result of such a mechanism, quite possibly apart from what anyone intends, is to make issues, personalities, and the paraphernalia of political life itself into symbols representing group membership. Part of this membership attachment is to partisan groups; but Parsons' more penetrating point is that participation in the overarching process of an electoral contest automatically generates attachment to the symbols representing the state in general. Although elections are rituals featuring argument and conflict as their content, the lengthy process of an electoral campaign eventually obscures the issues and leaves as its most permanent residue nationalist solidarity.

The model suggested by Parsons is one-sided and schematic, and deserves to be modified for various degrees and kinds of outcomes in terms of just how much solidarity ends up being attached to what social groups. But, as a general picture of elections, it rings truer than our usual instrumentalist interpretations, which always end up with *most* issues-oriented partisans, on whatever side, feeling that the "real issues" of the election were slighted. Nor does the ritual model of politics speak only to the conservative side. As a Trotskyite activist once commented to me, in the fervor of a 1960s election between what he regarded as two "lesser evils:" "voting is not a very political act."

In an even more explicitly Durkheimian vein, W. Lloyd Warner (1959) analyzed the patriotic ceremonies of Yankee City (the Fourth of July parade, Memorial Day for the war dead, and so forth) as rituals of social solidarity. However, in the context of Warner's analysis of the system of stratification, these ceremonies did not emerge as neutral, but as devices to identify the community with the upper class who could trace their lineage back to quasi-mythologized "heroic" ancestors, and with the Anglo–Protestant ethnic group. These rituals are weapons of ideological domination (though Warner did not use those terms) of traditional elites over lower classes and more recent ethnic migrants.

The most extensive model of politics as a conflict centered around rituals is found even further back, in the work of Durkheim's mentor, the historian Fustel de Coulanges.[9] As I have argued elsewhere (Collins 1985a), Fustel's *The Ancient City* gives a model of political conflict in the Greek and Italian city-states which makes ritual the analytical center of politics. This happens in two significant ways. First, religious ritual organizes the *units which can participate* in politics: initially families were religious cults under the patriarchal control of a male head; then the city itself was constituted as a coalition of families through the device of a joint religious cult. Ritual constitutes the component structures of politics: the solidarity groups which are the actors on the political stage, as well as the existence of the state itself. Durkheim appears to have acquired many of his basic theoretical ideas by abstraction from Fustel, including both a model of how a society of "mechanical solidarity" operated, and the underlying theory of ritual creating a moral order and the lines of group membership.

But for Fustel, ritual does not merely produce solidarity. His picture of ancient politics is not a pan-harmonic functionalism, but a history explicitly focused on "class conflict" and revolution. Fustel differs sharply from a Marxian view of classes (hence my ironicizing inverted commas around "class conflict"), in that the divisions of politics are not based on economics or other extrinsic divisions, but on the lines of participation in ritual itself. Hence the second point: ritual is a weapon of political domination, and hence a source of conflict. For Fustel, the first revolution of ancient times pitted the "clients," subordinate family lineages whose members did not control rituals of their own, and hence were excluded from participation in the coalition of families that made up the state, against the patriarchs who monopolized ritual leadership and hence political power. Whether one leads rituals or not creates a "class" division between political haves and have-nots, and hence itself results in a revolutionary political struggle. Fustel describes other waves of revolution, as yet other divisions of ritual participation and non-participation fractionated and mobilized further groupings and conflicts.

I have tried to show (Collins 1985b) that this line of analysis is capable of being expanded into a fully fledged model of politics in all times and places. The key points are that ritual is the mechanism by which solidarity groups are both formed and mobilized: hence that ritual creates the actors of politics; and that ritual is a weapon usable by some groups to dominate others, by manipulating emotional solidarity as well as the lines of group identification to the advantage of some and the disadvantage of others. Politics may thus be described as a struggle by, with, and over "the means of emotional production." For successful ritual depends upon certain material conditions: the ability to assemble a group physically, the paraphernalia to carry out impressive "stage management" (in the Goffmanian sense), the resources to re-enact and reproduce the symbols emotionally charged by participation in a history of past rituals. These resources are differentially distributed in society, depending upon its kind of stratification; hence the degree of inequality in the distribution of the "means of ritual production" is a major determinant of what groups can mobilize as political actors, and with what degree of success they can compel potential opponents to join their emotional and symbolic coalition. And some aspects of politics, usually covert, concern the critical struggle itself over the control of these means of ritual production.

There are various directions in which such a theory can be taken. For example, it gives some of the ingredients of a comparative model of political violence (Collins 1981c). Political violence is itself ritualistic; even warfare is not so much an effort at direct physical destruction as a symbolic use of violence in order to break the organizational solidarity of the opposing army. Armed violence between opposing forces is at one end of a continuum, in that it is a battle among opposing rituals, each striving to break the solidarity of the other. At the other end, we find violence used to exemplify pure domination, especially in the form of ritualized public tortures of victims whose absolute degradation is dramatized. The kind of moral order of society which encourages or prohibits such tortures is explainable by the kind of Durkheimian group structure underlying it.

A ritual theory of politics is especially fitting for the analysis of aspects of politics that are not immediately focused on economic and other material group interests. Thus it connects with a theory of nationalism (which for Weber was a crucial dynamic in producing legitimacy: see Collins 1985b), and potentially should give us some leverage towards a much-needed *general* theory of ethnic loyalty. Durkheimian ritual theory meshes in a similarly useful fashion with Weberian theory of Church organization to produce a general theory of heresy disputes ("Some Sociological Principles of Heresy, Religious and Secular," in Collins 1985b); and if ritual is an analytical key to politics in general, such theory has applications, as I have attempted to show, not only to historical religious disputes but to equivalents of heresy and orthodoxy in modern secular politics. The theme of alienation, which plays a major mobilizing role in the politics of modern intellectuals, can also be understood in terms of a Durkheimian ritual theory of politics ("Alienation as Ritual and Ideology," in Collins 1985b).

Despite the existence of various fragments, I would be the first to admit that a ritual theory of politics has barely begun to crystallize. Nevertheless I believe its potential is considerable for moving conflict theory onto the grounds of ideal and emotional elements in politics, without backsliding either into a euphemistic pan-functionalism of the German neo-evolutionist sort, or the free-floating idealism that reintroduces itself into the "structurationism" of Giddens. For the Durkheimian tradition, ideas and emotions are resources that can be transferred from situation to situation, and used to reproduce earlier structures; but they themselves are always produced by the material organization of social situations in rituals of varying degrees of intensity, and the very "storability" and "transferability" of symbols to subsequent situations is itself a materially stratified process. (In Bourdieu's metaphor (1977), it might well be called "cultural capital.")

The advantage of a ritual theory of politics is that it simultaneously proposes the conditions which divide groups for conflict; which differentially mobilize them; and which determine their degree of emotional and symbolic hegemony over others. A theory of this sort is not concerned merely with the "left-overs" which remain after the hard material conditions of economic struggle. Rather, it is properly poised to understand economic conflict itself. The fundamental social reality in all economic conflict, property, is itself a peculiarly Durkheimian entity. When examined from the point of view of its micro-reality in everyday life, property is not only fundamental in structuring social interactions: it is itself enacted and re-enacted as a basic emotional reality (Collins 1948). It is built into the taken-for-granted routines of everyone's relationships with others *vis-à-vis* their physical surroundings; but the "ethnomethodological" character of this routine quickly takes on a Durkheimian character when violations of the property routine bring forth moral outrage and appeals for social solidarity or enforcement of property against violators. This is only one thread in the labyrinth, but I believe it is a crucial one that may eventually make possible a thorough-going conflict theory of all dimensions of politics, economic as well as symbolic and moral.[10]

Durkheimian theory of sex and gender

Finally, it is worth noting that Durkheimian theory has much to offer in the relatively new studies of inequality pertaining to sex and gender. It is true that Emile Durkheim himself was a sexist of a rather traditional sort. He campaigned against liberalization of French divorce law in his own day, citing its deleterious effects of undermining family solidarity (and thus promoting suicide and other features of anomie) (Lukes 1973). He reviewed a book on the history of the family written by Marianne Weber, the wife of Max Weber, and severely criticized it for its feminist doctrine (Durkheim 1906–9). Nevertheless, we are not constrained by Durkheim's own political biases from applying his analytical apparatus to understand sexual domination. Nor is it necessary to accept the functionalist theory of the family, as an agency for socializing and legitimating children, as the only consequence of the Durkheimian perspective.

Instead, the Durkheimian intellectual lineage itself provides many of the ingredients of a conflict theory of the family. The family can be defined as various arrangements of "sexual property" (Collins 1975), which can be relatively more unilaterial or bilateral in character, more male-dominated or egalitarian. The basic concept of "sexual property" comes from Kingsley Davis (1949), and from Claude Lévi-Strauss (1969[1949]), two theorists working in the Durkheimian tradition. It was only necessary to give this less of the connotation of a permanent structure, and to see it as historically fluid as well as a set of variations on male and female inequality, to make it into a conflict theory of the family.[11]

The Durkheimian elements in a theory of sexual stratification are particularly useful because they connect to prominent historical changes in the structure of the family, as well as to the subjective and emotional side of male–female relationships. A property theory connects naturally to exchange theories of the family. Lévi-Strauss initiated anthropological alliance theory by his analysis of sexual property exchanges as binding together tribal societies in various structural forms. The historical shift to the more recent individually based marriage market brought about changes both in the form of male–female stratification and in its ideology, namely the modern cult of individual love. The structural, exchange or market side is not disconnected from the social definitions of maleness and femaleness and of the family, nor from the kinds of emotions experienced by individuals in these various structures. This is most easily seen in the case of the distinctively modern phenomenon of love.

Precisely what is modern about love is its pervasiveness, the ideal that all marriages ought to be based upon it, as well as its actual incidence in real lives. Feminist theorists (for example, Firestone 1970; Rubin 1975) have argued that love is a major source of ideological bondage, that it covers up and apologizes for the inequality of male and female power both in economic careers and in the home. Such theories however lack an explanatory mechanism. My conflict theory of the family proposed that love itself is the result of a Durkheimian ritual (Collins 1981b). A couple in modern courtship are structurally isolated as a dyad, put in each other's company and intensely focused upon each other to the exclusion of outsiders; the ritual mechanism takes over and intensifies whatever emotions are present (more on these below), and attaches them to symbols of the relationship itself. These symbols generally are the persons of the couple: the dyad is made into a sacred object, and each "beloved" is the special object of secular worship on the part of the other. Goffman (1967: 95) once proposed that the individual self is the pre-eminent sacred object in modern secular society, the object of little acts of worship in the deference and demeanor rituals of everyday life. Perhaps equally important is our cult of the dyad, of the idealized couple which gives personal meaning to our lives as well as constituting the major bond of the modern family.

This idealization of the dyad is not merely a matter of popular literature and entertainment (of which, indeed, it makes up the leading part). Love is not simply foisted upon the public by the mass media, but results from the structure of interpersonal relationships itself. Historically, the removal of political and military powers from the traditional patrimonial household of the upper classes, and of the locus of economic production from most other households, left individuals increasingly free to negotiate their own private household (and sexual) arrangements. But aggregates of individual choices, as everywhere, take the form of a market. As in capitalist markets, marriage markets (or for that matter, friendship markets, or markets for short-term sexual liaisons) are inevitably full of strains upon their individual participants. One's attraction to others is not automatically matched by a reciprocal attraction of them to us; and as one moves to different locations in the opportunity pool of social contacts, one's sexual ego is liable to emotional inflations and deflations. Part of the emotion that goes into making love a ritual, then, is the sense of having reached a more or less stable plateau, a haven from the ups and downs of the interpersonal market that comes when one meets a person whose degree of attraction to oneself is approximately equal to the attraction in the opposite direction. The equilibrating of two individuals' market positions (as stated, for example, in Walster's [1978] "equity theory" of love) is what sets off the special emotional appeal of well-matched lovers. This, together with erotic emotions themselves which are enhanced in the situation of intimacy, provides the emotional ingredient which the Durkheimian ritual process transforms into the basis for a symbolic, as well as moral, tie.

Love thus works through and in a sense because of the stratification system, played out individually in an interpersonal market of relative attractions. It also works within a situation of gender stratification, in which males and females come to the market with unequal economic resources. From this follow many differences between the ways in which males and females orient towards the sexual marketplace: males more spontaneously guided by external appearances and their own emotions, females more by deliberate efforts at controlling their emotions, to ensure that any resulting marriage is economically feasible (Safilios-Rothschild 1977). Love is indeed the ideological lynchpin of the modern system of gender stratification. In the terms of conflict theory, it is the 'emotional property' that goes along with sexual property. As a product of Durkheimian ritual, emotional and sexual property is symbolically charged with a substratum of moral sentiment; this ordinarily manifests itself in positive bonds, perhaps only taken-for-granted routine. But when violated (by sexual or affectional disloyalty), the moral force of possession bursts out in righteous anger, and hence is behind much of the violence of spouse abuse (Dobash and Dobash). The phenomena of modern sexism are deep, not in the sense that they are inevitable, but because they rest upon ritual foundations which operate with moral sentiments, below the level of ordinary reflection.

One implication of this line of analysis is that as the structural ingredients that go into the modern marriage market change, the relationships of emotional and sexual property between males and females also change. Women with greater economic leverage because of their careers have a different stance on the marriage market, with greater opportunities to treat both sex and love in ways that were previously reserved only for men. It appears, too, that men's behavior on such a sexual marketplace also shifts in some ways towards women's styles of behavior (such as in the declining incidence of the use of prostitutes) (Collins 1985c). The ideology is not autonomous; one is not stuck in a given traditional set of sex and gender roles; instead these change with structural shifts in the line-up of resources.

I believe that this view casts some light, and an optimistic light at that, on current discussions about deep-seated differences in male and female cultures. Gilligan (1982), for example, amasses some psychological evidence to show that women's moral sensibility is more person-oriented, while males' is more abstract, rule-following, and impersonal. Reversing a theme in traditional twentieth-century moral philosophy, Gilligan argues that the universalism of the male moral codes is unfeeling towards individuals, insensitive to situational variations, and thus actually less desirable than the more person-oriented female moral mode. Gilligan's theory is in keeping with other arguments, stemming from at least part of the feminist intellectual world, that women are not merely shaped differently from men by circumstances, but are a fundamentally different culture (Bernard 1981; Rossi 1984). Some theories do not make these differences intrinsic (for instance Chodorow [1978] rests them upon early childhood experiences, analyzed via neo-Freudian theory of object relations), but they agree in seeing the female mode as person-oriented, affectional, warm and maternal, in opposition to the cold, impersonal, rule-and-thing-oriented, striving male world.

Let us leave aside the question of whether the "female" traits are morally superior to the "male" traits (a theme argued strongly by Gilligan and others), and take up only the issue of the accuracy of this formulation. I would question the one-sidedness of this view of male–female differences; the degree of person-orientedness, abstraction, ambition, and so forth are only relative differences at most, with plenty of the "opposite sex" traits among both males and females. More importantly, this line of feminist theory seems to me to be inadequately sociological. For there is a line of theory to account for such cultural differences, to the extent that they occur, not in terms of intrinsic sexual differences, or deep-seated early childhood experiences, but of variations in social structure that individuals experience throughout their lives. This theory, in fact, is a variant on the Durkheimian theory. Earlier in this chapter, I demonstrated its application to the generation of class cultures. It applies equally well to producing traditional "female" and "male" personality types and moral styles.

The "female" culture that Gilligan and others describe, with its emphasis on personal solidarity rather than abstract rules, is essentially the culture of Durkheim's "mechanical solidarity." As I have argued above, it is more characteristic of the localized structure inhabited by the working classes than of the cosmopolitan networks in which the upper classes live; for that reason, orientation to abstract rules and to achievement rather than persons is itself *variable among males* rather than a universal male culture. (Gilligan herself used a sample heavily biased towards the middle class, and hence missed the extent to which working-class males would not necessarily share the "universalistic rules" moral code.) An alternative, and far more sociological, way to explain predominant female culture, then, is to see that it is the product of the more localized circumstances in which women often live. The woman who is a housewife is even more localized than a working-class man, parts of whose life at least take him somewhat beyond neighborhood circles. The greater restrictiveness with which girls were traditionally brought up meant that the sheer social and moral density surrounding a female was greater than that surrounding a male, even in childhood. Thus one could say, as a generalization of typical tendencies, that the typical "female" cultural style is merely an extreme version of the "mechanical solidarity" type which is found in varying degrees in the male society as well.

This erases any fundamental distinction between female and male cultures. The differences, matters of degree in any case (because of the empirical mixture of social circumstances in individual lives), are not fundamental, but follow from where men and women have typically been in the surface structure of historical societies, including our own. Some aspects of this have actually been studied on the micro-level; where girls' patterns of interaction are more localized and focused on a small friendship group, their cultural styles do indeed come out differently from boys whose interaction takes place more in organized complex groups such as team sports; but also from girls whose interaction takes place more in the "organic soldarity" pattern (Lever 1978). I have no doubt that further research can amply document the power of social structure in producing cultures, including gender cultures. These cultures are historically contingent and temporary.

Conclusion

I have provided a brief sketch of the connections of Durkheimian theory with conflict theory – or at least the kind of conflict theory that I espouse. In many ways, the Durkheimian intellectual lineage is its most distinctive theoretical component. It is true that the general themes of conflict sociology are owed especially to Marx and Engels; multidimensional conflict theory is the heir of Weber; and micro-oriented conflict theory draws on the various subjectivistic and phenomenological sociologies. But Durkheim provides a key element. His central model, of the generation of moral solidarity by structural arrangements of social interaction, and of the charging of symbols with emotional reactivity, especially via ritual, is what ties together the different elements of a multidimensional theory of stratification and conflict. It explains cultural and moral differences, between social classes as well as between genders; and it links both of these to the interaction ritual of everyday life. Via Durkheimian ritual theory, a connection is made between micro and macro levels of social structure, without making concessions to idealism. Durkheimian theory also provides a deeper view into the nature of property and of power, and of the conflicts organized by and around them. Obviously many of these formulations are imprecise, and much revision and development is needed. But Durkheimian theory is living theory in conflict sociology, capable of much further extension. It is a waste of its potential to make Durkheimian ideas merely the subject of polemics regarding the conservatism and functionalism prominent in much of this lineage, or to turn Durkheim over too quickly to be embalmed by historians.

Notes

1 Of course there are exceptions: that is what this chapter is about. Bloor (1976, 1983), for instance, has made brilliant use of Durkheimian theory of knowledge as a sacred object, and as social product.

2 See also an unjustly neglected book, Winston White, *Beyond Conformity* (1961), an application of this theory to twentieth-century American culture, as a Parsonian answer to David Riesman's *The Lonely Crowd*.

3 It is of little use to invoke a pure "conflict-reflex" theory of group solidarity, according to which conflict with an outside group creates in-group solidarity. Though this may be true, nevertheless it begs the question of what made this an "in-group" with its own identity in the first place. The Durkheimian model remains analytically central; and in fact I believe the conflict-promotes-internal-solidarity model is merely a special case of the Durkheimian theory of ritual solidarity: conflict is merely a very powerful form of ritual in that it focuses attention

and generates strong emotions, as well as strongly symbolizing group boundaries.

4 In another work (*The Rules of the Sociological Method*), Durkheim actually
describes punishments as rituals which reinstitute the solidarity of the group.
That is because they too fit the formula for a ritual: they assemble the group, focus
its attention, heighten a collective emotion, and finally attach it to symbols which
represent the group and its boundaries. In this case the criminal him/herself is a
kind of "negative sacred object," the mutual horror of which strengthens the
group ties.

5 See Joan Annett and Randall Collins, "A Short History of Deference and
Demeanor," in Collins 1975. I would also argue that Alexander's (1981) critique
of Dahrendorfian conflict theory picks on a weaker target, where the principles of
conflict are not treated at this appropriate level of analytical depth. In contrast, I
am suggesting that a conflict theory can be and is formulated at the fundamental
analytical level which Alexander espouses.

6 Strictly speaking, this should be the amount of conscious focus of attention
upon others and the amount of intercommunication, the sharing of viewpoints in
sustained conversational rituals. The supermarket checkout clerk interacts with a
large number and perhaps variety of persons, but in a psychologically unfocused
and superficial communication. Though this should no doubt have some effect
upon the degree of cosmopolitanism of that person, it likely does not move a
checkout clerk much beyond the level of more socially localized working-class
occupations, by comparison, say, to a technical professional who spends hours
poring over abstract communications from complex organizational settings.

7 Calhoun (1982) shows how these kinds of conditions affected class consciousness in the very workers' movements that Marx and Engels perceived in early
nineteenth-century England.

8 The concept of political ritual has been used by Paige and Paige (1981) in
their analysis of reproductive ritual in tribal societies. However, their theory is
not at all Durkheimian. My argument is not just that ritual can be used for political purposes – a phenomenon that Paige and Paige confine to stateless societies –
but that politics itself is ritual, in all societies.

9 Parsons was one of the few sociologists to recognize the significance of Fustel
for modern social thought, including him in his "canonical" *Theories of Society*
(1961). Parsons of course did not see Fustel as a conflict theorist.

10 Durkheimian theory has traditionally touched on property most closely in its
discussion of crime. Thus the degree of concern about "the crime threat" is itself
largely a matter of symbolic politics, since those persons least threatened with
crime, in a statistical sense, are most concerned with containing it (Collins
1981a). Donald Black (1984) has explored some of the Durkheimian dimensions
of crime.

11 Gayle Rubin (1975) similarly makes use of Lévi-Strauss to produce a feminist
theory of the family, although in this case with much less room for historical variation, and emphasizing a critique of the "compulsory heterosexuality" underlying all societies, including our own.

References

Alexander, Jeffrey. 1981. *Theoretical Logic in Sociology*. Vol. 1. *Positivism, Presuppositions, and Current Controversies*. Berkeley: University of California Press.

Bernard, Jessie. 1981. *The Female World*. New York: Free Press.

Bernstein, Basil. 1971–5. *Class, Codes, and Control*. London: Routledge.

Black, Donald, ed. 1984. *Toward a General Theory of Social Control*. New York: Academic Press.

Bloor, David. 1976. *Knowledge and Social Imagery*. London: Routledge.

   1983. *Wittgenstein: A Social Theory of Knowledge*. New York: Columbia University Press.

Bourdieu, Pierre. 1977. *Outline of a Theory of Practice*. New York: Cambridge University Press.

Calhoun, Craig. 1982. *The Question of Class Struggle*. Chicago: University of Chicago Press.

Chodorow, Nancy. 1978. *The Reproduction of Mothering*. Berkeley: University of California Press.

Collins, Randall. 1975. *Conflict Sociology*. New York: Academic Press.

   1981a. "The Normalcy of Crime." In Randall Collins, *Sociological Insight: An Introduction to Non-Obvious Sociology*. New York: Oxford University Press.

   1981b. "Love and Property." In Randall Collins, *Sociological Insight: An Introduction to Non-Obvious Sociology*. New York: Oxford University Press.

   1981c. "Three Faces of Cruelty: toward a Comparative Sociology of Violence." In Randall Collins, *Sociology Since Midcentury*. New York: Academic Press.

   1984. "Interaction Ritual Chains, Power, and Property." Paper delivered at German–American Conference on Sociological Theory, Giessen, Federal Republic of Germany.

   1985a. *Three Sociological Traditions*. New York: Oxford University Press.

   1985b. *Weberian Sociological Theory*. Cambridge and New York: Cambridge University Press.

   1985c. *Sociology of Marriage and Family: Gender, Love and Property*. Chicago: Nelson-Hall.

Davis, Kingsley. 1949. "Jealousy and Sexual Property." In Kingsley Davis, *Human Society*. New York: Macmillan.

Davis, Kingsley and Wilbert E. Moore. 1945. "Some Principles of Stratification." *American Sociological Review* 10: 242–9.

Dobash, R. Emerson and Russell Dobash. 1979. *Violence against Wives*. New York: Free Press.

Douglas, Mary. 1970. *Natural Symbols*. London: Routledge.

Durkheim, Emile. 1966 [1897]. *Suicide. A Study in Sociology*. New York: Free Press.

   1964 [1893]. *The Division of Labor in Society*. New York: Free Press.

   1982 [1895]. *The Rules of the Sociological Method*. New York: Macmillan.

   1906–9. Review of Marianne Weber, *Ehefrau und Mutter in der Rechtsentwicklung. L'Année Sociologique* 11: 363–9.

1961 [1912]. *The Elementary Forms of the Religious Life.* New York: Macmillan.

Erikson, Kai. 1966. *Wayward Puritans.* New York: Wiley.

Firestone, Shulamith. 1970. *The Dialectic of Sex.* New York: William Morrow.

Fustel de Coulanges. 1980 [1865]. *The Ancient City.* Baltimore: Johns Hopkins University Press.

Gans, Herbert. 1962. *The Urban Villagers.* New York: Free Press.

Giddens, Anthony. 1976. *New Rules of Sociological Method.* London: Hutchinson.

Gilligan, Carol. 1982. *In a Different Voice: Psychological Theory and Women's Development.* Cambridge: Harvard University Press.

Goffman, Erving. 1959. *The Presentation of Self in Everyday Life.* New York: Doubleday.

1967. *Interaction Ritual.* New York: Doubleday.

Kohn, Melvin L. 1977. *Class and Conformity.* Chicago: University of Chicago Press.

Lever, Janet. 1978. "Sex Differences in the Complexity of Children's Plans and Games." *American Sociological Review* 43: 471–83.

Lévi-Strauss, Claude. 1969 [1949]. *The Elementary Structures of Kinship.* Boston: Beacon Press.

Lukes, Steven. 1973. *Emile Durkheim, His Life and Work.* New York: Allen Lane.

Mills, C. Wright. 1956. *The Power Elite.* New York: Oxford University Press.

Paige, Karen Ericksen and Jeffery M. Paige. 1981. *The Politics of Reproductive Ritual.* Berkeley: University of California Press.

Parsons, Talcott. 1937. *The Structure of Social Action.* New York: Free Press.

1960. *Structure and Process in Modern Societies.* New York: Free Press.

1966. *Societies: Evolutionary and Comparative Perspectives.* Englewood Cliffs, NJ: Prentice-Hall.

Parsons, Talcott et. al., eds. 1961. *Theories of Society.* New York: Free Press.

Pope, Whitney. 1976. *Durkheim's "Suicide."* Chicago: University of Chicago Press.

Riesman, David. 1950. *The Lonely Crowd. A Study of the Changing American Character.* New Haven: Yale University Press.

Rossi, Alice. 1984. "Gender and Parenthood." *American Sociological Review* 49: 1–18.

Rubin, Gayle. 1975. "The traffic in Women: Notes toward a Political Economy of Sex." In Reyna Reiter, ed., *Toward an Anthropology of Women.* New York: Monthly Review Press.

Safilios-Rothschild, Constantina. 1977. *Love, Sex, and Sex Roles.* Englewood Cliffs, NJ: Prentice-Hall.

Swanson, Guy E. 1962. *The Birth of the Gods.* Ann Arbor: University of Michigan Press.

Turner, Jonathan H. 1983. *The Emergence of Sociological Theory.* Homewood, Ill.: Dorsey.

Walster, Elaine and G. William Walster. 1978. *A New Look at Love.* Reading, MA: Addison-Wesley.

Warner, W. Lloyd. 1959. *The Living and the Dead*. New Haven: Yale University Press.
White, Winston. 1961. *Beyond Conformity*. Glencoe, Ill.: Free Press.

6 Social structure and civil religion: legitimation crisis in a later Durkheimian perspective

Hans-Peter Müller

Introduction

In the last decade there has been an intense debate on legitimation problems[1] in democratic–industrial societies. The discussion of a crisis of legitimacy referred to a societal configuration[2] which, to a greater or lesser degree, had emerged in the industrial part of the Western hemisphere in the last thirty years: a powerful and dynamic capitalist economy, technologically innovative, concentrated in big corporate units and producing for the world market; an interventionist state which in marked contrast to the classical liberal state is engaged in scientific, technological and economic affairs in multiple ways and contributes considerably to a smooth operation of economic activities; welfare-state agencies which distribute life chances to a considerable degree by economic transfers, social security programs, and infrastructural policies. This new configuration is closely associated with the rise of new values and aspirations in contemporary societies which refer not only to the economic standard of living and material well-being but to the quality of life and cultural well-being. These new needs and expectations entail diverse aspects like good health care, educational attainment, political participation and communication as well as the enactment of new and often unconventional lifestyles.

However varied this process of social change may have been in different nations and regions, the resulting configuration has one common feature: the state has gained the central part in contemporary society, and the liberal separation of economy, state and society has been replaced by a complex intermediation of economic, political, and social life. Consequently, the starting point for the legitimation debate was the pervasive role of the modern state and the possible delegitimizing consequences of this new form of political action.

We can distinguish three dimensions of political activity and, hence, three classes of delegitimizing effects.[3] First of all, the modern state's engagement in economic matters to sustain economic growth, maintain full employment, avoid inflation and uphold a balance between exports and imports may fail to such a degree that the society plunges into an enduring economic crisis. Lack of *economic performance* attributable to the political system may threaten a political order in which the state has taken over responsibility for the smooth operation of economy. Secondly, the center of the political system has to take into account various interests and claims of different groups in order to establish the agenda of important issues and enable widespread political participation. Lack of *political performance* in this narrow sense generates the impression that the state only represents powerful interests at the expense of the rest of society, with the consequence of segregation and malintegration of various groups. Finally, and this is the most intricate relationship, the state has to accomplish new needs and aspirations via public opinion and to maintain active communication with the public. Lack of *sociocultural performance* in this sense opens up a gap between new objectives and aims of the people on the one hand and the traditional values and conventions of the political center on the other hand.

Economic, political, and sociocultural performance are the basic dimensions of the legitimation of a political system and constitute the principal sources of delegitimating effects. Throughout this chapter, I refer to *legitimacy*[4] as the acceptability of a political order according to a valued standard (justice, fairness, appropriateness). *Legitimation*, then, is the process by which political action, that is, certain issues and policies, are factually accepted as binding by the people. The problematic questions in the legitimation debate, then, were threefold: What is the actual and legitimate role of the modern state in contemporary society? What are the criteria defining legitimacy and which processes generate legitimation? What are the thresholds where legitimation problems end up in a legitimacy crisis?

To answer these questions several approaches emerged in the course of the legitimation debate, and I will detail these in the following sections. They usually focused on one of the specified delegitimating effects and built up their respective theory on this basis. Each provided some particularly valuable insights, but because they failed to take into consideration the whole range of economic, political and cultural aspects they remained one-sided.

In order to attain a better and more comprehensive understanding I suggest a return to Emile Durkheim's approach. The classical French sociologist, I believe, can contribute instructive insights to the multifaceted role of the modern state, to the complex institutional setting of modern societies and its relationship with the value system, and, finally, to the problem of the legitimation of a political order. More precisely, we can infer from Durkheim's writings that a crisis of legitimacy always points to an underlying moral or value crisis and that this crisis is usually due to the gap between existing values and the social structure of society. What follows is obvious – this gap can be closed only by institutional reforms which can be vehicles for value realization; without such value reform, the social identity of a society as well as the social integration of its members into society will be threatened. By returning to Durkheim, of course, I do not claim that he may provide us with a ready-made answer to the pernicious legitimation problem. His work does, however, point us in a new and important direction: to the *constitutive* relationship of cultural system, institutional order and individual conduct and to the *complementary* consideration of the interplay between the legitimacy of the political order and the cultural values of a society.

In spelling out Durkheim's contribution to the "religio-political problem" (Bellah 1980a: vii) of a legitimate order, I take four steps: (1) I describe the theoretical focus of the debate and give an outline of the different approaches put forward; (2) I turn to the functionalist-formalist view in its three variants and argue that they do not provide an adequate answer for the problem at stake; (3) I reconstruct the normative-practical view in three variants and give an extended interpretation of an alternative, Durkheimian approach; (4) in conclusion, I relate Durkheim's contribution to the other approaches and make a final assessment of the significance of the legitimation debate.

The theoretical core of the legitimation debate

As already mentioned, the starting point for the discussion of legitimation problems is the pervasive role of the modern state in regulating nearly all spheres of society. Whatever the labels used to characterize the modern state – for instance the "social eudaemonic welfare state" (Gehlen 1955), the "comprehensive maintenance State" (Forsthoff 1971), the "rational achievement State" (Hondrich 1973; Münch 1976) – the degree of overall agreement about the distinctive traits of the modern state among contemporary sociological scholars is impressive. Universal competence, an enormous bureaucratic staff, and a great burden of binding decisions are held to be the characteristics of modern political systems.[5]

What is highly controversial, however, is where and in which way legitimation problems arise, which consequences they have, and how they can be managed. In order to systematize the various approaches and contributions it seems appropriate to introduce an initial frame of reference for the subsequent discussion. In fact, we can detect two basic underlying views (Kopp and Müller 1980) throughout the widespread debate on legitimation problems: the functionalist-formalist and the normative-practical view. They differ in many respects – about the role of cultural values, the consequences of rationalization and secularization, the role of power and law, the evaluation of causes and sequences of legitimation problems and, of course, about their solution.

The *functionalist-formalist* view regards modern democratic-industrial society as a rationalized and secular order in which the disenchantment of the world has not only debased a religiously infused common value system of all of its meaning, but has demonstrated the differences, even contradictions, of various ultimate value systems. The legitimacy of a political order, therefore, does not rest upon a shared value system, but upon the organization of political processes and the performance of the state. According to this view, the political-administrative system itself generates general support for its policies through such devices as institutional procedures, symbolic manipulation and ideological mobilization of people's loyalty. This common view, however, covers perspectives which themselves differ considerably about the causes and sequences of a potential legitimation crisis and about whether to stress the economic, political or cultural performance of the state. One version, which emphasizes institutional and symbolic ritualism, declares the emergence of legitimation problems as a contingent, yet unlikely event; a second version suggests that ungovernability is likely, arguing that an overload of the political system's regulating ability will occur; a third version asserts that the incompatibility between economic accumulation and political legitimation is the main source of delegitimation.

Starting from the perspective of the system – the ruler in the Weberian frame – these perspectives are interested, above all, in the organization and stability of modern rule. They refer to the economic and political performance of the state without invoking the impact of a common value system. With respect to the sociological classics, this position is based upon the thinking of Karl Marx and even more on Max Weber, who gave this view its first and still most cogent expression.

While the functionalist-formalist view concentrates primarily upon the perspective of the system, that is, on the production and maintenance of general support for the political system, the *normative-practical* view relies upon the perspective of the actors – the ruled in Weber's term – emphasiz-

ing motives and reasons for the acceptability of a political order as legitimate. According to this view political action must be able – at least in
principle – to be legitimized in the light of relevant societal values and
practical institutional norms. Although the normative-practical position
basically shares the same characterization of modernization as the
functionalist-formalist view, it differs radically with the latter's evaluation of secularization. For the normative–practical position, rationalization does bring about a secular order and deprive traditional religions of
their formerly dominant role as the agency which arbitrates legitimacy by
providing the ultimate rules of conduct. According to this view, however, rationalization neither eliminates the sacralization of secular ideals
nor the "religious" quality of highly prized cultural values. Even modern
societies, therefore, convey an abstract cultural code which regulates the
legitimate expectations of people; this code allows for multiple ways to
"spell out" and institutionalize the common set of abstract ideals. From
this perspective, then, a crisis of legitimacy may arise if the economic and
political performance of the state ignores the cultural imperatives of the
social order.

Beyond this general level of agreement, however, the normative-
practical view has been spelled out in different ways. At least three different readings of the causes and sequences of legitimation problems have
emerged. One approach emphasizes the replacement of demands for
material gratifications by symbolic demands; it predicts that welfare
societies will face a crisis of legitimacy if new values – like the "symbolic"
quest for intrinsic meaning – will be addressed to a state which has been
conceived of primarily as a redistributive agency for material resources.
A second approach emphasizes the interplay of civil religion and national
state, suggesting that, especially in times of moral crisis, the availability
of civil religion on the level of national societies may help to overcome
civil strife and conflict. Finally, there is a third approach, which emphasizes the correspondence between moral values and institutional setting.
This argument is more multidimensional. It suggests that a moral crisis
can only be solved by institutional reforms which re-establish social solidarity and by cultural reforms which promote a viable civil religion.
Despite the diversity of these three explanations, they all share the
common normative-practical view. Starting from the perspective of
the actors, they are concerned above all with the acceptability of modern
rule. Without neglecting the impact of the economy, they concentrate
on the political and cultural performance of the state. With respect
to the sociological classics, this view is based upon Emile Durkheim's
legacy.

I will now consider the contributions of the functionalist-formalist view in its three main variants: the contingency approach of institutional and symbolic ritualism, the neo-Marxist approach of capitalistic crisis management by the modern state, and the system theoretical approach of overload and ungovernability. After this, I turn to the normative-practical view in its three variants: the approach of critical theory which stresses the interplay of legitimation and motivation crisis, the neo-functionalist approach of civil religion and, finally, what I see as Durkheim's own, more elaborated version of civil religion and institutional reform.

The functionalist–formalist view

The common core and the usual starting point for the entire functionalist-formalist doctrine is Max Weber's legal-rational type of rule and its problematic legitimacy. In his sociology of domination, Weber (1972) distinguished three pure types of rule according to three kinds of legitimacy criteria. Whereas traditional domination rests upon traditional beliefs and sentiments and charismatic rule is founded upon the extraordinary personal qualities of the charismatic leader, a legal-rational rule seems to be based upon the belief in the proper procedural production of a political decision. Rational legitimacy, in this sense, rests solely upon legal procedures. Although qualified as pure types – and in reality, therefore, always intermixed – Weber regarded the positivistic belief in procedural legitimation as the dominant type and unique source of the legitimacy of a modern political order. While he endorsed human rights as significant, he discussed them as ideological tools for modern democracies.[6]

Empty ritualism: legitimation through procedure and the symbolic uses of politics

Weber's theoretical conceptualization, and the prevalence in his scheme of a purely positivist notion of "rational legitimacy," deeply embarrassed students of political legitimation. The history of exegesis by secondary interpreters[7] can be read as the attempt to lend this type a substantive basis. Luhmann broke radically with this exegetical tradition. He looked for the institutional mechanisms that make a "legitimacy of legality" (Luhmann 1972: 261) sociologically possible. The complexity and hence contingency of the modern world, he believed, has considerable consequences for the legal, administrative and political system. In a temporal sense there is the difficulty of maintaining the continuity of functional decisions and the efficiency of regulating capacities. More substantively, there is simply the enormous number of issues to be decided and the problems of conflict and consensus deriving from divergent interests. Luhmann maintains that this complexity excludes any recourse to shared values and norms. He stresses, instead, a variety of procedures which register and manipulate the immediate interests of the participants and which, in this way, secure their acceptance of a system's results. Political elections, for example, allocate political roles while allowing for only minimal participation in the form of yes/no alternatives. Legislation transforms complex demands into concrete programs, the result of which also decreases participation. Judicial processes absorb temporary frustrations by permitting a high degree of precisely structured participation in specific procedural roles.

Yet, while such a procedural system may be conceived as a necessary prerequisite, Luhmann himself does not see it as a sufficient condition for the stability of a modern political order. In order to generate the positive functional consequences, it has to be backed up by more substantive means. Luhmann analyzes ideology[8] and trust[9] as subsidiary mechanisms of the procedural system. But whereas he readily admits the auxiliary relation between procedural legitimation and system trust, he makes no attempt to investigate the constitutive nature of this relationship.[10] As a result, the crucial issue of the relation between the political and cultural performance of the state is left open. Luhmann does not, in other words, offer a proper theory of political legitimation. Formal political procedures are not convincing if they are considered from the point of view of the affected people. After all, participating in institutional procedures does not necessarily lead citizens to accept contingent outcomes but to hope for positive results. Over and above purely formal concerns, in other words, there is a value and an interest component. In Western societies procedures are held to be legitimate if they realize democratic order and if they provide adequate institutional means for realizing group interests.[11]

To incorporate such a value and interest component into his system-theory would, however, undermine Luhmann's ambition to base a modern theory of legitimacy simply upon complexity and the need for reducing the contingency of action which is endemically produced. For Luhmann, there are only free-floating values on the one side, and highly individualized persons on the other side. An individual can use a value for a specific opportunity today and abandon it in favor of another, even contradictory one, tomorrow.[12]

One way to combine such purely procedural ideas with an interest component is to acknowledge "the symbolic uses of politics" by different social groupings. Murray Edelman (1964, 1971), for instance, focuses exclusively upon the expressive-symbolic side of institutional procedures and investigates the "set of predominant values, beliefs, rituals and constitutional procedures that operate systematically and consistently to the benefit of certain persons and groups at the expense of others" (Bachrach and Baratz 1970: 43). He distinguishes between two aspects of political reality. On the manifest and objective side, the cognitive content of a political issue and its objective consequences are taken at their face value. The latent side, which is concealed beneath the surface, generates manipulative effects. This ambiguity in political reality is supported by the high degree of differentiation between the political center and the societal periphery. On the one hand, the complexity of social reality causes anxieties among people who long for politically induced harmony through exonerating symbols and rituals. On the other hand, the officially offered symbolic patterns of interpretation cannot be controlled or approved by the people because the structural distance between them and government generates a loss of reality. With the ambiguity and complexity of political reality in mind, Edelmann tries to demonstrate the nearly endless manipulative facilities available to the political and business elites at hand.

While Edelmann's approach seems to be able to discover the structures of the "mobilization of bias" (Schattschneider 1960: 71) which are responsible for the uneven distribution of material and symbolic capital, this approach nevertheless comes perilously near to an empty, even facetious kind of symbolic ritualism. Because it fails to hypothesize the limits of symbolic manipulation or to envision the demasking of official dramaturgy, this symbolic-political theory seems unable to demarcate conditions under which the supposed relations between political behavior and symbolic fraud actually will be valid. In this way, Edelmann's approach becomes a direct correlate to the theory of legitimation through procedure – with the sole exception of an opposite moral-evaluative sign.[13] They both imply that democratic institutions and political performance do very well with a minimal amount of the subjectively implied "legitimacy," since general support for political action is produced by the institution itself. In this harmonic picture of political life, however, a crisis of legitimacy is a contingent event unlikely ever to happen. Fixed by the perspective of the system itself, this view is devoid of broader societal context and ignores the impact of economy and culture. As a result, it is unable to specify the causes and sequence of a potential legitimation crisis.

Contradiction: economic efficiency versus political legitimation

Within the domain of functionalist-formalist thinking, there are two approaches which are more directly concerned with legitimation crisis. These are the neo-Marxist one and system-theoretical theories.

According to neo-Marxist reasoning,[14] the source of legitimation problems is located in the interplay between the economic and political performance of the state. This is due, so their central thesis maintains, to an inherent contradiction between capitalistic accumulation and the political legitimation of the interventionist state. The state intervenes in the economic process to compensate for the dysfunctional consequences of the capitalist economy. The more the state subscribes to "exchange value" oriented *economic* strategies to promote sustained economic growth, the more obvious it becomes that this economic success increases disproportionately the profits of the bourgeois class. Hence, social harmony in society is undermined and political legitimacy threatened. On the other hand, the more the state tries to expand "use value" oriented *political* strategies, the more it is forced to impair the rules of capitalistic accumulation and to apply socialist instruments of planning. Entrepreneurial resistance and economic failure, therefore, reveal the inherent restrictions of political planning[15] and the typical limits of reform policies. The thesis points to the dichotomy of accumulation and legitimation, explaining legitimation problems by a "structural and increasing '*imbalance*' of *legitimacy* and *efficiency*" (Offe 1975b: 257).

The dichotomy thesis, however, is not convincing. In the first place, sustained growth and full employment improve the economic and social situation of the entire people, and this holds true even if the results of economic growth are unequally distributed throughout society. The general improvement of the standard of living not only mitigates the alleged antagonistic class differences between employers and employees, but dissolves and eventually melts away what remains of the proletarian milieu.[16] On the other hand, in periods of economic crisis the interventionist state possesses several means of reducing its role in, and thereby its political responsibility for, the economy – reprivatization, restoring confidence in the self-regulating ability of the market and cutting off welfare transfers are only some of the ways by which the state can exonerate itself from responsibility and avoid delegitimation. In sum, it is fatal for the neo-Marxist approach to rely upon such one-dimensional logic. The state's strategic repertoire as well as the public's values, aspirations, and attitudes cannot be ignored.

Ungovernability: political overload and people's rising expectations

This last point, the relationship of political performance and people's aspirations, is the center of the ungovernability approach.[17] The focus here
is on the concrete situation of the interventionist state which is called
upon to meet a myriad of economic and social demands at the same time.
The overload of political tasks and the rising inflation of public expectations by interest groups and voters have two consequences. The first
is an inherent ungovernability, the second is inevitably frustrated
expectations and uneasiness *vis-à-vis* state, parties, and politics.
If the state reacts to this dilemma of overload versus disappointed
expectations by extending its competences, the spiral of task enlargement
and expectation inflation is pushed one step further. In this case, the
individual autonomy of citizens will be undermined by massive state
intervention.

The thesis of ungovernability, then, regards legitimation problems as
an unintended consequence of the political action of the welfare institutions themselves. This view, however, overlooks the fact that the welfare state itself was the reaction to new social needs and aspirations.
Concentrating upon the allegedly insatiable desires and wants of the citizens, this perspective fails to see how state interventions actually stimulate the flow of economic production and how welfare transfers can
support the consumption capacity of the masses. It interprets historical
processes in a distorted, psychologistic manner, without the necessary
reference to either systemic processes or cultural patterns.

The normative-practical view: social identity, civil religion and institutional setting

While the functionalist-formalist view adopts the perspective of the
system, the normative-practical position starts from the actor's point
of view. This change of perspective entails, of course, different accents
and a shift from the economic-political to the political-sociocultural
performance of the state. Despite this different perspective both sets
of approaches share some basic problems, assumptions and theoretical
orientations.

Social identity: legitimation and motivation crisis

This is especially true for the comprehensive and integrative critical theory of Jürgen Habermas, who set the stage for the discussion on legitimation problems.[18] Basically, he shares the neo-Marxist assessment of late capitalistic economy and interventionist state, but locates legitimacy strains in the realm of political performance and people's demands. Like the ungovernability approach, he concentrates upon the values, aspirations, and attitudes of the people. But unlike their assumption of "utilitarian animals" with insatiable materialistic desires, he conceives of conscientious citizens with idealistic values who engage in political participation and intellectual discourse. Not the endless enhancement of their economic standard of living, but the improvement of the quality of life seems to be their dominant motivation.

Habermas (1973: 104) argues that delegitimation will only occur if the welfare state's dominant gratification, money, no longer is accepted, and if the majority of citizens demand culturally informed meaning orientations in their place. This strong thesis rests upon the empirical observation that a growing part of the population lives outside the market realm, is alienated from the state, and finds its basic life experience not in the occupational but the educational world. In the latter, new orientations develop which go beyond the conventional bourgeois lifestyle, centered on educational attainment, occupational achievement, social prestige, and family orientation. Yet even if Habermas' claims about the emergence of entirely new, alternative *Lebensformen* are valid, it remains to be shown why and how these alienated minorities would question political legitimacy. Without the rise of new social movements – which could present a new "revolutionary subject" after the embourgeoisement of the working class – there is little empirical evidence of this kind to challenge the stability of late capitalist rule.

Theoretically, however, this thesis is of more interest. At least the replacement of material gratifications (money) by symbolic orientations (meaning) locates the emergence of legitimation problems in the interplay between the political and cultural performance of the state. Not the incompatibility between economic efficiency and political legitimation *per se*, but the insoluble conflict between the redistribution of material gratifications and the distribution of symbolic rewards marks a legitimacy crisis. In this sense, then, a crisis of legitimacy can be traced back to a motivation crisis (Habermas 1973:105) or, in the more Durkheimian terms I am developing here, to a moral crisis.

Functionalist civil religion: political strife and social integration

Although Bellah's and Habermas' views converge on the intimate relationship between loss of legitimacy and value crisis, they differ substantively in their assessment of the role of a modern value system. As a true disciple of Max Weber, the German sociologist rejects the idea that the modern state can rely upon a universalistic value system that can be institutionalized on a national scale. As a disciple of Durkheim, Bellah argues that just that is possible. He tries to show how the state's political action can be oriented towards the core of a "civil religion" which conveys obligatory meaning.

Yet, at least in his recent work, Bellah's starting point is the deep civil crisis into which the United States was plunged as a consequence of racial conflict, the war in Indo-China, and the Watergate affair. In Peter Berger's (1980:66) view, these events certainly delegitimated the American state. They created a "crisis for the polity" and a "comparable crisis of credibility in the American religious community" – "there has been a hollowing out of the beliefs and values on which the polity depends for its continuing credibility, a failure of nerve paralyzing both action and imagination."

At first sight the appeal to the basic American creed of civil religion in the midst of such a credibility crisis would seem to amount to nothing more than an ideological effort to shore up traditional values. For Bellah (1970:168), however, the concept of civil religion[19] is not just "an idolatrous worship of the American nation." While Parsons (1973, 1974) quite readily takes civil religion to be the hard core of the American cultural system, Bellah conceives it to be a social phenomenon in the Durkheimian sense. Defining it as a "public religious dimension [that] is expressed in a set of beliefs, symbols, and rituals," Bellah (1980a:xi) studies it in a strictly historical and comparative manner. He believes that three basic conditions favored the development of civil religion in America. First, because Puritanism was dominant in the formative period of the United States, there emerged a widespread inner-worldly obsession with establishing "the kingdom of God on earth." Not only early Americans but their nineteenth- and twentieth-century descendants viewed this first new nation as "God's new Israel." The second and third conditions relate to the secularization of this religious conceptualization. In the unique American situation, the enlightenment facilitated a process of secularization that could deny to "traditional denominational bodies any official status" (Parsons 1974:205) and relegate them safely to the private sphere. This tendency toward religious individualism and privatism was complemented by the manner in which the Puritan's commitment to religious liberty legitimated the peaceful separation of church and state. This combination of secularization, individualism and pluralism marks, in Bellah's (1980a:xi) view, a unique constellation of conditions that opened up "the possibility that a distinct set of religious symbols and practices [could] arise that address issues of political legitimacy and political ethics but that are not fused with either church or state."

Even if we accept Bellah's historical interpretation of the American civil religion, however, several critical questions have to be raised.

1. Is the old rhetoric of civil religion still alive in the United States? While Bellah seems to assert this,[20] he is by no means able to show that it is. Demonstrating successfully the formation of a value system is not equivalent to proving its successful operation in contemporary society.

2. Furthermore, and in more theoretical terms, even if the viability of civil religion is assumed, one has to show more precisely the connection between the levels of cultural system, institutional order and individual action. How do the values of individualism, liberalism and tolerance penetrate the political institutions? How are they realized in the particular conduct of politics? Do people actually rely upon the terms of civil religion in evaluating the legitimacy of the American political order? Questions of this kind seem to reach far beyond the scope of Bellah's historically based concept. This is why he has been severely criticized for his claim about the importance and operation of civil religion in contemporary American society.[21] Empirical criticism has claimed that only small evidence exists of such a public religious dimension.[22] Theoretical criticism points to deep conceptual ambiguities.[23]

Durkheimian civil religion: institutional setting and individual autonomy

Although a true disciple of Durkheim, Bellah dislocates the concept of civil religion from the underlying development of society's social structure. With this strategy, ironically, he deprives himself of a solution to the very problem he sets out to study. Durkheim's own normative-practical view, by contrast, contains a theoretical position that is more multidimensional. Durkheim's theory integrates the levels of culture, institution, and individual in a way that elucidates the interplay between them – between the secular religion of moral individualism, the institutional configuration of a differentiated social order, and the contours of individual autonomy.

When Durkheim began his intellectual career a hundred years ago,

France faced a legitimacy crisis[24] much as that of Bellah's America today, but on a much vaster scale. Because of the unfortunate coincidence of confessional, political, and ideological cleavages, the Third Republic became divided into three irreconcilable political camps. Conservatives and radicals both fought against the republicans, one for monarchical restoration, the other for socialist revolution. It is not surprising, therefore, that Durkheim's choice of vocation coincided with his practical interest in developing for this young republic a secular, yet religiously infused public creed,[25] a fitting configuration of institutional order,[26] and, as a consequence, not only the philosophical promise but the practical exercise of individual autonomy.[27]

Durkheim's first step represented an attempt to come to grips with the structural make-up of modern societies in order to identify the source of the persistent moral crisis. What are the causes for the strife in the social order and the repressive denials of personal autonomy? For an answer, Durkheim (1967a [1893]) turned to the division of labor as the crucial feature of modern society. Is it an overall integrative force and, in addition, a source of self-realization, as the individualism of Adam Smith's *laissez-faire* theory would hold? Or is it a disruptive force and a source of alienation, as Karl Marx and the socialists would maintain? Durkheim believed he could compromise between individualism and socialism. Integration would be achieved not because of the miraculous invisible hand but because of regulated moral cooperation. He substantiated this thesis by comparing archaic and modern societies. In the latter, Durkheim believed, one finds a functionally differentiated institutional order which combines a complex division of labor with a regulating but minimal collective conscience. The result is the cooperation Durkheim called organic solidarity. Yet the relationship between structural heterogeneity and organic solidarity remained somewhat obscure. Does the division of labor, that is, the differentiation and the interdependence of functions, automatically lead to organic solidarity? If not, what are the sufficient conditions for a successful process of cooperation?

Much of Durkheim's subsequent work can be regarded as an attempt to throw new light upon this unresolved connection between structural differentiation and social integration. Theoretically, this implied the necessity to clarify the following three classes of problems. First, what is the role of the collective conscience, or rather, as this concept became transformed in his later writing, collective representations? Are they bound to be minimalized or can they adopt another form – a version that would be more in line with Durkheim's powerful later thesis about the eternal religious dimension of social life?[28] Second, what is the role of the state? Is it just a mechanical product of the process of differentiation, as Durkheim contends when he argues against Comte's position, which designated the state as the religio-political, integrative center of society? Or will the state be the central organ of social life, as Durkheim holds against Spencer's position, which regards the state as a superfluous institution which is destined to wither in the long run?[29] Finally, what is the role of the various parts of a society? Whereas Durkheim emphasizes throughout *The Division of Labor* the relation of individual and society,[30] he later gave up this simplifying assumption and elaborated the intermediate role of secondary groupings.[31]

The crucial intellectual experience which allowed Durkheim to clarify these problems was the new understanding of religious phenomena which emerged after *The Division of Labor*.[32] He now more clearly understood that the collective consciousness consisted of representations – ideas and values which are relatively independent of their morphological basis.[33] In preparing his later work, *The Elementary Forms of the Religious Life*, Durkheim studied the laws of collective ideation.[34] He conceptualized the formation, role and functional consequences of the simplest religious ideas and sentiments in order to throw light upon the cognitive, evaluative and expressive elements of constitutive religious symbolism per se.[35] Separating radically the sacred and profane spheres, Durkheim came to believe that there are group situations in which religious beliefs and sentiments can be generated and recreated. These collective commitments are both a cognitive representation of society and the evaluative and expressive dramatization of society – or, in Geertz's (1973) terms, both the "model of" and the "model for" society.[36] It is this symbolic differentiation which allows the civic religion to integrate its adherents into a moral community.

There is no doubt that Durkheim had the understanding of modern society in mind when he formulated his theory of archaic religion.[37] He dramatically stated that the understanding of modern man was his central aim,[38] that the religious dimension in social life is eternal,[39] and that no difference existed between archaic rituals and the celebration of the French Revolution.[40] He also expressed his hope that a creative effervescence in the future would generate a new set of beliefs to overcome the present state of "moral mediocrity."[41] Instead of simple analogies, however, one must examine Durkheim's thought for what would be specific to the role of modern religion. Durkheim insisted, from the outset, on symbolic differentiation. In modernity, cognitive symbolism belongs to the domain of science, evaluative symbolism becomes a matter of law and morality, and expressive symbolism reigns in the sphere of art and literature. Yet, while Weber treats such differentiation and secularization as identical with the retreat of religion from the public side of society to the private sphere of intimate personal relationships,[42] this is for Durkheim not at all the case.

While Durkheim concedes the loss of cognitive symbolism to science and expressive symbolism to art, he retains the sacred quality of evaluative symbolism. Behind this view lies a different assessment of secularization. It does not imply the disenchantment and degradation of all values to mere ideologies. The laws of collective ideation are still operative in a modern secular order; they allow a continued idealization of central values, which lends to them a sacred status. So secularized social orders still sacralize a culture's core, which in turn defines the social identity of society and specifies the regulating norms for the social integration of its members. For Durkheim, then, sacralization is (to use Parsons' term) an "evolutionary universal," a constant component in human societal development whether there is tradition or modernity.

This constancy of the religiously infused, sacred quality of evaluative symbolism – the ethical code of a society – is accompanied, however, by historical variations in the scope and substance of value systems. Although Durkheim usually employs the dichotomy of archaic and modern societies, he actually developed a tripartite differentiation. For each phase he considered the nature of the predominant cult and the prevalent kind of social formation. Archaic societies adhered to a cult of the group whose undifferentiated religious symbolism ruled the entirety of social life. Medieval societies followed a cult of the state based upon the differentiation of cognitive and religious symbolism. Modern societies are characterized by a cult of the individual, which lends to human beings in general a sacred status. In Durkheim's eyes these three cults present an evolutionary sequence in which the cult of the individual is morally "higher." As he had already stated in *The Division of Labor* (1967a [1893]: 404), an ideal is higher not because it is more transcendent, but because it offers a more comprehensive perspective. In this sense, then, Durkheim seems to assume a shift in the symbolic embodiment of the sacred from diffuse things (such as emblems and totems) to abstract transcendent entities (gods), to the transcendental man (the individual in general). At the same time, there is the movement on the institutional reference from group to state and then to the individual level.

This contraction of the sacred and its concentration upon the abstract modern man goes along with the multiplication of concrete morals which elaborate and vivify this ethic in real life. The morality of family, friendship, and professional groups is infused with a contagious individualism which moves an abstract cultural ideal into the center of social life. There is, in short, a shift from rigid regulation via traditional religion and cultural system to open regulation via the institutional order. There develops a new distribution of moral competences through the different institutions in modern society. New functional devices are also required, for institutions now have to regulate themselves – according to their own specific criteria – without reference to standards formerly mandated by the sacred tradition of religious life.[43] It follows, of course, that at the individual level persons cannot be socialized in an unreflective way by the diffuse traditional beliefs and the ritual calendar of former times. They now must be cognitively and morally trained, through moral education,[44] to live up to the demanding individual cult. Far from leading to the loss of morality, then, functional differentiation and secularization lead in the late Durkheimian perspective to a moral decentralization of social life *and* to an intensive regulation of the differentiated institutions by specific morals.[45]

The institutional setting Durkheim proposed for modern society is outlined in *Professional Ethics*. In discussing this course of lectures, it will be possible to answer the second and third questions left open in *The Division of Labor*, namely the role of the state and intermediary groupings. Durkheim argued here that occupational groups should be introduced to the economy on a national scale. He assigned to these groups representative, coordinative, and regulative functions in regard to such issues as the relationships of employers and employees, work conditions, and wages. The different professions, he believed, should be grouped into a hierarchical organization, with an administrative council assembling representatives of all occupations at the top. This administrative council should be in close contact with the state, which would articulate the general principles of industrial legislation.

In order to foster organic solidarity in the economy, this regulative center of social life would have to be an active welfare state. This state would grasp, canalize and systematize the diffuse collective representations of society, translate them into political programs, execute policies, and decide conflicting issues. But its task, above all, would be to represent the ideal of moral individualism. Thus, among the multiple tasks of the modern state, Durkheim focused not so much on the economic and political but on the socio-cultural performance of modern democracy. In fact, he came to see this politicized "cult of the individual" as the secular equivalent of the religious collective conscience. Historically the last religious ideal, this cult was morally the highest. Committing the state to protecting and enlarging individual rights, it would become a kind of civic, or rather civil, religion in a modern society.

On the other hand, with the French tradition in mind, Durkheim was very well aware of the authoritarian possibilities of a modern central state holding power and financial resources. Only a democratic state could fulfill the functions he laid out. Only democracy could properly organize communication between state and society, allow for citizens' participation, and establish a power between state, social groups, and individuals. Durkheim envisioned a corporative society in which professional organization overcame economic anomie in the economy, welfare institutions combined economic efficiency with social justice in the polity, and democracy restructured communication and restored checks and balances throughout. Only such a corporative society could establish a legitimate order with organic solidarity and individual autonomy – at least in the long run.

Despite its realistic ambitions and multidimensional frame, however, Durkheim's model for a corporative society is not backed up by a political sociology proper. He does not elucidate the conditions for institutionalizing his normative ideas; he gives no precise analysis of political actors, parties and their interest structure; he does not describe the institutional procedures and mechanisms involved. Still, the contours of the interplay between the economic, political and socio-cultural performance of the state – and the relationship of value system and individual autonomy – are quite clear. As this conception attests, Durkheim is far from simply emphasizing the existence of an abstract value system, as Bellah and Parsons do when they assume but do not explain how important such commitments are for institutional formation and individual conduct. Instead, Durkheim's reflections upon a secular civil religion are embedded in the institutional infrastructure of modern societies. His program for institutional reform revolves around the relation of economy and state, state and moral education, professions and individuals. We can sum up his basic insights into the interplay of cultural system, institutional order, and individual conduct in three points.

1. The interrelation between secularization, differentiation and individual autonomy, Durkheim believes, leads to a plurality of institutions which perform functionally specific duties (its *secular* aspect) and which are regulated by specified moral duties (its *sacred* aspect).[46] Individual autonomy, then, is accomplished under two conditions. On the one hand, the plurality of different roles enables the individual to evade the despotism of particular groups,[47] while on the other, a plurality of moral milieus provides patterns of normative orientation for the meaningful conduct of individual life.[48]

2. The state's economic performance introduces regulating norms in the economy in order to overcome anomie and to sustain organic solidarity; politically, it engages in multiple welfare activities to secure social peace and to attain social justice; socioculturally, it aims at an equilibrium between structural dynamics and value commitments via political communication with the public and the protection and enlargement of indi-

vidual rights. This theoretical strategy is superior, I believe, to a mere value-integrationist perspective of the type promoted by functionalist notions of civil religion, which presupposes the binding capacity of a value system *vis-à-vis* institutional order and individual conduct.[49]

3. Durkheim sociologized Kant's ethical ideal of individual autonomy by showing how individual autonomy is possible in the midst of a differentiated institutional order.[50] The cult of the individual is the abstract core of the modern cultural code. In order to lend this collective ideal the vivid moral authority of a common civil religion, this moral individualism has to be spread throughout the multiple web of specific morals and to be anchored institutionally. The more the individualistic ethic is morally and institutionally anchored, the more it contributes to a legitimate social order.

Conclusion

Throughout the recent legitimation debate Durkheim has played no important part. Yet this entire debate revolves around the relationship of value systems to legitimacy problems. The functionalist-formalist view rests upon the assumption of secularization and disenchantment, the pluralization of antagonistic value systems and the impossibility of legitimating modern political systems by common values. Insofar as this has occurred, a modern democratic order can dispense with a great amount of legitimacy. Rational legitimacy through a system of legal procedures is, indeed, sociologically possible in periods of prosperity and consensus. Yet, this does not mean that legitimacy by common values is superfluous. Quite the contrary, Durkheim argues that the smooth operation of a modern political system is itself due to the correspondence between cultural code and political order in normal periods. It is because political institutions are held to be legitimate that the political costs for decision-making are low and that people can become as engaged in their occupational and family lives as in their civic roles. The latent relationship of common values and political legitimation, moreover, becomes fully apparent in times of crisis. When political legitimacy is deeply questioned, the demand for unifying values expands exponentially. But the supply is not arbitrarily produceable. It is this fact which explains Durkheim's lifelong interest in a modern civil religion and in the emergence and development of value systems, an interest which came to theoretical fruition only in his later work.

In light of the framework which Durkheim established in his later writings, Habermas' insistence on the consensual founding of new values through discourse free of social and political determination seems more than ever like a philosophical abstraction. It is only because individuals adhere to a moral community that they are able to agree upon rationally generated norms and decisions. It is their faith in the moral superiority of reason, not their insight into the cognitive superiority of reason, which enables individuals of a modern society to engage in rational action. Only this can explain the difficulties which are generated when common moral codes are disrupted and groups establish themselves on the basis of incompatible ideas. To maintain a moral consensus on a legitimate order, therefore, is not simply a matter of rational persuasion, but the product of communal moral convictions.

Yet this is not to suggest merely essentialism by another name. Surrounding the hard core of common values – in Durkheim's terms, the transcendental component – is a protective belt which fluctuates according to changes in a society's social structure. This explains the multiple forms of value realization which exist within a given society as well as the refraction of the ethical code into diverse concrete morals. Not the abstract validity of the symbolic code, as Bellah often seems to assume, but the code in conjunction with specific morals is what constitutes the value efficacy and, hence, the legitimacy of a social order. The more the morality of family, peer-groups, and occupational groups is infused with the spirit of individuality – the more viable and well-entrenched the new civil religion is in society – the more legitimate the social system is *vis-à-vis* the dominant code. It is only by keeping such considerations firmly in mind that a theory of civil religion can be articulated which is faithful to the cultural and social insights of Durkheim's later work.

Notes

1 In the enormous body of literature on legitimation problems, it is difficult to single out certain publications. Central to the actual discussion, however, are the texts by Habermas (1973, 1976); Hennis (1976); Offe (1972, 1973, 1975a and b, 1976); and Luhmann (1965, 1972, 1974, 1975); an overview of the discussion is given by Ebbighausen (1976); Kielmansegg (1976); Kopp and Müller (1980); and Heidorn (1982).

2 This societal configuration can be found in most diagnoses of modern societies, e.g. the two-volumed book by Habermas (1981a and b) or Münch (1984).

3 This analytical distinction follows the main functions of the state, as discussed in the literature. For comparable classifications see Offe 1973; Easton 1965, 1967; Habermas 1973; Hirsch 1974; Miliband (1972).

4 Cf. Kopp and Müller 1980: 4. Throughout the debate, there was a consider-

able confusion on the central terms. Legitimacy, in our view, is not directed toward the level of single political decisions, policies or a government, but toward the institutional level of regime. Closest to our conceptualization is Gurr's (1971: 185) definition: "regimes are said to be legitimate to the extent that their citizens regard them as proper and deserving of support."

5 Cf. for this characterization Easton (1965, 1967), Luhmann (1974), Münch (1976), and Poggi (1978).

6 This discussion is in his sociology of law. Cf. Weber 1972: 502.

7 For example, Winckelmann 1952; Loos 1970; Habermas 1973: 133ff; Mommsen 1974a and b; Stallberg 1975; Schluchter 1979: 122ff; and Kopp and Müller 1980: 28ff.

8 See Luhmann 1974: 178ff.

9 See Luhmann 1973.

10 For such an attempt see Münch 1976: 80ff.

11 This is the critique of Luhmann's proposal by Kielmansegg (1971) and Offe (1976).

12 In Luhmann's eyes this scenario expresses a progressive social order. Yet a closer look at his oeuvre reveals that his position seems to have gradually changed in this respect: In early publications he regarded common values as a normative basis of democratic society – see for instance Luhmann 1965; in a late article on "human rights as civil religion" (Luhmann 1981: 293ff) he nevertheless treats civil religion ironically as an old and outdated European idea disposed to satisfy intellectual needs of harmony but scientifically useless to explain the functional appearance and operation of a differentiated society.

13 This is spelled out by Offe's introductory remarks to the German edition of Edelman's (1976: x) book.

14 See for this position and its different variants Altvater 1972; Gündel et al. 1967; Hirsch 1974; Lindberg et al. 1975; Miliband 1972; O'Connor 1973; Wolfe 1977. For a critical evaluation see Wirth 1972; valuable introductions are given by Esser (1975) and Kostede (1980). A principle critique of historical materialism as the core of neo-Marxist reasoning is forwarded by Habermas (1976: 144ff) and Giddens (1981:203ff). For a critique of the neo-Marxist state theory see Greven et al. 1975 and Guggenberger 1974, 1975.

15 They are discussed in Ronge and Schmieg 1973, Grottian and Murswieck 1974, and Mayntz 1980. An excellent case study is Offe 1975a.

16 This is convincingly shown by Gorz (1982); cf. Beck 1983.

17 For the widespread discussion on governability problems, see Binder et al. 1971; Crozier et al. 1975; Frei 1978; Grew 1978; Hennis et al. 1977; Kaltenbrunner 1975; King 1976; Rose 1978; and Scheuch 1977. Cf. Offe 1979 for an excellent critique.

18 Cf. Habermas' seminal works ranging from the earliest version (1968) to the main formulation (1973) and discussion (1976) as well as refinement (1981a and b).

19 He has made numerous attempts to study civil religion in all of its varieties; see Bellah 1970, 1975, 1976, 1980a–e.

20 This seems to be so, yet Bellah's early optimistic tone (see 1970) changes on account of the "broken covenant" and, as he (1980e: 186) admits, "a revitalization of the revolutionary spirit of the young republic at present seems utopian."

21 Cf. Bellah's (1980a) resigned statement: "In 1967 I published an essay I have never been allowed to forget."

22 Much of the debate was in literal, philosophical and even theological terms; this is one reason why there is only a small share of empirical investigations. Above all, the empirical findings are somewhat contradictory: Thomas and Flippen (1972: 218ff), who took a nationwide sample of newspapers of 4 July 1970 (Honor America Day), revealed no appeal to any dimension of Bellah's concept in their content analysis. On the other hand, Wimberley et al. (1976: 890ff) discovered a civil religious dimension apart from the Church religious dimensions like religious belief, religious behavior and religious experience.

23 Cf. the contributions in Cutler 1968; Wilson 1979; and for the general difficulty to specify religious functions see the still valuable essay of Eister (1957). Bellah (1980b: 3) himself readily admits that "the term 'civil religion' has spread far beyond any coherent concept thereof." Further conceptual refinement was developed by Coleman (1970) and Hammond (1974, 1980a–e).

24 This is pointed out as an important impact on Durkheim's sociology by Bellah (1973: xvi), Giddens (1977: 238), Müller (1983: 16ff), and Tiryakian (1978: 195).

25 Durkheim's standard argument points to the necessity of establishing a new moral order! Cf. for instance Durkheim 1967a [1893]: 461.

26 In Durkheim's eyes, to build up a new moral order is equivalent to an institutional reform of society. Cf. Durkheim 1969a [1897]: 446.

27 This intention is revealed in his sociology of law and politics as well as in his sociology of education. Cf. Durkheim 1969c [1950], 1963 [1925].

28 Cf. Durkheim 1967a [1893]: 396 for the first, and ibid.: 148 for the second line of interpretation.

29 Cf. Durkheim 1967a [1893]: 350 for his discussion of the Comtean position, and ibid.: 257ff for his debate of Spencer's position.

30 This is the basic relation for Durkheim (1967a [1893]: 138, note), which he sticks to for reasons of simplification.

31 Although there are remarks towards the growing importance of professional organizations, the theorem of intermediary groupings is worked out in the Second Foreword of *The Division of Labour* and *Professional Ethics and Civic Morals*. For valuable discussions of his political writings see Alexander 1982; Bellah 1973; Giddens 1977; Lacroix 1977, 1981; Müller 1983; Prager 1981; and Wallwork 1972.

32 Cf. Durkheim's (1907 and 1975a: 401ff) letter to the "Directeur de la Revue neo-scolastique" which reveals the great impact of Robertson Smith's writings upon his thinking.

33 Cf. *Representations individuelles et representations collectives* (1898a and 1967b: 1–38).

34 It was in this essay of 1898 that he called for a special branch of sociology to study the laws of collective ideation.

35 Therefore Durkheim's *Elementary Forms* are at once a sociology of knowledge, a sociology of religion and a sociology of aesthetics.

36 The idea of a creative effervescence includes the production *and* reproduction of normative ideas and values and hence the maintenance *or* change of a society's identity.

37 Thus, the decisive critiques of Goldenweiser (1915, 1917), Lukes (1973: 1ff, 250ff, 506ff) and Stanner (1967) are in some sense irrelevant to Durkheim's main project.

38 See Durkheim 1968 [1912]: 1.

39 A proposition which can be found in his earliest writings (cf. 1887 and 1975b: 156) as well as in late statements (cf. 1914 and 1970: 305ff).

40 This analogy is most cogently expressed in *L'Individualisme et les Intellectuels* (1970 [1898b]: 261ff). Cf. Müller 1983; 163ff, 1986: 92ff.

41 Cf. the conclusion of *The Elementary Forms* (1968 [1912]).

42 Cf. Weber 1973: 612.

43 Cf. for example Durkheim's (1967a [1893]: 183f) statement that all social life is religious in the early days of societal evolution. For a discussion of this statement see Parsons 1973.

44 This pedagogical interest explains Durkheim's preoccupation with the history, systematics and the practical conclusions of cognitive and moral education. See Durkheim 1969b [1938], 1963 [1925], 1966 [1922] and for valuable expositions of his moral and educational theory cf. Bertram 1980, 1986; Cherkaoui 1976; Müller 1986; and Wallwork 1972.

45 Therefore Durkheim (1969c [1950]) is primarily concerned with the "physique des moeurs et du droit."

46 This dialectics of secularization and sacralization is Durkheim's message of his sociology of religion: while secularization has to be regarded as an irreversible process depreciating every religion with universal claims on the one hand, there will always be counteracting processes of sacralization lending ideals of great value sacred status.

47 Cf. his countervailing power-model of his theory of democracy, where this insight is formulated and then used in the sociology of education. See Durkheim 1969c [1950]: 96ff.

48 Cf. Durkheim's (1969a [1897]) discussion of the types of suicide pointing to the prerequisite of a moral milieu.

49 Durkheim has been interpreted in such a misleading manner: cf. for instance Foskett's (1940:51) statement: "[Durkheim] failed to provide any further clue as to the nature of the social factor other than to emphasize the importance of common ends or goals in human conduct. . . . This left him with common moral elements as the sole basis of social order." From this interpretation it was often a small step to the charge of an inherent conservatism in Durkheim's thought. See Coser 1960; Nisbet 1965, 1970; and Zeitlin 1968.

50 Cf. Parsons 1968, 1973, 1978, Münch 1981 and Müller 1986.

References

Alexander, J. C. 1982. *Theoretical Logic in Sociology.* 4 vols. Berkeley and Los Angeles: University of California Press.

Altvater, E. 1972. "Zu einigen Problemen des Staatsinterventionismus." *Probleme des Klassenkampfes* 3: 1ff.

Bachrach, P. and M. S. Baratz. 1970. *Power and Poverty. Theory and Practice.* New York: OUP.

Beck, U. 1983. "Jenseits von Klasse und Stand?" In R. Kreckel, *Soziale Ungleichheiten,* pp. 35–74. Göttingen: Schwartz.

Bellah, R. N., 1970: *Beyond Belief. Essays on Religion in a Post-Traditional World.* New York: Harper and Row.

    1973. ed. Introduction to *Emile Durkheim on Morality and Society.* Chicago: Chicago University Press.

    1975. *The Broken Covenant: American Civil Religion in a Time of Trial.* New York: Seabury Press.

    1976. "The Revolution and the Civil Religion." In J. C. Brauer, ed., *Religion and the American Revolution,* pp. 55–73. Philadelphia; Fortress Press.

    1980a. Introduction. In: R. N. Bellah and P. E. Hammond, *Varieties of Civil Religion,* pp. vii–xv. San Francisco: Harper and Row.

    1980b. "Religion and the Legitimation of the American Republic." In R. N. Bellah and P. E. Hammond, *Varieties of Civil Religion,* pp. 3–23. San Francisco: Harper and Row.

    1980c. "The Japanese and American Cases." In R. N. Bellah and P. E. Hammond, *Varieties of Civil Religion,* pp. 27–39. San Francisco: Harper and Row.

    1980d. "The Five Religions of Modern Italy." In R. N. Bellah and P. E. Hammond, *Varieties of Civil Religion,* pp. 86–118. San Francisco: Harper and Row.

    1980e. "New Religious Consciousness and the Crisis of Modernity." In R. N. Bellah and P. E. Hammond, *Varieties of Civil Religion,* pp. 167–87. San Francisco, Harper and Row.

Bellah, R. N. and P. E. Hammond, 1980. *Varieties of Civil Religion.* San Francisco: Harper and Row.

Berger, P. L. 1980. "Religion and the American Future." In S. M. Lipset, ed., *The Third Century. America as a Post-Industrial Society,* pp. 65–77. Stanford: Stanford University Press.

Bertram, H. 1980. "Moralische Sozialisation." In *Handbuch der Sozialisationsforschung,* pp. 717–44. Edited by K. Hurrelmann and D. Ulich. Weinheim and Basel: Beltz.

Bertram, H. 1986. *Gesellschaftliches Zwang und moralische Autonomie.* Frankfurt-am-Main.

Binder, L. et al. 1971. *Crises and Sequences in Political Development.* Princeton, NJ: Princeton University Press.

Cherkaoui, M. 1976. "Socialisation et conflit: les systèmes educatifs et leur histoire selon Durkheim." *Revue française de sociologie* 17 (2): 197–212.

Coleman, J. A. 1970. "Civil Religion." *Sociological Analysis* 31: 67–77.

Coser, L. A. 1960. "Durkheim's Conservatism and its Implications for his Sociological Theory." In K. H. Wolff, *Emile Durkheim*, pp. 211–32. Ohio: Ohio University Press.

Crozier, M., S. P. Huntington and J. Watanuki. 1975. *The Crisis of Democracy.* Report on the Governability of Democracies to the Trilateral Commission. New York: New York University Press.

Cutler, D. R., ed. 1968. *The Religious Situation.* Boston: Beacon Press.

Durkheim, E. 1887. Review of Guyau, M., "L'irreligion de l'avenir." *Revue philosophique* 23: 299–311.

1898a. "Représentations individuelles et répresentations collectives." *Revue de metaphysique et de morale* 6: 273–302. Repr. in *Sociologie et Philosophie*, 1–48 Paris.

1898b. "L'individualisme et les Intellectuels." *Revue bleue*, 4th series, 10: 7–13. (Repr. in Emile Durkheim, *La Science Sociale et l'Action*. Edited by J. C. Filloux. Paris, 1970: 261–78).

1907. "Lettres au directeur de la Revue néoscolastique." In *Revue néoscolastique* 14: 606–7 and 612–14.

1914. 'L'Avenir de la religion". (Repr. in *La Science Sociale et l'Action*. Edited by J.-C. Filloux. Paris, 1970: 305–13).

1963 [1925]. *L'Education Morale.* With Preface by Paul Fauconnet. Paris: PUF.

1966 [1922] *Education et Sociologie.* With Introduction by Paul Fauconnet. Paris: PUF.

1967a [1893] *De la division du travail social.* Paris: PUF.

1967b. *Sociologie et Philosophie.* 3rd edn. Paris: PUF.

1968 [1912]. *Les Formes élémentaires de la vie religieuse. Le système totémique en Australie.* Paris: PUF.

1969a [1897]. *Le Suicide. Étude de sociologie.* Paris: PUF.

1969b [1938]. *L'Evolution pedagogique en France.* Introduction by Maurice Halbwachs. Paris: PUF.

1969c [1950]. *Leçons de sociologie. Physique des moeurs et du droit.* Preface by H. N. Kubali. Introduction by G. Davy. Paris: PUF.

1975a–c. *Textes*, 3 Vols. Edited by V. Karady. Paris: Les Editions de Minuit.

1970. *La Science Sociale et l'Action.* Ed. and with Introduction by J. C. Filloux. Paris: PUF.

Easton, D. 1965. *A Framework for Political Analysis.* Englewood Cliffs: Prentice Hall.

1967. *A Systems Analysis of Political Life.* New York, London and Sydney: Wiley.

Ebbighausen, E., ed. 1976. *Bürgerlicher Staat und Legitimation.* Frankfurt-am-Main: Suhrkamp.

Edelmann, M. 1964. *The Symbolic Uses of Politics.* Urbana: University of Illinois Press.

1971. *Politics as Symbolic Action, Mass Arousal and Quiescence.* Chicago: Markham.

1976. *Politik als Ritual. Die symbolische Funktion staatlicher Institutionen und politischen Handelns.* Edited by Claus Offe. Frankfurt-am-Main and New York: Campus.

Eister, A. W. 1957. "Religious Institutions in Complex Societies: Difficulties in the Theoretic Specification of Functions." *American Sociological Review* 22 (4):387–91.

Esser, J. 1975. *Einführung in die materialistische Staatstheorie.* Frankfurt-am-Main – New York: Campus.

Filloux, J.-C. 1970. Introduction. In Emile Durkheim, *La Science Sociale et l'Action,* pp. 5–68. Paris: PUF.

Forsthoff, E. 1971. *Der Staat der Industriegesellschaft.* Munich: Beck.

Foskett, J. D. 1940. "Emile Durkheim's Contribution to the Problem of Social Order." *Research Studies of the State College of Washington* 8.

Frei, D., ed. 1978. *Überforderte Demokratie?* Zürich: Schulthess.

Gertz, C. 1973. *The Interpretation of Cultures. Selected Essays.* New York: Basic Books.

Gehlen, A. 1955. "Buchbesprechung von J. Winckelmann, *Legitimität und Legalität in Max Webers Herrschaftssoziologie,* Tübingen 1952." *Deutsches Verwaltungsblatt* 70.

Giddens, A. 1977. *Studies in Social and Political Theory.* London: Hutchinson.

1981. *A Contemporary Critique of Historical Materialism.* London: Macmillan.

Goldenweiser, A. A. 1915. Review of Durkheim 1912. *American Anthropologist* 17: 719–35.

1917. "Religion and Society: A Critique of Durkheim's Theory of the Origin and Nature of Religion." Reprinted as part 4, ch. 1 of *History, Psychology and Culture.* New York, 1933.

Gorz, A. 1982. *Farewell to the Working Class. An Essay on Postindustrial Socialism.* Tr. M. Sonnenscher. London: Pluto Press.

Greven, M., B. Guggenbergen and J. Strasser. 1975. *Krise des Staates? Zur Funktionsbestimmung des Staates im Spätkapitalismus.* Darmstadt: Luchterhand.

Grew, E., ed. 1978. *Crisis of Political Development in Europe and the United States.* Princeton: Princeton University Press.

Grottian, P. and A. Murswieck, eds. 1974. *Handlungsspielräume der Staatsadministration.* Hamburg: Hoffmann and Campe.

Guggenberger, B. 1974. *Wem nützt der Staat? Kritik der neomarxistischen Staatstheorie.* Stuttgart, Berlin, Cologne and Mainz: Kohlhammer.

1975. "Herrschaftslegitimierung und Staatskrise. Zu einigen Problemen der Regierbarkeit des modernen Staates." In Greven et al. *Krise des Staates?,* pp. 9–59.

Gündel, R. et al. 1967. "Zur Theorie des staatsmonopolistischen Kapitalismus." *Schriften des Instituts für Wirtschaftswissenschaften der DAdW zu Berlin* 22.

Gurr, T. R. 1971. *Why Men Rebel.* Princeton: Princeton University Press.

Habermas, J. 1968. *Technik und Wissenschaft als Ideologie.* Frankfurt-am-Main: Suhrkamp.

1973. *Legitimationsprobleme im Spätkapitalismus.* Frankfurt-am-Main: Suhrkamp.
1976. *Zur Rekonstruktion des historischen Materialismus.* Frankfurt-am-Main; Suhrkamp.
1981a and b. *Theorie des kommunikativen Handelns.* Vols. 1 and 2. Frankfurt-am-Main: Suhrkamp.
Hammond, P. E. 1974. *Religious Pluralism and Durkheim's Integration Thesis.* In A. W. Eister, ed., *Changing Perspectives in the Scientific Study of Relgion,* pp. 115–42. New York, London, Sydney, Toronto: Wiley.
1980a. "The Conditions for Civil Religion: A Comparison of the United States and Mexico." In R. N. Bellah and P. E. Hammond, *Varieties of Civil Religion,* pp. 40–85. San Francisco: Harper and Row.
1980b. "The Rudimentary Forms of Civil Religion." In R. N. Bellah and P. E. Hammond, *Varieties of Civil Religion,* pp. 121–37. San Francisco: Harper and Row.
1980c. "Pluralism and Law in the Formation of American Civil Religion." In R. N. Bellah and P. E. Hammond, *Varieties of Civil Religion,* pp. 138–63. San Francisco: Harper and Row.
1980d. "Civility and Civil Religion: The Emergence of Cults." In R. N. Bellah and P. E. Hammond, *Varieties of Civil Religion,* pp. 188–99. San Francisco: Harper and Row.
1980e. "The Civil Religion Proposal." In R. N. Bellah and P. E. Hammond, *Varieties of Civil Religion,* pp. 200–5. San Francisco: Harper and Row.
Heidorn, F. 1982. *Legitimität und Regierbarkeit.* Berlin: Duncker and Humblot.
Hennis, W. 1976. "Legitimität. Zu einer Kategorie der bürgerlichen Gesellschaft." *Merkur* 332 (30): 17 ff.
Hennis, W. et al., eds. 1977. *Regierbarkeit. Studien zu ihrer Problematisierung.* Vol. 1. Stuttgart: Illett.
Hirsch, J. 1974. *Staatsapparat und Reproduktion des Kapitals.* Frankfurt-am-Main: Suhrkamp.
Hondrich, K. O. 1973. *Theorie und Herrschaft.* Frankfurt-am-Main: Suhrkamp.
Kaltenbrunner, G. K., ed. 1975. *Der überforderte schwache Staat. Sind wir noch regierbar?* Freiberg: Herder.
Kielmansegg, P. Graf von. 1971. "Legitimität als analytische Kategorie." *Politische Vierteljahresschrift* 12: 367–401.
ed. 1976. "Legitimationsprobleme politischer Systeme." *Politische Vierteljahresschrift* 17, special edition 7. Opladen: Westdeutscher Verlag.
King, A. S., ed. 1976. *Why is Britain Becoming Harder to Govern?* London: BBC.
Kopp, M. and H.-P. Müller. 1980. *Herrschaft und Legitimität in modernen Industriegesellschaften.* Münich: Tuduv–Verlagsgesellschaft.
Kostede, N. 1980. *Staat und Demokratie. Studien zur politischen Theorie des Marxismus.* Darmstadt and Neuwied: Luchterhand.
Lacroix, B. 1977. "Dynamique sociale et subordination relative au politique selon Emile Durkheim." *Cahiers internationaux de sociologie* 62: 27–44.
1981. *Durkheim et le politique.* Paris: Presses de la Fondation Nationale des Sciences Politiques, and Montreal: Presses de l'Université de Montréal.

Lindberg, L. et al. 1975. *Stress and Contradiction in Modern Capitalism*. Lexington: Lexington Books.

Loos, F. 1970. *Zur Wert- und Rechtslehre Max Webers*. Tübingen: Mohr-Siebeck.

Luhmann, N. 1965. *Grundrechte als Institution. Ein Beitrag zur politischen Soziologie*. Berlin: Duncker and Humblot.

1972. *Rechtssoziologie*, Vols 1 and 2. Hamburg: Rororo.

1973. *Vertrauen*. Stuttgart (Trans. 1979 in *Trust and Power*). New York: Wiley.

1974. *Soziologische Aufklärung. Aufsätze zur Theorie sozialer Systeme*. Vol. 1. Opladen: Westdeutscher Verlag.

1975. *Legitimation durch Verfahren*. Neuwied–Berlin: Luchterhand.

1981. "Grundwerte als Zivilreligion." In N. Luhmann, *Soziologische Aufklärung*, Vol. 3. *Soziales System, Gesellschaft, Organisation*, pp. 293–308. Opladen.

Lukes, S. 1972. *Emile Durkheim. His Life and Work. A Historical and Critical Study*. London: Allen Lane.

Mauss, M. 1928. *Introduction to Emile Durkheim, Le Socialisme*. Paris (repr. 1971, 27–31)

Mayntz, R., ed. 1980. *Implementation politischer Programme*. Königstein-Taunus.

Miliband, R. 1972. *Der Staat in der kapitalistischen Gesellschaft*. Frankfurt-am-Main: Suhrkamp.

Mommsen, W. 1974a. *Max Weber und die deutsche Politik 1890–1920*. Tübingen: Möhr-Siebeck.

1974b. *Max Weber. Gesellschaft, Politik und Geschichte*. Frankfurt-am-Main: Suhrkamp.

Müller, H.-P. 1983. *Wertkrise und Gesellschaftsreform. Emile Durkheims Schriften zur Politik*. Stuttgart: Erike.

1986. "Gesellschaft, Moral und Individualismus. Emile Durkheims Moraltheorie." In Hans Bertram, ed., *Gesellschaftlicher Zwang und moralische Autonomie*, pp. 71–105. Frankfurt-am-Main.

Münch, R. 1976. *Legitimität und politische Macht*. Opladen: Westdeutscher Verlag.

1981. "Socialization and Personality Development from the Point of View of Action Theory, the Legacy of Emile Durkheim." *Sociological Inquiry* 51: 3–4, 311–54.

1984. *Die Struktur der Moderne*. Frankfurt: Suhrkamp.

Nisbet, R. 1965. *Emile Durkheim*. Englewood Cliffs, NJ: Prentice Hall.

1970. *The Sociological Tradition*. New York: Basic Books.

O'Connor, J. 1973. *The Fiscal Crisis of the State*. New York: St Martin's Press.

Offe, C. 1972. *Strukturprobleme des kapitalistischen Staates*. Frankfurt-am-Main: Suhrkamp.

1973. "'Krisen des Krisenmanangements': Elemente einer politischen Krisentheorie." In M. Jänicke, ed., *Herrschaft und Krise*, pp. 197–223. Opladen: Westdeutscher Verlag.

1975a: *Berufsbildungsreform. Eine Fallstudie über Reformpolitik*. Frankfurt-am-Main: Suhrkamp.

1975b: Introduction to Part III: "Legitimacy versus Efficiency." In L. Lindberg et al., *Stress and Contradiction in Modern Capitalism*, pp. 245–59.

1976. "Überlegungen und Hypothesen zum Problem politischer Legitimation." In R. Ebbighausen, *Bürgerlicher Staat und Legitimation*, pp. 30ff. Frankfurt-am-Main.

1979."'Unregierbarkeit'. Zur Renaissance konservativer Krisentheorien." In J. Habermas, ed., *Stichworte zur "Geistigen Situation der Zeit"*. Vol. 1. *Nation und Republik*, pp. 294–318. Frankfurt-am-Main: Suhrkamp.

Parsons, T. 1968 [1937]. *The Structure of Social Action*. Vols. I and II with a new introduction to the paperback edition. New York: Free Press.

1973. "Durkheim on religion revisited: another look at the elementary forms of the religious life." In C. Y. Glock and P. E. Hammond, eds. *Beyond the Classics? Essays in the Scientific Study of Religion*, pp. 156–80. New York: Harper and Row.

1974. "Religion in Postindustrial Society. The Problem of Secularization." *Social Research* 41: 193–225.

1978. *Action and the Human Condition*. New York, Free Press.

Poggi, G. 1978. *The Development of the Modern State. A Sociological Introduction*. Stanford: Stanford University Press.

Prager, J. 1981. "Moral Integration and Political Inclusion: A Comparison of Durkheim's and Weber's Theories of Democracy." *Social Forces* 59 (4): 918–50.

Ronge, V. and G. Schmieg. 1973. *Restriktionen politischer Planung*. Frankfurt-am-Main: Athenäum Verlag.

Rose, R. 1978. *Ungovernability: Is there Fire behind the Smoke?* Glasgow: University of Strathclyde.

Schattschneider, E. 1960. *The Semi-Sovereign People. A Realist's View of Democracy*. New York: Holt, Rinehart and Winston.

Scheuch, E. K. 1976. *Is Germany Becoming Ungovernable?* Trans. E. C. Page. Glasgow: University of Strathclyde.

Schluchter, W. 1979. *Die Entwicklung des okzidentalen Rationalismus. Eine Analyse von Max Webers Gesellschaftsgeschichte*. Tübingen: Mohr-Siebeck.

Stallberg, F. W. 1975. *Herrschaft und Legitimität. Untersuchungen zur Anwendung und Anwendbarkeit zentraler Kategorien Max Webers*. Meisenheim-am-Glan: Anton Hain.

Stanner, W. E. H. 1975. "Reflections on Durkheim and Aboriginal Religion." In W. S. F. Pickering, ed., *Durkheim on religion. A Selection of Readings with Bibliographies*. London: Routledge and Kegan Paul.

Tiryakian, E. A. 1978. "Emile Durkheim". In T. Bottomore and R. Nisbet, eds., *A History of Sociological Analysis*, pp. 187–230. New York: Basic Books.

Thomas, M. C. and C. C. Flippen. 1972. "American Civil Religion: An Empirical Study." *Social Forces* 51: 218–25.

Wallwork, E. 1972. *Durkheim: Morality and Milieu*. Cambridge, MA: Harvard University Press.

Weber, M. 1972. *Wirtschaft und Gesellschaft*. Tübingen: Mohr-Siebeck.

1973. *Gesammelte Aufsätze zur Wissenschaftslehre.* Edited by J. Winckelmann. Tübingen: Mohr-Siebeck.

Wilson, J. F. 1979. *Public Religion in American Culture.* Philadelphia: Temple University Press.

Wimberly, R. C. et al. 1976. "The Civil Religious Dimension: It it there?" *Social Forces* 54: 890–900.

Winckelmann, J. 1952. *Legitimität und Legalität in Max Webers Herrschaftssoziologie.* Tübingen: Mohr-Siebeck.

Wirth, M. 1972. *Kapitalismustheorie in der DDR.* Frankfurt-am-Main: Suhrkamp.

Wolfe, A. 1977. *The Limits of Legitimacy – Political Contradictions of Contemporary Capitalism.* New York: Free Press.

Zeitlin, I. M. 1968. *Ideology and the Development of Sociological Theory.* Englewood Cliffs, NJ: Prentice Hall.

Ritualization and public life

7 Articulating consensus: the ritual and rhetoric of media events

Daniel Dayan and Elihu Katz

To Barbara Myerhoff

Festive television

Televised events are advertised to the public as grandiose and unique.[1] But, despite their individual qualities, many of these events seem to echo each other, to answer one another. They belong to a common genre. They share common rhetoric. Thus the coronation of Elizabeth II not only predates other "royal" events such as the wedding of Prince Charles and Lady Diana, or the funeral of Lord Mountbatten, it also displays a profound kinship with events apparently far removed both thematically and geographically, such as the visit of Anwar al-Sadat to Jerusalem, the first Moon landing, the Polish pilgrimage of Pope John Paul II. All these events share a consistent set of characteristics – semantic, syntactic, and pragmatic. Their kinship is perceived not only by sociologists but by those in the industry as well. Television organizations, for example, circulate from event to event updated lists of practical recommendations, technical handbooks, catalogues of dangers and mistakes. Viewers, too, experience their festive character; they invoke a sense of occasion.

Televised ceremonies
Semantically, these events are presented as celebrations of consensus, proclaiming in effect the charter of what is now called "civil religion." Durkheim would agree.[2] "What essential difference is there" asks Durkheim, "between an assembly of Christians celebrating the principal dates of the life of Christ, or of Jews remembering the exodus from Egypt or the promulgation of the decalogue, and a reunion of citizens commemorating the promulgation of a new moral or legal system or some great event in the national life?" Durkheim would not be surprised to learn how the televis-

ing of such events can contribute to "the upholding and reaffirming . . . of the collective ideas which make up [a society's] unity and its personality." He might be surprised, however, to hear his critics argue that such events also make room for the conflicts that divide a society in addition to the common themes that unite it.

Indeed, we shall argue that media events are heavily burdened with ambiguities that demand resolution. Sometimes they present conflict, hoping that a consensus will emerge; sometimes they present consensus, hoping that an underlying conflict will be overriden; sometimes they serve as "trial balloons" to propose an idea of social order that transcends, even repudiates, the very social order from which the event arose, just as a glimpse of the messianic order might threaten any extant system of stratification and administration.[3] Media events may do all of these since they contain the semantic seeds of multivocality.

Durkheim had the idea that these "moral remakings," like holidays, punctuate the calendar at "regular intervals."[4] He would be surprised, therefore, to learn that they may be irregular as well as regular; indeed, that they may even be one-time events. But, regular or irregular, these events may be characterized *syntactically* as interruptions. Postponing their programs to make room for the occasion, the networks interrupt social life, depriving it of the rhythms conferred by non-stop broadcasting in its function as collective clock or daily agenda. This disorganization and the slight sense of chaos which accompanies it fulfill a major dramatic function: television's most powerful gesture consists precisely in interrupting the continuous flow of its programs; in dismantling its own "supertext."[5] The event is presented not only as a triumph *of* television, but as a triumph *over* television, direct access to the real world. As if to confirm this realistic ambition, the event is transmitted "live," and although it interrupts, it will never itself be interrupted.

The *pragmatic* dimension of these events (the circumstances in which they are received or understood) is equally exceptional. The space of leisure – home and its privacy – is no longer the antithesis to the public dimension of social life. Public space invades the home. People no longer undress to watch television; they may actually dress up. The event becomes the occasion for a spectatorial contract. Friends are invited in to watch the show. The apathetic television viewer described by so many television theorists as drifting from program to program in an endless and shapeless "strip," vaguely ashamed to be caught in front of his television screen, is replaced by an active viewer, a sociable being full of purpose, ready to assume his role as a spectator. Social pressure has inverted its sign. It is no longer "watch television and avoid reality." The only escape now is *not* watching. The event calls for witnesses. These witnesses

summon other witnesses to prove they have attended. We are far removed from television as "moving wallpaper."

Continuing in the realm of the pragmatic, we shall find support in the
Durkheimian tradition – with its dialectical emphasis on the social dimension of religiosity, and on the religious dimension of sociality itself – for
maintaining that media events may sometimes extend or redefine the
social boundaries of collective sentiments. Celebrations of this particular
form of civil religion sometimes break out of the traditional boundaries of
community or nation to produce new social configurations.

Totalitarian media events, democratic media events
Media events display a specific character in Western democracies that is
different from those in the Eastern bloc, both in terms of ideological content and ceremonial style.

Televised events in the West are often prospective, and not only commemorative. The occasions they celebrate are typically "unexpected,"
"unheard of," or even "unimaginable." Their unexpectedness, their
interruptive status, are among their most celebrated features, those
usually associated with the word "historic." Used here as an absolute su-
perlative, "historic" carries a millenarian tone, suggesting a passage
beyond history. The event – we are told – will introduce us to a new era. In
contrast, media events of East European television are usually retrospective commemorations. History is not the site of the unexpected, but the
focus of pre-planned expectations. It does not allow for original
experiences, only for reiteration and confirmation. Political ceremonies
in the East are mere diagrams or illustrations complementing a highly
structured ideological discourse.

Media events in the West have a much more powerful role by being
dramatic examples substituted for the coherence of a discursive ideology.
From each event, a fragment of ideology can be inferred, but one must
note that the ritual performance precedes its exegesis, its after-the-fact
justification or rationalization. Like sacred texts, media events are not
expressions of a given, exclusive meaning. They trigger, instead, hermeneutic attitudes, inviting multiple commentaries. Media events call for
ideology to caption them. The corpus of our media event consists of symbolic gestures presented ceremonially to enlist consensus. But there exists
an ambiguity in the consensus they celebrate; the object of the consensus
often remains in question, even though its presence can hardly be doubted.

Media events in Eastern Europe are also defined in terms of consensus,
but of a pre-existing sort which is authoritatively pronounced effective.
The party and its leaders are, by definition, the expression of popular
will. As a result totalitarian media events offer displays of control, or

manifestations of obedience. They are characteristically "monologic." The relationship suggested between political leaders and the public is that of a choreographic oneness. Organized in gigantic tableaux, the mass audience is transfigured into the face of Lenin or the body of Mao.[6] There can be no dialogue, because there is no distinction between leader and led. They are ideologically and scenographically interwoven. All are supposed to speak in the same voice. Consensus is not needed, because it is posited *a priori*. Masses are not cast as the interlocutors of political communication; they compose its kinetic message.

Much the opposite, the ceremonies of the West which concern us advertise their dialogic form. They often herald the introduction of major change which popular agreement is called upon to legitimize. The essence of these events lies in the mobilization of consensus, more prospective than retrospective. Without consensus, ceremonies lose their meaning and fail; they turn into empty forms. They are disdained proposals, "void performatives."[7] Underlying such occasions is a dramaturgic, rather than choreographic model which requires the presence of two distinct and complementary roles: performer and respondent. Performance and reaction are largely simultaneous, but they are theoretically independent. Their dialogue may be simulated or futile. Such a dialogue is nevertheless essential to the nature of the proposed fiction and to the metaphoric nature of the ceremonial display.

As pointed out by Eric Rothenbuhler, the sacred centers of society, and the symbolic situations in which they manifest themselves, serve totalitarian systems as providers of a constant justification of the regime. Practices are equated with extant norms, and celebration of norms. Political ceremonies propose the sacralization of institutions. In democratic societies, on the other hand, the current state of society is "held up to judgement by the sacred, its leaders are seen as striving for standards, not justified by them."[8] Thus, in Western ceremonies, the leaders are the spectacle, and the led are the watchers, whereas in totalitarian regimes – in spite of their theoretical oneness – the public constitutes a spectacle offered to the glance of the leaders.

Consensus or conflict: ambiguous event

Describing the riots of May 1968 in France, Roland Barthes[9] stresses the clarity of the signs used to express the conflict. Although emphatically confrontational the situation was, nevertheless, based on an underlying consensus. Everybody agreed on the repartition of each camp's emblems: French flag versus black or red flag; the "Marseillaise" versus the "International"; the Champs Elysées versus the Bastille, and more generally, right bank versus left bank.

The conflictual ceremonies discussed by Lukes[10] are of this order too. Ostensibly disagreeing with Durkheim – or, more precisely, with Durkheimians – he protests that a theory of the ceremonial mirroring of a society ought to make room for its conflicts as well as its consensus. But Lukes ignores the consensual implication of the very institution of ceremoniality, even when the ceremony addresses conflict. A labor strike is indeed a demonstration of social difference and disruption, but it is also an occasion on which the conflicting parties agree to abide by ceremonial rules such as the choreography of the picket line, the rhetoric of the posters, the advertising and the chanting, and the etiquette of the televised confrontation between labor and management.[11] Indeed, it is the rules of the game that are celebrated. The event shapes the conflict; it confines it. In articulating it, the conflict is shown, not incorrectly, as part of an underlying consensus.

As discussed by Alexander[12] and by Lang and Lang,[13] the live broadcasting of the Senate Watergate hearings may be seen not only as a public outbreak of bitter conflict but also as an appeal to, and celebration of, the rules by which the system is governed, and in terms of which society reflects upon and evaluates itself. This reflective mood is characteristic of all holidays that detach us from daily concerns and cause us to commune with some central value of society. Events such as Watergate, rather than simply celebrating a value or its personification in a heroic person, remind us that the values are guidelines to behavior and invite their application. The consensus around the rules, and the reassertion of faith in the institutions, overcame the Watergate conflict even to the point of enlisting the allegiance of the vanquished leader himself.

Even events that are much more manifestly consensual – those that celebrate not conflict but its resolution – are not as unequivocal as they seem. Being live, even their organizers and spokespersons – even the network presenters – cannot be certain how they will proceed. Often enough, they have more than one organizer with conflicting motives – such as Begin and Sadat, or the pope and the Polish government – each vying for his own outcome and his own image of consensus. Once produced the events call for different interpretations. The Royal Wedding is in danger of being jeered at; the Olympics may be perceived in terms of international conflict rather than as a ceremonial appeasement of conflict. True, crowds are electrified and the home audience is busy celebrating the event. But what are they celebrating? Always grandiose, full of pomp, media events may be numbered among the major monuments of this part of the century. But they are ambiguous monuments because they do not only display and reaffirm an already established consensus. They are engaged, rather, in the business of defining a new consensus, either by proposing new symbols for an existing core of values, or, more profoundly, by modifying the nature of articulation of such values. Thus, symbolic events may be said not to be "mirrors" of consensus, but means of *articulating* or *rearticulating* it, and the passage from the mirror metaphor to that of construction reminds us that consensus is not simply there waiting an official call but must be produced. This production is not exempt from conflictual aspects, and progression through social space, from center to periphery, from inception to reception is a sequence of negotiations, amendments and rearticulations leading to, then based on, the televised text of the event. Let us first take a closer look at this text.

The event as text: rhetorics of consensus

Media events are ceremonial hybrids: part spectacles, part festivals, part texts, part performances. This complex character affects the roles of all participants. Organizers and public are no longer exclusively characterized by their positions at both ends of the communication process. They are engulfed in the media event; they become part of the television text.

Expanding events
The festive broadcast is not a neatly shaped object circulating from emitter A to receiver B. Rather, like an oil stain, it characteristically expands, and ends up by including the circumstances of its broadcasting and reception. Thus the original (and limited) ceremonial performance is not much more than a starting point for the much larger performance engineered by television. Once on the air, the event progressively incorporates its entire context, including the space from which it is watched. Spectators are filmed on the ceremonial site, but they are also filmed at home, or in distant celebrations staged as "answers" to the event. Matching the sights of the ceremony itself, constantly expanding "reverse shots" abandon the direct ceremonial audience, depict increasingly larger publics, and finally include, at least by metonymic representation, the whole of society. For analytic reasons, let us however distinguish between shot and reverse shot, between text and context, between the ceremonial action and the reaction it elicits.

Stripped to the essential, ceremonial action consists of a "presentation of self" performed by a given society for its own members and those of other societies.[14] This presentation highlights what the society considers its essence, its official identity. Symbols to which Edward Shils attributes

the power of resisting centrifugal forces (and which he defines consequently as society's "center") are ceremonially displayed.[15] But this presentation is more than solemn. It is also what Victor Turner[16] would call
"subjunctive."

Events as subjunctive exercises
Within any culture, subjunctive attitudes can be opposed to practices in
the "indicative." The subjunctive emerges at exceptional moments
during which the rules of daily life are temporarily suspended. The new
rules correspond to the domains of the "potential," or the "desirable."
Norms are no longer ideal constructions, inaccessible models, lofty
guidelines, both revered and neglected because of their unattainability.
When it accedes to the subjunctive mode, a society becomes, at least temporarily, what it ought to be. It enacts its professed objectives, reiterates
its own principles. Subjunctive behaviors thus call for ceremonial displays. Being universalizable, or at least generalizable within a given cultural universe,[17] they are ideal occasions for self presentation.

Media events are celebrations of subjunctive situations or of situations
proposed as subjunctive. Anwar al-Sadat enters unarmed into the enemy
camp, to propose peace. The Israeli government welcomes the man responsible for the Yom-Kippur War. The Polish government takes the
risk of inviting the head of the Catholic Church. In each case, a conflict of
interests is presented as if it had been resolved in concordance with norms
which transcend these interests. Without using this phrase in a pejorative
sense, media events are "symbolic manipulations." They display a striking affinity to the techniques used in therapeutic contexts by traditional
"shamans."[18] Through ceremony, a problematic situation is redefined,
transcribed in another language, transposed from the "indicative" of conflict to the subjunctive of conflict resolution.

Symbolic manipulations do not always appease the conflicts they
address. Thus the passage of the Watergate episode from the columns of
the *Washington Post* to live television not only reflects the deepening of the
crisis, but leads to its further escalation. Transferring the situation from a
given genre (investigation of a scandal) to another genre (televised celebration, or "media event") has a characteristic result. The very ceremoniality of the genre, its subjunctiveness, its normative "ambition,"
reinforce the position of the Senate Judiciary Committee and weaken that
of the White House defendants. The irregularities under investigation can
no longer be presented as regrettable but insignificant. They are by now in-
escapably symbolic; emblems of the whole regime. By translating the
event in the subjunctive register of political norms, the televised broadcast of the Senate Watergate hearings creates an irreversible situation. As

Alexander suggests it leads to the eventual impeachment of the president, but also to a new and little celebrated equilibrium.[19] A tacit reconciliation takes place between the "silent majority" and the outspoken left, to which the event gives the opportunity of abandoning an entrenched – and finally sterile – position outside the consensus, and of enunciating the basic values of American democracy. Functioning as a *rite de passage*, the event confirms that "the war is over," allows adversary factions to move from their uncompromising positions towards a possible dialogue. Assuming a judiciary form, this dialogue is far from peaceful. It nevertheless invokes accepted rules and shared values.

Subjunctive transcriptions of crisis usually allow symbolic control over them. John Kennedy is assassinated, but his funeral, with its disciplined pageantry and the martyred image, announces that democracy is safe. The sacrificial metaphor proposes the death of the president as an additional guarantee of the survival of the system. Death becomes a tribute, a price to be paid. When subjunctive transcription is turned into a rhetorical instrument, it encourages sophistry, of course. Thus, in a virtuoso homily, the Archbishop of Canterbury manages to portray Prince Charles and Princess Diana as normative ideals, rather than narcissistic models. A narrative casuistry can guarantee pathos by rephrasing a situation in terms of surmounted conflict.

A grammar of media events

This does not necessarily mean that all evoked conflicts are imaginary, and all proposed solutions cosmetic. Based on principles which it might be useful to describe in terms borrowed from Propp or Greimas,[20] tele-ceremonies progressively develop a refined grammar. Their rhetoric includes three ritual "subgenres" which we call "contests, conquests and coronations."[21]

"Contests" (Olympic Games, presidential debates, Watergate) are ceremonial competitions, miniaturized confrontations, that oppose matched individuals or teams equally worthy of respect, competing in good faith, and in accordance with a shared set of rules. Beyond winner and loser, contests are celebrations of these rules. Their relevance is affirmed no matter who wins. Indeed these events do mirror conflict as Lukes would have it, but they also reveal the underlying solidarity which allows the conflicting parties each to perform its part, and, in so doing, to discover the rules that govern both conflict and its reconciliation.

"Conquests" (Sadat's visit to Jerusalem, visit of the pope to Poland, the first moon landing) also involve the domain of rules, but they do so quite differently. They correspond to the moment when an established rule, either a historical habit (hostility between Israel and the Arab world; irreconcilable distance between socialist Poland and the Vatican) or a natural law (inaccessibility of the moon) is reformulated in the wake of an advance of technology, or abolished in the name of a higher ethical norm. "Conquests" are live broadcasts of great human achievement. Their protagonists are not mere champions; they are heroes confronted by apparently insuperable odds. They acquire a mythical status, the power of reconciling opposites, the privilege of reformulating rules in the name of laws which transcend them. The victory of a "conqueror" is much more than a personal or partisan triumph. It calls for the conversion of his opponents, and is therefore presented as a victory for all parties concerned. Thus the American victory in the space-race is converted into a "giant step for mankind."

Theoretically, "coronations" represent the highest moment of the heroic curriculum. Often (funerals of Nasser, Kennedy, Mountbatten) – they are consecrations of a dead hero. The departed is ceremonially transferred from the world of the living to the realm of norms. Symbol among symbols, he[22] enters the Shilsian "center". His life is transcribed, according to the rules of hagiography, into an educational program, a matrix of desirable behaviors, a catalogue of virtues. However, coronations do not always benefit from the remarkable semiotic plasticity of defunct heroes. Instead of being metaphoric, they may be literal. Think of Queen Elizabeth's coronation or of the wedding of Prince Charles; they are uneasy transfigurations of living subjects.

Our three ceremonial types do not exhaust the genre; recent examples prove the existence of televised ceremonies with no narrative continuity and no individualized hero.[23] Nor do they exclude each other: most of the events we have encountered combine, in various ways, elements of the three. However, in most cases, one type seems to dominate the telling of the event.

We should finally stress that from our point of view these three types are not equally worthy of interest. "Contests" are a normal, if not routine part of the functioning of institutions. They correspond to what Greimas[24] would call a "qualifying task," and are regularly, if not frequently, repeated; they allow, for example, for the renewal of political leadership. "Contests" lack the unexpectedness, the transfigurative character which confers an almost messianistic coloration on certain media events.

"Coronations" are often electrifying, but they are relatively repetitive. Their occurrence is predictable even though one can hardly anticipate their timing. (Nobody could foresee the date of Enrico Berlinguer's death, or the impressive nature of the reactions it triggered throughout Italy.) Yet, leaders have to enter the political arena and they must exit some day. "Contests" and "Coronations" thus function as *rites de passage*, scanning social life at infrequent, but repetitive, intervals.

"Conquests" on the other hand, are mostly unpredictable, and may have no equivalent except in the "falling-in-love" which Francesco Alberoni situates at the beginning of all major, political or religious movements.[25] Typically oriented towards the future, true "conquests" often radiate an extraordinary intensity, an intensity which relies on the "conqueror's" charisma, but involves much more. "Conquests" provoke conversations to new ways of seeing. The event may challenge the beliefs which provide meaning to historical experience, leaving room for the possibility of different beliefs, for the rearranging of the world in patterns theretofore unthinkable and for which the event is a testing ground.

The event as process:
conflict surmounted

Often, the very existence of an event has to be paid for with so many compromises that the final result is a riddle, a masterpiece in elusive ambiguity. While proclaiming its consensual ambition, the event turns into a definitional battlefield. Concerned parties keep arguing long after the event is over. Sometimes the arguing infiltrates the event itself and the ceremonial invocation of consensus hardly camouflages a juxtaposition or even a confrontation of distinct performances.

Let us then move from the global, monolithic aspect presented by media events when considered as "texts" to another perspective which stresses their processual nature.

A chain of endorsements

The event on screen has an obvious symbolic value. However, it can be read, not only as a symbol, but as a process involving a series of performances. These performances are logically consecutive, but temporarily simultaneous. Each incorporates the previous one, and comments upon it. Each can be described as an adoption and an "endorsement" of the previous performance.

Initially, one finds a ritual of limited scope, or even a purely pragmatic situation. The Prince of Wales and the woman of his choice pronounce the vows of marriage. An American missile leaves Cape Canaveral and lands on the moon. The event, possibly important, possibly insignificant as well, is endorsed by state authorities. The endorsement elevates it to a symbolic dimension: the event's protagonists are associated with the august repertory of society's "central" values. By now, the original situation is transformed into an official ceremony and proposed to the public as worthy of celebration.

The first concerned audience is made of those physically present on the ceremonial grounds. Swimmers on the Florida beaches applaud when they get a glimpse of Apollo XI. Crowds mass in the London streets to cheer and hail the princely couple in their horse-drawn carriage. By their presence, they confirm the validity of the ceremony; they legitimate the decisions made by the officals who took the risk of organizing it.

The ceremony, at this stage, includes an original situation (ritual or not), its endorsement by state authorities, and, responding to this endorsement, the reaction of the crowd. Television – either national or private – is now called upon to play its part; that of endorsing the whole of the occasion and of transcribing it as a spectacle. In response, spectators gather in ad hoc parties as viewing communities who translate the television spectacle back into a ceremony of sorts by inscribing it in the festive context improvised at home. This new endorsement is followed by that of foreign television audiences whose access to the event depends, of course, on an additional endorsement: that of foreign television networks.[26]

The sequence of endorsement does not stop here. One must also take into account the role of the written press. Concerning the ceremony itself, the role of the written press seems "marginal." It ushers in the event, and retrospectively analyzes it. (Willy-nilly, editorial writers are transformed into television critics.) One must not underestimate the importance of these "marginal" contributions. Ushering of the event by the press is essential to its success, since it determines its magnitude, builds up its following. Post facto assessment retrospectively shapes public perception. Moreover, the mobilization of the written press deserves attention in and by itself. This unusual convergence in regard to certain events clearly involves – as stressed by Philip Elliott – a ceremonial dimension.[27] The press, of course, may fail to respond, but its failure may also lead to failure of the event, which takes us back to the issue of consensus.

Let us, however, limit ourselves to the essential articulations of the ceremonial event. Such an event requires at least: (a) an organizing entity; (b) an audience gathered on the ceremonial site; (c) television networks to broadcast it; and (d) a viewing public reached by these networks. Thus, there is an organized event, an attended event, a broadcast event, and the experience of this broadcast event. Note that the event presents itself, not as a text, but as a series of texts grafted onto each other.[28] Each text includes the previous one; each proposes for ceremonial celebration that which, in the previous stage, was already an answer to a former proposal. Thus, the royal wedding is a ritual performance cast within a ceremonial performance, framed in a popular celebration, transmitted in a televised spectacle, which in turn is incorporated into home celebrations. Some of these home celebrations are themselves filmed so that the televised spectacle ultimately includes even the reactions it has itself elicited. The broadcast now tells and shows its own reception![29]

In our view, each successive adoption represents the potential emergence of a specific conflict. The progression of the event seems therefore characterized by a constant negotiation. It is a succession of cease-fires, amendments and compromises. Within a democratic framework, events cannot simply be imposed. Their success is never guaranteed. Media events do not take place in a controlled void. Success depends at each stage on agreement of the parties concerned. Let us review these stages.

Organizers: monophony or babelic polyphony

State authorities control festive calendars. It is their privilege to determine suitable themes or occasions for ceremonial events, and to promote only those which correspond to their professed values. And yet, once the event is triggered, state authorities lose control. Ceremony is taken over and remodelled by television, in view of the transformed nature of the public space it commands.[30]

But, even before the intervention of television, we must realize that the authorities who sponsor the event do not necessarily constitute a homogeneous entity. A distinction can be made between the events' actors – the protagonists of the original, circumscribed, action or gesture – and the organizers of the state ceremony. The actors are often used by the organizers to express the latter's views. Often they are already dead and thus available for any symbolic manipulation. Sometimes, they have no other identity than that conferred upon them for the occasion. Tom Wolfe reminds us that the astronauts of the first moon landing were chosen as much for their ambassadorial qualities – good looks, American-type, clean-cut geniality – as for their technical talents.[31] Their virtues were impressive but useless given the nature of their actual mission: before being turned into a ceremonial prop symbolically unfit for anything but "the right stuff," Apollo XI was supposed to be "manned" by chimpanzees.

In this case the event's "actors" are no more than emanations of the organizers' intentions. Their image-like quality[32] provides absolute freedom to ceremonial planners. The organizing entity thus remains perfectly monophonic. At other times, however, this entity is not only polyphonic but frankly divided, either because there are many, and differently-minded, organizers, or because actors have their own scripts and do not intend to follow anyone's directives, or for both reasons.

Thus, on his visit to Poland, Pope John Paul II goes to his home-country as a "pilgrim." But throughout his visit, the pontiff trespasses the strict liturgical boundaries assigned to his presence by the event's co-organizer, the Polish government that invited him. His visit is ratified by the civil authorities. It is a state visit. It is also a game of hide-and-seek. Firmly invited to distribute in advance the text of his speeches, he complies, but throws in last-minute improvisations which take his censors by surprise. In similar manner, President Sadat actively contributes to the effusive rhetorics which mark his state visit to Israel.[33] He salutes the Israeli flag, the memory of the victims of the holocaust, the grave of the unknown soldier; he accepts flowers, gifts and children's greetings. Yet, at the Knesset, he also pronounces a rigid, intransigent, maximalist speech and further distances himself from his hosts by delivering it in Arabic, constraining the Israeli prime minister to respond in Hebrew, although he would have preferred the exchange to be in English.

These various expressions of tension manifest a fundamental disagreement on the meaning of the visit, a disagreement which the Israeli public, reluctant to give up the euphoric feeling created by the visit, chose to ignore.[34]

For one of its organizers – the Israeli government – the long-awaited gesture of recognition was what was most wanted and thus the fact of the visit would have sufficed either in itself or as a preamble to future negotiations. For the other organizer and main actor, President Sadat, the visit was part and parcel of the negotiation. With the real danger that it meant to his political and physical survival, the visit was in fact his contribution to a negotiating event he conceived as a public display of sacrifices and counter-sacrifices. Israelis conceived the situation in terms of quiet "diplomacy." Sadat proposed a spectacular exchange. They offered a quid pro quo. He started a "potlatch."

Yet the event took place. It did celebrate consensus, but, there were two of them. Through Egyptian and Israeli voices, the event paid a similar homage to peace. It did so in idioms not only distinct but hardly compatible.

It is easy to see, therefore, how the boundaries originally defined for an event by its organizers can be redefined – indeed, can go awry – as an event proceeds. The Polish government and its state-controlled television allowed the pope to make a "pilgrimage" to show the world that a Polish pope was welcome in his homeland. It could not foresee that solidarity between socialist workers and Church might be the result, or that the pope – by showing in pilgrimage after pilgrimage that national boundaries are only enclaves of the universal Church – would fuel the yearning for reunion of Eastern and Western Europe. Similarly, the hope of Premier Begin for a consensus between Israel and Egypt failed to foresee that the heroic image of President Sadat would so influence opinion in the United Sates that the Arab leader and his nation would come to be perceived as a Western-style ally, equal to, or better than, Begin and Israel.

Crowds: absence, fervour, riot, carnival

In any ceremony, and especially in the case of one intended as a mass ceremony, the physical absence of a public represents definitional failure. Such a failure may be avoided through authoritarian measures. One may limit access to the event; failure is then unverifiable. One may also force crowds to gather on the ceremonial site; failure is then impossible. Yet, because of geographical configurations which rule out any direct audience, some events are hardly transposable into ceremonies. In response to the moon landing of Apollo XI, bathers stand on Florida beaches, applauding with the best of will an event so distant as to make their gathering slightly absurd. Similarly, the engineers at Cape Canaveral start rejoicing in the unseemly company of their controls, monitors and knobs. Bathers and engineers are as close to the event as one can imagine, but not enough to be ceremonially part of it.

The presence of a crowd on the site of an event is necessary to its ceremonial existence, but it does not automatically guarantee its success. A crowd may be both present and hostile. It may protest the event instead of legitimating it; it may turn celebration into riot, endorsement into challenge. In less extreme situations, the public on the site may choose to misunderstand the event, to read it wrong, to reformulate or to pervert its values. Thus the wedding of Prince Charles is stripped of its solemnity when punk members of the audience start identifying princely pageantry with their own kitsch and consequently behave in a carnival manner. While television cameras coyly avert their gaze, a discrete negotiation – mostly tut-tutting on the part of policemen – brings the stray sheep back to the concert of straightforward cheers. But even when television enters into play, and does some well-meaning touching of the situation, it is not necessarily uncritical. The nature of its endorsement of the event may openly clash with the organizers' intents.

Television: fiction, journalism, liturgy

In certain circumstances, television networks may refuse to broadcast "live" an event proposed by government authorities. This refusal is easiest in the case of private networks; the reasons for not covering an event live generally derive from box-office preoccupations.[35] Yet, one finds cases when such a refusal is ideological. The event is shown but within the framework of everyday news,[36] and without the privileges attached to the status of a media event. The situation is acknowledged, but its ceremoniality and the consensus it invokes are refused. Ceremony is seen here as a cosmetic reshuffling, a minor variation on the *status quo ante*. Its symbolic power is denied or simply credited to the wishful thinking of the organizers.

Such attitudes almost always characterize broadcasters' treatment of the ceremonial events of other countries. Of course the events proposed by the established authorities of the broadcaster's own station are markedly privileged. But privilege, here, has limits. Let us try to analyze what happens when a network agrees to provide full ceremonial treatment for a given event.

The first problem encountered is one of organization. To whom can the event be entrusted? To the journalists in charge of news? To special teams recruited from sport and entertainment programs? To ceremonial experts? The recourse to special teams – take for example the productions of Michael Lumley for the BBC; the commentaries of Nicholas Dimbleby for the same BBC, or those of Leon Zitrone for France's TFI – has advantages. It avoids journalists who are feared for their potential irreverence or criticism. Yet, whenever an event has a political dimension – and all major events do – one can hardly dispense with journalistic expertise.

Journalists therefore are often called upon to contribute. They face an almost impossible task. Are they to keep their critical stance, the distance usually associated with objectivity, or will they agree to become custodians of the event's success like "wedding photographers" whose task is to smile to the guests while portraying them from the best angles? More exactly (and since the event cannot really take place without them), will they become the priests whose charge it is to conduct the ceremony? If so, what distance can they maintain when an event becomes part of their own performance?

The problem turns up frequently and in dramatic terms. Take the Camp David peace treaty, for example. While the celebration is taking place on the lawns of the White House, noisy demonstrators, massed at a short distance, can be heard in protest. Should one cover the whole situation, including the booing and mistreatment of the ceremony? Despite an obvious lack of symmetry – three heads of state, whole governments on one side; a determined but not necessarily representative group of protesters on the other – this would amount to framing the event as a "conflict" between "supporters" and "opponents" of a peace treaty. Or should one, on the contrary, respect the consensual character of the ceremony, protect its text, and exclude any reference to the demonstrators? The choice is not easy. Caught between consensual imperatives and journalistic norms, the various networks represented on the site vary in their choices. Their dilemma repeats itself from event to event. In some cases consensus is favored: the BBC builds a protective barrier around the wedding of Prince Charles, silencing, for the duration of the event, all echoes of the Toxteth riots. Similarly, and despite an extraordinary potential for scandal, the assassination of Lee Harvey Oswald during the funeral of his presumed victim, President Kennedy, tends to be mini-mized. In the commentary of CBS's closing program on the event, Oswald's death is described as a "grotesque" interlude in the midst of a tragedy.[37] The point here is clearly to avoid mixing styles.

Sometimes, though, the accent is put on conflict and the ceremoniality of the event is abandoned. Thus the networks covering the 1968 Conven-tion in Chicago lose interest in the ritual of nominations, move their cameras outside the Convention halls and start filming in the streets where young radical demonstrators face the brutal repression organized by Mayor Daley's police force. Journalists may be turned into priests for a moment but they remain journalists.

Even when journalists stick to their priestly role, the possibility of con-flict is not altogether eliminated. There are many ways of performing a ritual, many ways of broadcasting a ceremony. Thus, television treat-ment may fall short or go beyond the wishes of the organizers: Kurt and Gladys Lang, describing the triumphal welcome offered to General MacArthur by the population of Chicago, underline the active inter-vention of television, its success in making this welcome much more triumphant on screen than it was in the streets.[38] But official intentions may also be perverted or subverted. Astonishingly, such is the case with *Olympia*, a film on the Berlin Olympics produced by Leni Riefensthal for the Nazi regime. At the peak of "Aryan" racial theories, *Olympia* cele-brates at length the prowess of a black athlete, Jesse Owens.[39] Such is also the case for the parade organized in 1946 by the British government to celebrate the conclusion of the Second World War. This "victory parade" was conceived in homage to the virtues of the British people, and, especially, as a glorification of the courage displayed by the civilian popu-lation. The BBC radio production played down the civilian role, high-lighted that of the army, turning the event into a military parade. The organizers' intentions were trampled to the accompaniment of brasses and drums.[40]

Sometimes enhancing the performance of the event, sometimes altoge-ther rejecting its claims, television provides an active and often partisan reading. It displays what is less a report than a reaction to the event. How is this reaction received in turn by television spectators?

Television spectators: commitment, avoidance, desecration
Watching a media event is a social act. To attend this type of broadcast is
like inviting the event home. Home, for the occasion, is turned into an
open house. Media events provoke innumerable invitations to "come and
watch television with us"; they trigger epidemics of gatherings. By so
doing, those who participate in these gatherings enter an informal contract. They commit themselves to watching. Not only does the event constitute a "phatic" link between the society's center and its "periphery,"
but it reactivates all sorts of affinity networks among spectators. Provok-
ing a flurry of telephone calls, it increases sociability within the periphery
itself.

Members of the audience may also commit themselves not to watch.
They may organize themselves in actively hostile parties, or decide to
ignore the event altogether. What is relevant here is the social, almost
"public" nature of their behavior. In view of the collective pressure
which calls upon one to be a witness of the event, one cannot simply skip
its transmission. The fact of not showing up in front of the television
screen is more than the expression of individual preference or personal dis-
interest; it is a gesture of near defiance, an action for which one is responsible. One must account for disassociating oneself from a mobilized
society. This is why the contractual dimension of the proposed spectacle
never vanishes into thin air. The refusal to watch has to turn into a collective decision to ignore the event. To flee from Prince Charles' wedding, a
party of British anti-royalists charter a ship to Boulogne, where they
drink (champagne) to accompany their escape from an omnipresent ceremony. Through this slightly histrionic gesture, the event is not merely
overlooked; it is emphatically disdained.

Hostility may go further and provide a new ceremony in order to
demean, deride or denigrate the proposed event. Spectators no longer display their lack of concern, but actively concern themselves with desecration. They generate a counter-event, often pardoxically ceremonial. A
practical joker dressed as Prince Charles marries a drag queen imperson-
ating Lady Diana. More sinister in tone is the hanging of Sadat's effigy in
the streets of Baghdad where this effigy is insulted, defiled and set on fire.

Watching the event has little to do with the passivity generally at-
tributed to television spectators.[41] Passivity, in this case, seems to be
replaced by an active attitude confirming the exceptionality of the event,
its "liminal" character, the passage it represents from "structure" to
"anti-structure."[42] A television ceremony exists only potentially
without its mass audience. It needs to be seen in order to exist. To watch
it is to commit oneself in its favor, to enter into the contract proposed by
the ceremony. Let us now delineate the major features of this contract.

The event as a contract

The witnesses of a traditional ceremony bring it into full being by engaging their presence in it. Thus is defined a double performance: the ritual itself and its validation by the public.

In the case of media events, three partners are involved. In addition to the authorities who set the event in motion, and the audiences who do (or do not) subscribe to it, the media play a relatively independent part. This part can be described as condensing the two previous ones. First, the media must intervene for the ceremony to take place as a mass ceremony. Television thus becomes part of the entity that launches the event; it represents an extension of the organizers by transmitting their proposal to the public. But television also anticipates the role of the public, since it confers on this proposal, by the very fact of transmitting it, a first validation. Television thus appears, not only as a go-between, not only as a partner, in its own right, but as the major protagonist in this whole interaction. Its role consists less in transmitting the event than in stimulating it.

Ceremonial pathology: external
The contractual nature of this threesome becomes clear when one examines the reasons why a given event runs adrift or flounders. The pathology of televised events can actually take two main forms. The ceremonial contract may be refused; it may also be broken.

Breaking the contractual nature of media events determines a pathology that might be called external. This type of pathology deviates from the democratic ideals. Through coercion, one of the three protagonists in the event is eliminated or replaced.

The first victim of this process may be the entity organizing the event. Following the kidnapping and slaughter of the Israeli athletes, broadcasting of the Munich Olympics moves out of the control of the Olympic Committee. They are forcefully turned into a tribune where what is preached is no longer brotherhood among peoples, but the necessity of excluding some of them. The event has been kidnapped, its program reformulated. The role of the organizers has been usurped.

The next candidate for elimination is the public. Whenever public reactions – be they enthusiastic or negative – are judged dangerous, audiences are kept at bay. The exclusion concerns first of all the in-person audience: the crowds massed on the site of the ceremony. Fearing a reaction of indifference, or even hostility, to the funeral of President Sadat, vice-president Mubarak orders the army to surround the Cairo suburb where the event is due to take place. Egyptians are kept away from the site, filtered, admitted one by one. Filmed by cameras both awkwardly static and too few for the task, the announced funeral turns into a furtive, barely ritualized burial.

The elimination of the audience may also apply to the immense majority of spectators who stay at home and attend the event on their television screens. During Pope John Paul II's visit to Poland, state television authorities not only managed to suppress all the shots depicting crowds, they also chose to confine live broadcasting to the areas where the filmed ceremonies were actually taking place, areas which clearly did not need these broadcasts, since in most cases their population was already gathered around the pontiff. To these spectators, the broadcast was useless. Others had no access.

Forceful elimination may finally affect the media, and television in particular. Surrounded with frenetic rejoicing, Khomeini's return to Iran after a long exile is, at the outset, broadcast live on Iranian television. Following a mysterious power cut, the broadcast is interrupted after a few minutes. In this case, as in the previous examples, the event-as-a-contract has been broken. The ceremonial exchange has been prevented or pre-empted.

Ceremonial pathology: internal
Televised ceremonies may also suffer internally, so to speak, from a pathology which is more specific to their own nature. Their failure may be provoked, not from an external violation of the ceremonial contract but by the legitimate refusal of this contract by one of the concerned parties. State authorities have the privilege of organizing events. They can propose them. In the west, at least, they cannot impose them. Events may be refused by the media. Thus, all three major American channels decline President Reagan's 1983 invitation to broadcast the festivities he organized for a day of solidarity with Poland. They judge this manifestation too meek.

Once accepted by the media, and consequently broadcast, events may be rejected by the public. Spectators may ignore altogether the circumstance and its solemnity. Such is the fate of President Nixon's visit to communist China. The visit marks a historic reconciliation. It is broadcast live. The television event is a failure. In fact, the situation does not even antagonize the audience; it leaves it only indifferent.

Events which are attended by huge audiences obviously do not encounter this apathetic response. The contract proposed by the organizing authorities, and endorsed by the media, is, in such cases, accepted by the last major protagonist: the public. But the contract is not always clear.

Monuments of the possible: The performance of the public

Ceremonial proposals are necessarily ambiguous since they are made essentially in gestural form. To accept an event is to recognize its subjunctiveness, and to invest the situation it proposes with a ceremonial value. This acceptance does not require a total understanding, and the event often remains elusive, despite its own claims to obviousness and the clarifying captions offered by the media. Television succeeds more in suggesting an attitude towards events than in spelling out their signification. Indeed, instant exegesis is often an impossible task, given the "babelic" nature of many events, and also given the historical ambitions they display.

If these historical ambitions are to be taken seriously, the text of the occasion, the proposed event, represents only half the event. The historical dimension of the event really concerns what the public does with the proposal. Anthropologists – Barbara Myerhoff, in particular – point to the fact that religious traditions cannot be transmitted according to a "take it or leave it" model; that they have to be negotiated, translated, adapted to the particular styles of specific collectivities or generations. The orthodoxy represented by the "big traditions" has to be reformulated in the idioms specific to the "little traditions" which govern the practices of actual worshippers.[43] Similarly, our one-time events cannot impress on the public the intentions of the organizers, even when these intentions are reasonably clear. As suggested by Stuart Hall and by David Morley, audience members can accept dominant readings, but they can also construct "oppositional readings,"[44] or simply submit an event, by displaying their indifference to it, to a "critique of silence." But, even when the public joins in the "dominant reading," the nature of what is read can not be known in advance. The actual, realized meaning of the event can only be assessed historically, that is in retrospect.

We propose a minimal definition of the acceptance of the event. To accept the event, is to accept its "subjunctive" value; to withhold doubts, as least for a while, concerning its importance and the sincerity of its professed motives. Thus, the subjunctive mood accompanying Sadat's visit in Israel also consists in *not* projecting a Machiavellian frame on the visit, and in not denouncing the reasons behind Sadat's gesture as deceitful, as some Israelis did, refusing the subjunctive. Seeing the event as subjunctive meant accepting it as a bona fide gesture towards peace.

Subjunctiveness refuses cynicism, but is not uncritical. It entails the reevaluation of an existing consensus. The sacred occasion is the moment for re-evaluation of political practices and institutions. By inviting Sadat to Jerusalem, Begin takes the risk of allowing his political career and many of the historical choices made by Israel to be criticized. The emergence of the sacred confronts daily political practice with the norm it is supposed to embody; it invites questioning of the status quo. Not only does exposure of deviant practices strengthen the norm, as Durkheim points out;[45] the subjunctive re-evaluation of daily practice may even allow re-definition of the norm. As shown by Alexander,[46] a new political covenant emerges from the Watergate hearings. Subjunctiveness permits a rearticulation of the center, which emerges not from the proposed event alone but also from the public reaction to it.

Let us watch the Israelis as Sadat arrives. His plane has landed, but the president has not yet made any statement. The order of things in the Middle East seems to have changed, but no one knows how. Traditional Israeli stands are obviously inadequate for the occasion, but nothing, for the time being, seems able to replace them. Puzzlingly, the moment has freed itself from all familiar references. For a short while it swarms with potentialities.

The experience is brief. It is, to use Turner's phrase, "liminal," an interstitial moment of freedom between strong definitions of reality. Despite its brevity, it is heavy with consequences. No matter how fugitive, other possibilities did unquestionably beckon. Projectively, these possibilities were translated by the public into concrete hopes, into demands until then unvoiced. Shouldn't Israeli leadership be able to transform this opportunity into a reality? Shouldn't it be held accountable if it fails to do so? The sacred form of the event invites the exercise of reflexivity. Civil religion is thus invoked, but not as a political or social straight-jacket, not just as a ritualistic reiteration of some pre-existing consensus.

Ostensibly, the multivocality of media events is alienating or mystifying. Functionally, however, this ambiguity may be the dynamic condition from which an actual consensus arises as the public responds to an event: the event displays symbols. The public produces their meaning, and in so doing proceeds to a remapping, and updating of consensus. Ceremonial events may make room for change. Often, they catalyze profound transformations in historical consciousness. Monumental and elusive, they herald the possible.

Media events and civil religion

Media events in democratic societies differ both from their counterparts in non-democratic societies and from the consensual ceremonies portrayed by Durkheim and other students of civil religion. Let us summarize here some of their most original features.

Media events present themselves as historical celebrations but the history they celebrate is not one which is already sacralized and treasured in collective memory. It is a history in the making. The symbols it provides are from events in progress, or actions that are still being enacted and have not yet become what Victor Turner calls "root-paradigms," "structures of thought and feeling," examples of desirable behaviors. An event can be unexpected and still connected to the symbolic "center" of society.[47] Civil religion here displays its capacity for absorbing new situations. Thus the most impressive of our examples are not calendar fixed, but improvised, irregular and non-repetitive.

As opposed to other expressions of civil religion which are retrospective and commemorative, media events are characteristically prospective, anticipatory. At their best, they celebrate the multiple possibilities of a future that has yet to emerge clearly, beyond the turning points they claim to constitute.

As much as media events mirror an existing consensus, they can be said to "produce" and articulate new consensus. This rearticulation may be attempted in the text of the proposed event, but their full realization depends on the performance of the public, on how the public reads the event. Media events have a certain ambiguity, an untriedness. Even when successfully mobilizing audiences on a scale hitherto unknown, media events do not speak for themselves. The broadcasters speak for them, but even that is not enough and the consensus they map remains unclear. The event thus serves as a catalyst for ideological formulation or reformulation. The interruption it represents triggers social reflexivity.

This reflexivity is articulated around "subjunctive" themes. These themes serve as a basis for the critique, or evaluation – not justification – of political practice, and may lead to a reorientation of practice.

Clearly oriented towards the future, media events most differ from religious events in that their legitimation derives not only from *tradition* – from what Elias Canetti describes as "the two invisible masses of the already dead, and of the yet unborn" – but also and essentially from their huge, simultaneous, spatial *expansion*.[48] Media events are often last-minute improvisations, but they acquire a planetary dimension, spreading across national or continental boundaries.

The size and multiplicity of their international publics suggests that the performative aspect of media events does not consist merely in articulating or rearticulating social relations within a given society.[49] While displaying symbols connected to the center of a national society, media events reach out to constitute or to delineate entirely new social formations, surpra- or meta-societies which transcend the limits of established nations and provoke planetary groupings of publics.

Consider the moon landing or the Live Aid rock concert for Ethiopia.

Could Durkheim have foreseen how the collective sentiments shared by tribe, community or nation might be uprooted from their natural habitat, and – if only for a fleeting moment – reapportioned among a new global constituency? Unlike the other events of civil religions, media events refuse to be confined to a given community of collective sentiments. Are they the civil religion of emerging social entities, the constantly shifting center of communities whose boundaries are as yet undetermined?[50]

Notes

1 An earlier version of this chapter, "La Télévision et la rhetorique des grandes cérémonies," was published in Marc Ferro, ed., *Film et Histoire* (Paris, 1984). We must thank for their suggestions and their remarks, Jeffrey Alexander, Barbara Myerhoff, Eric Rothenbuhler, Marc Ferro, Pierre Motyl, Janet Cheng, Steve Weissman and Carol Horn
    The "Media Events" project is funded by the John and Mary R. Markle Foundation.
2 The quotes are from Durkheim, *The Elementary Forms of the Religious Life* (New York: Free Press, 1965 [1912], pp. 474–5) as discussed by Lukes and Rothenbuhler. Rothenbuhler credits Bellah and Hammond for the attribution to Durkheim of the tradition of research on the sociology of civil religion, and we credit Rothenbuhler for making explicit the connection between Durkheim's moral ceremonies and our media events. See Steven Lukes, "Political, Ritual and Social Integration." *Sociology* 9, 1975; Eric W. Rothenbuhler, "Media Events, Civil Religion and Social Solidarity: the Living Room Celebration of the Olympic Games," Doctoral Dissertation. Annenberg School, USC, 1985 and Robert N. Bellah and P. E. Hammond, *Varieties of Civil Religion*. San Francisco: Harper and Row, 1980.
3 One can understand such events, in reference to Victor Turner's opposition of "structure" and "antistructure," and to Don Handelman's opposition between events that "present" and events that "represent." See Victor Turner, *The Ritual Process: Structure and Anti Structure*. (Ithaca, 1977), and Donald Handelman, "Presentation, Representing and Modeling," unpublished paper, Department of Sociology and Anthropology, Hebrew University of Jerusalem (1983).
4 His reference to "commemorating the promulgation of a new moral system or some great event in the national life" likely refers more to regular commemoration than to the inauguration of such a system or the first anniversary of such an event. While inclusive of commemorative and repeated events as well, our media events are heavily biased towards original, one-time events.
5 Nick Browne, "Introductory Statement," Panel on *Television Theories*, 50th Anniversary Conference, MLA NY (Dec. 1983).
6 Paul Virilio, *Vitesse et politique* (Paris, 1977).
7 J. L. Austin, *How To Do Things With Words* (Oxford, 1962).

8 Eric Rothenbuhler, "Media Events, Civil Religion and Social Solidarity."

9 Roland Barthes, "L'Écriture de l'evénement," *Communications* 12 (Paris: Seuil, 1968).

10 Steven Lukes, "Political Ritual and Social Integration."

11 See Eric Rothenbuhler, this volume.

12 Jeffrey Alexander, "The Symbolic Meaning of Watergate," International Sociological Association, Panel on Media Events, World Congress of Sociology, Mexico, 1982. Reprinted as "Culture Form and Political Substance: The Watergate Hearings as Media Ritual," in Sandra Ball-Rokeach and Muriel G. Cantor, eds., *Media, Audience and Social Structure* (Newbury Park: Sage Publications, 1986).

13 Kurt Lang and Gladys Engel Lang, *The Battle for Public Opinion* (New York: Columbia University Press, 1983).

14 Our reference to "presenting" ceremonies draws of course on Goffman, but also on Dan Handelman: "Presenting, Representing and Modeling."

15 Edward Shils, *Center and Periphery, Essays in Macrosociology* (Chicago: University of Chicago Press, 1975).

16 Victor Turner, *The Ritual Process: Structure and Anti-Structure* (Cornell University Press, 1977).

17 Which usually encompasses quite a number of societies. For example, the Western bloc.

18 Claude Lévi-Strauss, "The Effectiveness of Symbols," in *Symbolic Anthropology* (New York: Basic Books, 1963).

19 Jeffrey Alexander, "Cultural Form and Political Substance" and "Three Models of Culture and Society Relations: Toward an Analysis of Watergate" in Alexander, *Action and its Environments* (New York: Columbia University Press, 1988).

20 V. Propp, *Morphology of the Folk-Tale* (Austin: University of Texas Press, 1986), and A. J. Greimas, *Semantique structurale* (Paris: Larousse, 1966).

21 Elihu Katz and Daniel Dayan, "Contests, Conquests, Coronations: On Media Events and Their Heroes," in C. Graumann and S. Moscovici, eds., *New Conceptions of Leadership* (New York: Springer, 1987).

22 "Her" biography in the cases of Golda Meir, and Indira Gandhi. But such coronations are still the exception.

23 For example, the televised ceremonies commemorating the civil war in Korea organized in 1983 by the Southern Korean state television (KBS) and centered on the drama of unexpected on-the-air reunions of families separated by war. Organized as a "telethon," the first commemoration of this type lasted nearly 70 hours over a whole week. The program ultimately led to the reunion of more than 10,000 families. See Suk Ho Jun and Daniel Dayan, "Family Reunion: Interactive Television Turns a Page in Korean History," *World Communication Association*, Atlantic Convention, San Juan, Puerto Rico, December 1984.

24 A. J. Greimas, *Semantique structurale*.

25 Francesco Alberoni, *Le Choc amoureux* (Paris: Ramsay, 1980).

26 Foreign television networks may either produce their own programs or adopt and retransmit images "fed" to them by national networks, which they make their own by providing their own sound tracks.

27 Philip Elliott, "Press Performance as Political Ritual," in D. C. Whitney, *et al.* eds., *Mass Communication Review Yearbook*, vol. 3 (Beverly Hills: Sage, 1982).

28 For very similar formulations which tend however to be more systematic in their ambition to characterize *all* television programs, see Eric Michaels' *T.V. Tribes*, Doctoral Dissertation, University of Texas, Austin, 1982 and Horace Newcomb's "Television Textuality; Defining the Problem," *Speech and Communications Association*, Los Angeles, California, November 1981.

29 Daniel Dayan and Elihu Katz "Rituels publics à usage privé," *Annales: Economie, Société, Civilizations* (Paris, 1983).

30 This is true even of totally state-controlled television organizations. But new ceremonial experts and chiefs-of-protocol are increasingly recruited among television specialists.

31 Tom Wolfe, *The Right Stuff* (New York: Bantam Books, 1980).

32 "Image-like" in Boorstin's sense. See Daniel Boorstin, *The Image: A Guide to Pseudo Events in America* (New York: Atheneum, 1972).

33 Actively, if not enthusiastically. Ephraim Kishon credits him with the following declaration: "No more war! No more bloodshed! No more kisses!"

34 "The reaction was, at first, one of disagreeable surprise; but we are a volatile people, and, as soon as we realized that we were in for a long haul, we changed the rules of the game and turned it into an oratorical contest . . ." Philip Gillon, *The Jerusalem Post*.

35 Fred Friendly, *Due to Circumstances Beyond Our Control* (New York: Vintage, 1967).

36 As we know, news is almost always devoted to accidents, conflicts, or scandals.

37 CBS, "Four Dark Days," videotape.

38 Kurt Lang and Gladys Engel Lang, *Politics and Television* (Chicago: Quadrangle Books, 1968).

39 Leni Riefensthal, *Olympia*, 1936.

40 See David Chaney, "A Symbolic Mirror of Ourselves. Civic Ritual in Mass Society," *Media, Culture and Society* 5 (1983).

41 Concerning this theme, see the analysis proposed by Beverly Houston in her "Television: The Metapsychology of Endless Consumption," *Quarterly Review of Film Studies* 1 (1984).

42 Victor Turner, *The Ritual Process*.

43 Barbara Myerhoff, Elihu Katz and Daniel Dayan, "Engineering Ceremonies," unpublished lecture. Hillel, USC, Los Angeles, November 1983.

44 David Morley, "The 'Nationwide' Audience: Structure and Decoding." London; BFI. Television monographs, No. 11, 1980.

45 As discussed by P. F. Lazarsfeld and R. K. Merton, "Mass Communication, Popular Taste and our Organized Social Action," in W. Schramm and D. F. Roberts, eds., *Process and Effects of Mass Communication* (Urbana: University of Illinois Press, 1971).

46 Jeffrey Alexander, "Cultural Form and Political Substance."

47 Edward Shils, *Center and Periphery, op. cit.*

48 Elias Canetti, *Masse et Puissance* (Paris, Gallimard, 1980).

49 We note a convergence on this theme of producing consensus with the work of Edward Gross, University of Washington.

50 One might think of McLuhan and his global village, or of Braudel and the world-wide markets he describes as "economical worlds" (*Weltwirtschaften*). The nature of the ideological communities defined by media events is difficult to apprehend in that they have no formal-political or legal-existence. Yet they share a string of consensual occasions, which, in spite of their unexpectedness, their irregular occurrences, and their diversity, constitute a corpus sufficiently homogeneous to be perceived as unified. See M. McLuhan, *Understanding Media*, and Fernand Braudel, *La Dynamique du capitalisme* (Paris: Arthaud, 1985).

8 Culture and political crisis: "Watergate" and Durkheimian sociology

Jeffrey C. Alexander

Durkheim's legacy has been appropriated by generations of social scientists in strikingly different ways. Each appropriation depends on a reading of Durkheim's work, of its critical phases, its internal crises and resolutions, and its culminating achievements. Such readings themselves depend upon prior theoretical understandings, for it is impossible to trace a textual development without seeing this part within some already glimpsed whole. The texts, however, have constituted an independent encounter in their own right, and new interpretations of Durkheim have given crucial impetus to the development of new theoretical developments in turn.

Almost every imaginable kind of sociology has been so inspired, for it is possible to see in Durkheim's development sharply contrasting theoretical models and presuppositions. Ecological determinism, functional differentiation, demographic expansion, administrative punishment and legal control, even the distribution of property – the study of each has been taken as sociology's decisive task in light of Durkheim's early work. From the middle and later work have emerged other themes. The centrality of moral and emotional integration is undoubtedly the most pervasive legacy, but anthropologists have also taken from this work a functional analysis of religion and ritual and a structural analysis of symbol and myth. None of these inherited exemplars, however, takes fully into consideration the actual trajectory of Durkheim's later and most sophisticated sociological understanding. Given Durkheim's classical stature, this failure is extraordinary, the possibility of remedying it equally so. To begin this remedialization is the point of the chapter which follows.

I

It has become more widely accepted in recent years that Durkheim's work shifted sharply toward the subjective as early as 1894. Indeed, it was in the very first chapter of *Rules* that Durkheim (1938 [1895]) suggested that ecological forces, or social morphology, actually consisted in conceptual and emotional interaction. In *Socialism* (1958 [1895–6]) and *Suicide* (1951 [1897]) this insight was elaborated, yet, in fact, by 1896 and 1897 Durkheim was already engaged in extensive revision of this decisive break. Emotional interaction, he now perceived, never occurred separately from the symbolization of ideational values. Religion, and particularly religious ritual, now became the model for Durkheim's understanding of social life. Interaction produces an energy like the "effervescence" of religious ecstasy. This psychic energy attaches itself to powerful symbols – things or ideas – which in turn crystallize critical social facts. Symbols, in turn, have their own autonomous organization. They are organized into the sacred and profane, the latter being mere signs, the former being symbols redolent with mystery, and this symbolic division constitutes authority. These sacred symbols, Durkheim came to believe, could themselves control the structure of social organization. The liquid character of sacredness makes it contagious and precious. Societies must elaborate rules to contain it, for it must be rigorously separated not only from impure substances but from profane ones. Complicated ceremonies, furthermore, must be developed for its periodic renewal.

Although many interpreters have discussed this movement toward the sociology of religion, none have appreciated its full significance. From 1897 onward, Durkheim's intention was not just to develop a sociology of religion but, rather, a religious sociology. In everything he turned his hand to after that transitional time, his intention was always the same: to transform his earlier, secular analyses into religious ones. The division of labor and theory of history, the explanation of social pathology and crime, the theory of law, the analyses of education and family, the notions of politics and economics, and of course the very theory of culture itself – Durkheim sought in his later years to explain all these by analogy to the internal structuring of religious life (Alexander 1982:259–98). Each institution and process was made strictly analogous to the ritual model. Each structure of authority was conceived of as sacred in form, a sacralization that depended upon periodic propinquity and emotion. The developmental processes of each were alternating phases of sacred and profane, and the attenuation of effervescence constituted, for each, the turning points of its development.

Only after the pervasiveness of this theoretical shift is understood can the challenge that Durkheim's legacy poses to contemporary social science be fully appreciated. Durkheim's challenge is to develop a cultural logic for society: to make the symbolic dimension of every social sphere a relatively autonomous domain of cultural discourse interpenetrated with the other dimensions of society. Few of Durkheim's own students picked up this gauntlet, some because they failed to understand it, others because they rejected it on some principled ground. It has taken the rest of us the better part of a century to come back to it. Durkheim's later religious sociology makes fundamental advances over the thought of his classical contemporaries. Marx developed scarcely any theory of contemporary culture, working instead at the other side of the epistemological continuum. Weber did make fundamental contributions to a theory of culture and society, but his historicist insistence on the modern destruction of meaning makes the incorporation of his insights extraordinarily difficult, though no less necessary for that. Durkheim alone insisted on the centrality of meaning in secular society, and only in his work does a systematic theory of contemporary cultural life begin to emerge. This theory also goes beyond the most important post-classical theory – functionalism – in significant ways. Functionalism either has closely tied cultural values to social structual strain or, in Parson's case, it has conceptualized culture's autonomy only by speaking of "values," a static and structuralist way of talking about meaning.

For all of this, however, it must be frankly acknowledged that Durkheim's religious sociology is difficult to understand. This difficulty does not reside simply in the interpreter; it rests also on deep ambiguities in the theory itself. Durkheim's religious sociology works on three different levels: as a metaphor, as a general theory of society, and as a special theory of certain social processes. It is necessary to separate these theories from one another and to evaluate them independently if the permanent contributions of Durkheim's later work are to be properly understood and incorporated into contemporary thought.

It is clear that, in one sense, Durkheim's insistence after 1896 that society *is* religion plays a metaphorical role. He has invented here a vigorous and compelling way of arguing for the value-imbeddedness of action and order. Far from being a mundane utilitarian world, modern society still has a close relationship to strongly felt ends that compel the acquiescence of powerful means. These supra-individual ends are so strong, indeed, they may be likened to the other-worldly ends established by God. This metaphor of "religious society" produces accompanying similes: social symbols are *like* sacred ones, in that they are powerful and compelling; the conflict between social values is *like* the conflict between sacred and profane, or pure and impure sacredness; political interaction is *like* ritual participation in that it produces cohesion and value commitment.

Considered as metaphor and simile – as, in other words, a series of rhetorical devices – Durkheim's religious sociology is "true." It effectively communicates the importance of anti-utilitarian qualities in the modern world. As a conceptual or theoretical vocabulary, however, basic problems remain. For as a general theory of society – the second level at which it operates – Durkheim's religious sociology is certainly wrong. It is wrong in the first place for epistemological reasons, because it inscribes a dualistic social life that reflects Durkheim's overwhelming idealism. But Durkheim's religious sociology *qua* general theory is also wrong on empirical grounds. To make a strict analogy between society and religion leads to an overly condensed, undifferentiated, all or nothing understanding of social life. It implies that values can be communicated only through intensive high energy symbols which generate awe and mystery. These symbols are held to be constituted through "social" experiences with a capital S, periods of renewal which are without conflict or material integument, whose integrative denouement is absolutely complete. This world of symbol and ritual, moreover, is conceived as opposed to a profane world of individuals, economic institutions, and merely material structures. Because they are profane these objects are held to be non-social, and because they are non-social they are seen neither as socially structured nor as sociologically comprehensible.

But highly energized symbols are not, of course, the only way values are generated and maintained in modern societies. The profane world, defined as the routine world of relatively reduced excitation, remains firmly value-directed. It is also decidedly social and as ordered as it is conflictual. The social experiences which constitute intense and awesome symbols, moreover, are not necessarily harmonious and thoroughly integrating. They may be subject to intensely competitive processes, to individuation and reflexivity, and they may integrate some parts of society rather than the whole.

As a general theory, indeed, Parsonian functionalism seems in all these respects to be superior to Durkheim's later theory, and Parsons expressly sought to incorporate this later theory into his own. Parsonian theory clarifies levels of generality and establishes the independent social logics of various spheres. Rather than dichotomizing culture and material life, it argues for the simultaneous independence and interpenetration of personality, social system, and culture. Symbolism and values, then, are always part of social and individual life. While social system processes are not usually highly effective or intense, the specificity of role relationships is dependent, nonetheless, on normative prescriptions of general cultural values. While functionalism acknowledges that value renewal occurs in time of crisis – though its analysis of such processes, I will argue, is seriously deficient – it also quite correctly sees that values are also acquired through more routine processes like socialization and learning, through leadership, and through exchange of the generalized media that facilitate communication between groups, individuals, and subsystems.

"Authority" presents a good example of the contrast between functionalism and Durkheimianism as general theory. For the religious theory authority is always numinous; to the degree that it is profaned and routinized it becomes meaningless, approximating mere power and force. By contrast, Parsonian functionalism draws upon Weber to argue that, in modern societies at least, routinized authority becomes "office." This designation implies a symbolic code that regulates power by condensing, indeed by secularizing previously vivid, longstanding religious values, values like the impersonal transcendence of God and the duty for all men to carry out His will. Through the concept of office, Friedrichs (1964) has argued, mundane legal forms like constitutions can ensure the value-regulation of "profane" political life.

If this were the full extent of Durkheim's later sociology, if it were merely successful metaphor and failed general theory, we could leave Durkheim's legacy alone, satisfied with Parsons and Weber. But that is not so. Durkheim's later work also presents us with a special theory referring to specified kinds of empirical processes. This specific theory is true and enlightening, and its implications have scarcely begun to be mined.

The ritualistic model of religious life which Durkheim developed in his later years is a hermeneutics of intense, direct value experience. It interprets the structure and effects of unmediated encounters with transcendent realities. The religious vocabulary of such experience, as Durkheim rightly insisted, derives not from the unique qualities of divine encounters but rather from the fact that such encounters typify transcendent experience as such. This religious experience, then, is one manifestation of a general form of social experience. These experiences are called religious simply because, in the course of human history, they have occurred most frequently in a religious form. In this sense, therefore, the "religious model" can indeed be taken as a strict analogy for certain universal processes of secular life.

Such a direct, unmediated encounter with transcendent experience is relevant to secular processes in at least two crucial ways. First, social system processes themselves are never thoroughly bound to normative prescriptions and differentiated roles. They are never, that is, completely routinized or profane. The terror and awe of simplified and general symbols – the purely cultural level that is experienced as religious or transcendent reality – always remains in the interstices of social life. We may continue here with our earlier example of political authority. While its use in modern societies is hedged in by elaborate norms of office, authority also carries with it the pregnant symbolism of sacred things. Roger Caillois (1959 [1939]) was the first Durkheimian to insist that sacredness often has the ecological correlate of centeredness, and that for this reason political power is often associated with the same kind of prohibitions and proscriptions as religious life. Edward Shils (1975) was the second Durkheimian to do so, and in his work the ambiguous interplay of the center's material and symbolic power is profoundly illuminated. Bernard Lacroix (1981) is the third to pick up this theme. Though he is wrong, I believe, to insist that Durkheim's own analysis is concerned with power in a political sense, he is quite right to urge that the categories of this religious theory have an important political application.

Since this religious quality of secular power often, for better or worse, overpowers the specific role obligation of "office," it is ironic that it recalls the religious qualities from which specifically office obligations were derived. This concealed dialectic points to the profound relationship that exists between normative obligations and the much more generalized value-creating processes of cultural life. Values are created and renewed through episodes of directly experiencing and re-experiencing transcendent meaning. While these experiences are never completely shut out by the walls of routinized life, the periods of peak experience constitute an independent mode of "religious" experience.

In periods of social conflict and strain, the broad cultural framework for specific role definitions itself becomes an issue for examination. Parts of societies, or even societies as such, may be said to experience a "generalization" (Parsons and Smelser 1957: ch. 7; Parsons and Bales 1955: 353–96; Smelser 1959 and 1963) away from the specificity of everyday social life. Though utilitarian factors like faction and interest are often crucial in determining the specific course of such generalized crisis, non-rational ritualization is the order of the day. This ritualization, which can occur massively or episodically, involves the direct re-experiencing of fundamental values (cf. Tiryakian 1967) and often their rethinking and reformulating as well as their reaffirmation. The classificatory system of collective symbols can sometimes be drastically changed through these experiences; the relation of social actors to these dominant classifications is always shifted and transformed. Cultural myths are recalled and extended to contemporary circumstance. Social solidarities are reworked. Yet, while solidarity is always the concomitant of ritual, it may be expanded or contracted, depending on the specific case. Finally, role relationships are certainly changed, not only in terms of the structure of opportunities and rewards, but in terms of subjective role definitions.

II

I would like at this point to introduce a case study which seeks to exemplify this secular relevance of Durkheim's religious sociology. My discussion of the Watergate crisis in the United States between 1972 and 1974 continues, in a more detailed and specific way, the analysis of authority which has been my empirical referent in the preceding discussion. After making this extended analysis of Watergate, I will return to a more general consideration of the specific explanatory structure of Durkheim's religious theory.

In June 1972, employees of the Republican Party made an illegal entry and burglary into the Democratic Party headquarters in the Watergate Hotel in Washington, DC. Republicans described the break-in as a "third-rate burglary"; Democrats said it was a major act of political espionage, a symbol, moreover, of more general demagoguery by the Republican president, Richard Nixon, and his staff. Americans were not persuaded by the more extreme reaction. The incident received relatively little attention, generating no real sense of outrage at the time. There were no cries of outraged justice. There was simply deference to the president, respect for his authority, and belief that his explanation of this event was correct despite what in retrospect seemed like strong evidence to the contrary. With important exceptions, the mass news media decided after a short time to play down the story, not because they were coercively prevented from doing so but because they genuinely felt it to be a relatively unimportant event. Watergate remained, in other words, part of the profane world in Durkheim's sense. Even after the national election in November of that year, 80 per cent of the American people found it hard to believe that there was a "Watergate crisis"; 75 per cent felt what had occurred was just plain politics; 84 per cent felt that what they had heard about it did not influence their vote. Two years later, this same incident, still called "Watergate," had initiated the most serious peacetime political crisis in American history. It had become a riveting moral symbol, one which initiated a long passage through sacred time and space and wrenching conflict between pure and impure sacred forms. It was responsible for the first president voluntarily to resign his office.

How and why did this perception of Watergate change? To understand this we must see first what this extraordinary contrast in these two public perceptions indicates, namely that the actual event, "Watergate," was in itself relatively inconsequential. It was a mere collection of facts, and contrary to the positivist persuasion, facts do not speak. Certainly, new "facts" seem to have emerged in the course of the two-year crisis, but it is quite extraordinary how many of these "revelations" actually were already leaked in the pre-election period. Watergate could not, as the French might say, tell itself. It had to be told by society; it was, to use Durkheim's famous phrase, a social fact. It was the context of Watergate that had changed, not so much the raw empirical data themselves.

To understand how this telling of a crucial social fact changed, it is necessary to bring to the sacred/profane dichotomy the Parsonian conceptualization of generalization. There are different levels at which every social fact can be told (Smelser 1959, 1963). These levels are linked to different kinds of social resources, and the focus on one level or another can tell us much about whether a system is in crisis – and subject, therefore, to the sacralizing process – or is operating routinely, or profanely, and in equilibrium.

First and most specific is the level of goals. Political life occurs most of the time in this relatively mundane level of goals, power and interest. Above this, as it were, at a higher level of generality, are norms – the conventions, customs, and laws that regulate this political process and struggle. At a still higher point there are values: those very general and elemental aspects of the culture that inform the codes which regulate political authority and the norms within which specific interests are resolved. If politics operates routinely the conscious attention of political participants is on goals and interests, that is, it is relatively specific attention. Routine, "profane" politics means, in fact, that these interests are not seen as violating more general values and norms. Non-routine politics begins when tension between these levels is felt, either because of a shift in the nature of political activity or a shift in the general, more sacred commitments that are held to regulate them. In this situation, a tension between goals and higher levels develops. Public attention shifts from political goals to more general concerns, to the norms and values that are now perceived as in danger. In this instance we can say there has been the generalization of public consciousness I referred to earlier as the central point of the ritual process.

It is in light of this analysis that we can understand the shift in the telling of Watergate. It was first viewed merely as something on the level of goals, "just politics," by 75 per cent of the American people. Two years subsequent to the break-in, by summer 1974, public opinion had sharply changed. From purely political goals Watergate was now regarded as an issue that violated fundamental customs and morals, and eventually – by 50 per cent of the population – as a challenge to the most sacred values which sustained political order itself. By the end of this two-year crisis period almost half of those who had voted for Nixon changed their minds, and two-thirds of all voters thought the issue had gone far beyond politics.[1] What had happened was a radical generalization of opinion. The facts were not that different but the social context in which they were seen had been transformed.

If we look at the two-year transformation of the context of Watergate, we see the creation and resolution of a fundamental social crisis, a resolution that involved the deepest ritualization of political life. To achieve this "religious" status, there had to be an extraordinary generalization of opinion *vis-à-vis* a political threat that was initiated by the very center of established power and a successful struggle not just against that power in its social form but against the powerful cultural rationales it mobilized. To understand this process of crisis creation and resolution we must integrate Durkheim's ritual theory with a more muscular theory of social structure and process. Let me lay these factors out generally before I indicate how each became involved in the instance of Watergate.

What must happen for a society to experience fundamental crisis and ritual renewal?

First, there has to be sufficient social consensus so that an event will be considered polluting, or deviant, by more than a mere fragment of the population. Only with sufficient consensus, in other words, can "society" itself be aroused and indignant.

Second, there has to be the perception by significant groups who participate in this consensus that the event is not only deviant but that its pollution threatens the "center" of society.

Third, if this deep crisis is to be resolved, institutional social controls must be brought into play. However, even legitimate attacks on the polluting sources of crisis are often viewed as frightening. For this reason, such controls also mobilize instrumental force and the threat of force to bring polluting forces to heel.

Fourth, social control mechanisms must be accompanied by the mobilization and struggle of elites and publics which are differentiated and relatively autonomous from the structural center of society. Through this process there begins to be the formation of counter-centers.

Finally, fifth, there have to be effective processes of symbolic interpretation, that is, ritual, and purification processes that continue the labeling process and enforce the strength of the symbolic, sacred center of society at the expense of a center which is increasingly seen as merely structural, profane, and impure. In so doing, such processes demonstrate conclusively the deviant or "transgressive" qualities that are the sources of this threat.

In elaborating how each one of these five factors came into play in the course of Watergate, I will be indicating how, in a complex society, reintegration and symbolic renewal are far from being automatic processes.[2] Much more than a simple reading of Durkheim's work might imply, reintegration and renewal rely on the contingent outcomes of specific historical circumstances.

First, the factor of consensus. Between the Watergate break-in and the election, the necessary social consensus did not emerge. This was a time of subjectively intense polarization politically, though the actual social conflicts of the 60s had signficantly cooled. The Democratic candidate, McGovern, was the very symbol of "leftism" upon which Nixon had built the backlash and reactionary elements of his presidency. McGovern's active presence during this period, therefore, allowed Nixon to continue to promote the authoritarian politics that could justify Watergate. One should not suppose, however, that because there was no significant social reintegration during this period that no significant symbolic activity occurred. It is terribly important to understand that agreement in complex societies occurs at various levels. There may be extremely significant cultural agreement – e.g. complex and systematic agreement about the structure and contents of language – while more socially or structurally related areas of subjective agreement – e.g. rules about political conduct – do not exist. Symbolic agreement without social consensus can exist, moreover, within more substantive cultural arenas than language.

During the summer of 1972 one can trace a very complex symbolic development in the American collective conscience, a consensual development that laid the basis for everything that followed even while it did not produce consensus at more social levels.[3] It was during this four-month period that the meaning complex of "Watergate" came to be defined. In the first weeks which followed the break-in to the Democratic headquarters, "Watergate" existed, in semiotic terms, merely as a sign. The word simply denoted a single event. In the weeks that followed, this sign became more complex, referring to a series of interrelated events touched off by the break-in, including charges of political corruption, presidential denials, legal suits, and arrests. By August of 1972, "Watergate" had become transformed from a mere sign to a redolent symbol, a word that rather than denoting actual events connotated multifold moral meanings.

Watergate had become a symbol of pollution, embodying a sense of evil and impurity. In structural terms, the things directly associated with Watergate – those who were immediately associated with the crime, the apartment complex, the persons implicated later – were placed on the negative side of a polarized symbolic classification. Those persons or institutions responsible for ferreting out and arresting these criminal elements were placed on the other, positive side.[4] This bifurcated model of pollution and purity was then superimposed onto the traditional good/ evil structure of American civil religion, whose relevant elements appear in the following form. It is clear, then, that while significant symbolic structuring had occurred, the "center" of the American social structure was in no way implicated (see fig. 1).

This symbolic development, it should be emphasized, occurred in the public mind. Few Americans would have disagreed about the moral meanings of "Watergate" as a collective representation. Yet, while the social basis of this symbol was widely inclusive, the symbol just about exhausted the meaning complex of Watergate as such. While the term identified a complex of events and people with moral evil, the collective consciousness did not connect this symbol to particular significant social roles or institutional behaviors. Neither the Republican Party, President Nixon's staff, nor, least of all, President Nixon himself had yet been polluted by the symbol of Watergate. In this sense, it is possible to say that

Fig. 1. *Symbolic classification system as of August 1972*

The Watergate "structure"

Evil	Good
Watergate Hotel	Nixon and staff/White House
The burglars	FBI
Dirty tricksters	Courts/Justice Department's prosecution team
Money raisers	Federal "watchdog" bureaucracy

American civil religion

Evil	Good
Communism/fascism	Democracy
Shadowy enemies	White House–Americanism
Crime	Law
Corruption	Honesty
Personalism	Responsibility
Bad presidents (e.g. Harding, Grant)	Great presidents (e.g. Lincoln, Washington)
Great scandals (e.g. Teapot Dome)	Heroic reformers

some *symbolic* generalization had occurred but that value generalization within the social system had not. It had not because the social and cultural polarization of American society had not yet sufficiently abated. Because there was continued polarization, there could be no movement upwards toward shared social values, and because there could be no generalization, there could be no societal sense of crisis. Because there was no sense of crisis, in turn, it became impossible for the other forces I have mentioned to come into play. There was no perception of a threat to the center. There was no mobilization of social control, for these forces were afraid to act. There was no struggle by differentiated elites against the threat to and by the center, for these elites were divided, afraid and immobilized. Finally, no deep ritual processes emerged, for these could emerge only in response to tensions generated by the first four factors.

Yet in the six months following the election the situation began to be reversed. First, consensus began to emerge. The end of an intensely divisive election period allowed a realignment to begin which had been building at least for two years prior to Watergate. The social struggles of the 60s had long been over and many issues had been taken over by centrist groups.[5] Critical universalism had been readopted by these centrist forces without it being linked to the specific ideological themes or goals of the Left. With this emerging consensus, the possibility for common feelings of moral violation emerged and with it began the movement towards generalization *vis-à-vis* political goals and interests. Now, once this first resource of consensus had become available, the other developments I mentioned could be activated.

The second and third factors I mentioned were anxiety about the center and the invocation of institutional social control. Developments in the post-election months provided a much safer and less "political" atmosphere for the operation of social controls. I am thinking here of the activity of the courts, of the Justice Department, of various bureaucratic agencies, and special congressional committees. The very operation of these social control institutions legitimated the media's efforts to extend the Watergate pollution closer to central institutions. It reinforced public doubt about whether Watergate was, in fact, only a limited crime. It also forced more facts to surface. Of course, at this point the ultimate level of generality and seriousness of Watergate remained undetermined. With this new public legitimation, and the beginnings of generalization it implied, fears that Watergate might pose a threat to the center of American society began to spread to significant publics and elites. The question about proximity to the center preoccupied every major group during this early post-election Watergate period. Senator Baker, at a later time, articulated this anxiety with the question that became famous during the summertime Senate hearings: "How much did the President know and when did he know it?" This anxiety about the threat to the center, in turn, intensified the growing sense of normative violation, increased consensus, and contributed to generalization. It further rationalized the invocation of coercive social control. Finally, in structural terms, it began to realign the "good" and "bad" sides of the Watergate symbolization. Which side were Nixon and his staff really on?

The fourth factor I mentioned was elite conflict. Throughout this period, the generalization process – pushed by consensus, by the fear for the center, and by the activities of new institutions of social control – was fueled by a desire for revenge against Nixon by alienated institutional elites. These elites had represented "leftism" or simply "sophisticated cosmopolitanism" to Nixon during his first four years in office, and they had been the object of his legal and illegal attempts at suppression or control. They included journalists and newspapers, intellectuals, universities, scientists, lawyers, religionists, foundations, and, last but not least, authorities in various public agencies and the U.S. Congress. Motivated by a desire to get even, to revive their threatened status, and to defend their universalistic values, these elites moved to establish themselves as counter-centers in the years of crisis.

By May of 1973, then, all of these forces for crisis creation and resolution were in motion. Significant changes in public opinion had been mobilized and powerful structural resources were being brought into play. It is only at this point that the fifth crisis factor could emerge. These were the deep processes of ritualism – sacralization, pollution, and purification – though there had certainly already been important symbolic developments as well.

The first fundamental ritual process of the Watergate crisis involved the Senate Select Committee's televised hearings, which began in May and continued through August. This event had significant repercussions on the symbolic patterning of the entire affair. The decision to hold and to televise the Senate Select Committee hearings responded to the tremendous anxiety that had built up within important segments of the population. The symbolic process that ensued functioned to canalize this anxiety in certain distinctive, more generalized, and more consensual directions. The hearings constituted a kind of civic ritual which revivified very general yet nonetheless very crucial currents of critical universalism and rationality in the American political culture. It recreated the sacred, generalized morality upon which more mundane conceptions of office are based, and it did so by invoking the mythical level of national understanding in a way that few other events have in postwar history.

The Senate hearings were initially commissioned on specific political and normative grounds, their mandate being to expose corrupt campaign practices and to suggest legal reforms. The pressure for ritual process, however, soon made this initial mandate all but forgotten. The hearings became a sacred process by which the nation could reach a judgment about the now-critically judged Watergate crime. The consensus-building, generalizing aspect of the process was to some extent quite conscious. Congressional leaders assigned membership to the committee on the basis of the widest possible regional and political representation and excluded from the committee all potentially polarizing political personalities. Most of the generalizing process, however, developed much less consciously in the course of the event itself. The developing ritual quality forced committee members to mask their often sharp internal divisions behind commitments to civic universalism. And many of the committee staff who had been radical or liberal activists now had to assert patriotic universalism without any reference to specific left-wing issues. Other staffers, who had been strong Nixon supporters sympathetic to backlash politics, now had to forsake that justification for political action entirely.

The televised hearings, in the end, constituted a liminal experience (Turner 1969), one radically separated from the profane issues and mundane grounds of everyday life. A ritual communitas was created for Americans to share, and within this reconstructed community none of the polarizing issues which had generated the Watergate crisis, or the historical justification which had motivated it, could be raised. Instead, the hearings revivified the civic religion upon which democratic conceptions of "office" have depended throughout American history. To understand how liminality could be created it is necessary to see it as a "phenomenological world" in the sense that Schutz described. The hearings succeeded in becoming a world "unto itself." It was *sui generis*, a world without history. Its characters did not have rememberable pasts. It was in a very real sense "out of time." The framing devices of the television medium contributed to the deracination that produced this phenomenological status. The in-camera editing, the repetition, juxtaposition, simplification, and other techniques that made the mythical story were invisible. Add to this "bracketed experience" the hushed voices of the announcers, the pomp and ceremony of the "event," and we have the recipe for constructing, within the medium of television, a sacred time and sacred space.

At the level of mundane reality, two ferociously competitive political forces were at war during the Watergate hearings. For Nixon and his political supporters, "Watergate" had to be defined politically: what the Watergate burglars and cover-uppers had done was "just politics," and the anti-Nixon senators on the Watergate Committee (which, after all, was majority Democratic) were simply on a political witch-hunt. For Nixon's critics on the committee, by contrast, this mundane political definition had to be opposed. Nixon could be criticized and Watergate legitimated as a real crisis only if the issues were defined as being above politics and involving fundamental moral concerns. These issues, moreover, had to be linked to forces near the center of political society.

The first issue was whether the hearings were to be televised at all. To allow something to assume the form of a ritualized event is to give participants in a drama the right to intervene forcefully in the culture of the society; it is to give to an event, and to those who are defining its meaning, a special, privileged access to the collective conscience. In primitive societies, ritual processes are ascribed: they occur as preordained periods and in preordained ways. In more modern societies, ritual processes are achieved, often against great odds. Indeed, in a modern society the assumption of ritual status often poses a danger and a threat to vested interests and groups. We know, in fact, that strenuous efforts were made by the White House to prevent the Senate hearings from being televised, to urge that less TV time be devoted to them, and even to pressure the networks to cut short their coverage after it had begun. There were also efforts to force the committee to consider the witnesses in a sequence that was far less dramatic than the one eventually shown.

Because these efforts were unsuccessful, the ritual form was achieved.[6] Through television, tens of millions of Americans participated symbolically and emotionally in the deliberations of the committee. Viewing became morally obligatory for wide segments of the population. Old routines were broken, new ones formed. What these viewers saw was a highly simplified drama – heroes and villains formed in due course. But this drama created a deeply serious symbolic occasion.

If achieving the form of modern ritual is contingent, so is explicating the content, for modern rituals are not nearly so automatically coded as earlier ones. Within the context of the sacred time of the hearings, administration witnesses and senators struggled for moral legitimation, for definitional or ritual superiority and dominance. The end result was in no sense preordained. It depended on successful symbolic work. To describe this symbolic work is to embark on the ethnography, or hermeneutics, of televised ritual.

The Republican and administration witnesses who were "called to account for themselves" during the hearings pursued two strategies. First, they tried to prevent public attention from moving from the political/profane to the value/sacred level at all. In this way, they repeatedly tried to rob the event of its phenomenological status as a ritual. They tried to cool out the proceedings by acting relaxed and casual. For example, H. R. Haldeman, the president's hatchet man, actually let his hair grow long so he would look less sinister and more like "one of the boys." These administration witnesses also tried to rationalize and specify the public's orientation to their actions by arguing that they had acted commonsensically according to pragmatic considerations. They suggested that they had decided to commit their crimes only according to standards of technical rationality. Secret meetings were described not as evil, mysterious conspiracies but as technical discussions about the "costs" of engaging in various disruptive and illegal acts.

Yet the realm of values could not really be avoided. The symbol of Watergate was already quite generalized, and the ritual form of the hearings was already in place. It was within this value realm, indeed, that the most portentous symbolic struggles of the hearings occurred, for what transpired was nothing less than a struggle for the spiritual soul of the American republic. Watergate had been committed and initially justified in the climate of cultural and political "backlash," values which were in basic ways inimical to the universalism, critical rationality, and tolerance upon which any contemporary democracy must be based. Republican and administration witnesses evoked this subculture of backlash values. They urged the audience to return to the polarized climate of the 1960s. They sought to justify their actions by appealing to patriotism, to the need for stability, to the "un-American" and thereby deviant qualities of McGovern and the Left. They also justified it by arguing against cosmopolitanism, which in the minds of backlash traditionalists had undermined respect for tradition and neutralized the universalistic constitutional rules of the game. More specifically, they appealed to loyalty as the ultimate standard that should govern the relationship between subordinates and authorities. An interesting visual theme which summed up both of these appeals was the passive reference by administration witnesses to family values. Each witness brought his wife and children if he had them. To see them lined up behind him, prim and proper, provided symbolic links to the tradition, authority, and personal loyalty that symbolically bound the groups of backlash culture.

The senators, for their part, faced an enormous challenge. While they were virtually unknown outside the Senate, arrayed against them were representatives of an administration which six months before had been elected by the largest landslide vote in American history. This vote had been, moreover, partly justified by the particularistic sentiments of the backlash, the very sentiments that the senators were now out to demonstrate were deviant and isolated from the true American tradition.

What the senators did, in the first instance, was to deny the validity of such sentiments and motives out of hand. They bracketed the political realities of everyday life, and particularly the critical realities of life in the 1960s. Throughout the hearings the senators never referred to the polarized struggles of that day. By making those struggles invisible, they denied any moral context for the witnesses' actions. This strategy of isolating backlash values was supported by the only positive explanation the senators allowed, namely, that the conspirators were just plain stupid. They poked fun at them as utterly devoid of common sense, implying that no normal person could ever conceive of doing such things.

This strategic denial, or bracketing in the phenomenological sense, was coupled with a ringing and unabashed affirmation of the universalistic myths which are the backbone of the American civic religion. Through their questions, statements, references, gestures and metaphors, the senators maintained that every American, high or low, rich or poor, acts virtuously in terms of the pure universalism of the civic republican tradition. Nobody is selfish or inhumane. No American is concerned with money or power at the expense of fair play. No team loyalty is so strong that it violates common good or neutralizes the critical attitude towards authority that is the basis of a democratic society. Truth and justice are declared to be the main themes of American political society. Every citizen is rational and will act in accordance with justice if he is allowed to know the truth. Law is the perfect embodiment of justice, and office consists of the application of just law to power and force. Because power corrupts, office must enforce impersonal obligations in the name of the people's justice and reason. Narrative myths which embodied these themes were often invoked. Sometimes these were timeless fables, sometimes they were stories about the origins of English common law, often they were the narratives about the exemplary behavior of America's most sacred presidents. John Dean, for example, the most compelling anti-Nixon witness, strikingly embodied the American detective myth (Smith 1970). This figure of authority is derived from the Puritan tradition, and in countless different stories he is portrayed as ruthlessly pursuing truth and injustice without emotion or vanity. Other narratives developed in a more contingent way. For administration witnesses who confessed, the committee's "priests" granted forgiveness in accord with well established ritual forms, and their conversions to the cause of righteousness constituted fables for the remainder of the proceedings.

These democratic myths were confirmed by the senators' confrontation with family values. Their families were utterly invisible throughout the hearings. We don't know if they had families, but they certainly were not presented. Like the committee's chairman, Sam Ervin, who was always armed with the Bible and the Constitution, the senators embodied transcendent justice divorced from personal or emotional concerns.

Another confrontation that assumed ritual status was the swearing in of the witnesses. It served no real legal function because these were no legal proceedings. The swearing-in functioned instead as a form of moral degradation. It reduced the famous, powerful people who were involved to the status of "Everyman." It placed them in subordinate positions *vis-à-vis* the overpowering and universalistic law of the land.

In terms of more direct and explicit conflict, the senators' questions centered on three principal themes, each fundamental to the moral anchoring of a civic democratic society. First, they emphasized the absolute priority of office obligations over personal ones: "This is a nation of laws not men." Second, they emphasized the imbeddedness of such office obligations in a higher transcendent authority: "The laws of men" must give way to the "laws of God." Or as Sam Ervin put it to Maurice Stans, the ill-fated treasurer of Nixon's campaign committee, "Which is more important, not violating laws or not violating ethics?" Finally, the senators insisted that this transcendental anchoring of interest conflict allowed America to be a true *Gemeinschaft*, in Hegel's terms, a true "concrete universal." As Senator Wiecker put it in a famous statement: "Republicans do not cover up, Republicans do not go ahead and threaten . . . and God knows Republicans don't view their fellow Americans as enemies to be harassed [but as] human being[s] to be loved and won."

In normal times many of these statements would have been greeted with derision, with hoots and cynicism. In fact, many of them were lies in terms of the specific empirical reality of everyday political life, and especially in terms of the political reality of the 1960s. Yet they were not laughed at or hooted down. The reason was because this was not everyday life. This was a ritualized and liminal event, a period of intense generalization that had powerful claims to truth. It was a sacred time and the hearing chambers had become a sacred place. The committee was invoking the most sacred values, not trying to describe empirical fact. On this mythical level the statements could be seen and understood as true, and they were so seen and understood by significant portions of the population.

The hearings ended without laws or specific judgments of evidence, but they had, nevertheless, profound effects. They helped to establish and fully to legitimate a framework that henceforth gave the Watergate crisis its meaning. They accomplished this by continuing and deepening the cultural process which had begun before the election itself. Actual events and characters in the Watergate episode were organized in terms of the higher antitheses between the pure and the impure elements of America's civil religion. Before the hearings "Watergate" already symbolized the structured antitheses of American mythical life, antitheses which were implicitly linked by the American people to the structure of their civil religion. What the hearings accomplished, first, was to make this linkage to civil religion explicit and pronounced. The "good guys" of the Watergate process – their actions and motives – were purified in the resacralization process through their identification with the Constitution, norms of fairness, and citizen solidarity. The perpetrators of Watergate, and the themes which they evoked as justification, were polluted by association with civil symbols of evil: sectarianism, self-interest, particularistic loyalty. As this description implies, moreover, the hearings also restructured the linkages between Watergate elements and the nation's political center. Many of the most powerful men surrounding President Nixon were now implacably associated with Watergate evil, and some of Nixon's most outspoken enemies were linked to Watergate good. As the structural and symbolic centers of the civil religion were becoming so increasingly differentiated, the American public found the presidential party and the elements of civic sacredness more and more difficult to bring together (see fig. 2).

While this reading of the events is based on ethnography and interpretation, the process of deepening pollution is also revealed by poll data. Between the 1972 election and the very end of the crisis in 1974 there was only one large increase in the percentage of Americans who considered Watergate "serious." This occurred during the first two months of the Watergate hearings, April through early July 1973. Before the hearings, only 31 per cent of Americans responded to Watergate as a "serious" issue. By early July 50 per cent did, and this figure remained constant until the end of the crisis.

Although an enormous ritual experience had clearly occurred, any contemporary application of Durkheimianism must acknowledge that such modern rituals are never complete. In the first place ritual symbols must be carefully differentiated. Despite the frequent references to presidential involvement, and despite the president's shadow throughout the hearings, poll data reveal that most Americans did not emerge from the ritual experience convinced of President Nixon's involvement. In the second place, the ritual effects of the hearings were unevenly felt. The Senate hearings were most powerful in their effect on certain centrist groups and left-wing groups: (1) among McGovern voters whose outrage at Nixon was splendidly confirmed; (2) among moderate Democrats who even if they voted for McGovern were now outraged at Nixon, particularly after many had crossed party lines to vote for him; (3) among moderate or liberal Republicans and Independents who while disagreeing with many of Nixon's positions had voted for him anyway. The latter groups were particularly important to the entire process of Watergate. They were pro-

Fig. 2. *Symbolic classification system as of August 1973*

The Watergate "structure"

Evil	Good
Watergate Hotel	White House
The burglars	FBI
Dirty tricksters	
Money raisers	Justice Department
Employees of CREEP and	
Republican Party	
Former U.S. Attorney General and	
Secretary of Treasury	Special Prosecutor Cox
President's closest aides	Senators Ervin, Weicker, Baker
	Federal "watchdog" bureaucracy
	President Nixon

American civil religion

Evil	Good
Communism/fascism	Democracy
Shadowy enemies	White House-Americanism
Crime	Law
Corruption	Honesty
Personalism	Responsibility
Bad presidents (e.g.	Great presidents (e.g.
Harding, Grant) President Nixon	Lincoln, Washington)
Great scandals (e.g. Watergate)	Heroic reformers (e.g. Sam
	Ervin)

totypically cross-pressured, and it was the cross-pressured groups who along with radical McGovern supporters became most deeply involved in the hearings. Why? Perhaps they needed the hearings to sort out confused feelings, to clarify crucial issues, to resolve their uncomfortable ambivalence. Certainly such a relative stake can be found in the poll data. In the period mid-April 1973 to late June 1973 – the period of the hearings' beginnings and their most dramatic revelations – the growth among Republicans who thought Watergate "serious" was 20 per cent, and among Independents 18 per cent; for Democrats, however, the percentage growth was only 15 per cent.[7]

The year-long crisis which followed the hearings was punctuated by episodes of moral convulsion and public anger, by renewed ritualization, by the further shifting of symbolic classification to include the structural center, and by the further expansion of the solidary base of this symbolism to include most of the significant segments of American society. In the wake of the Senate hearings, a Special Prosecutors Office was created. It was staffed almost entirely by formerly alienated members of the left-wing opposition to Nixon, who with their assumption of office made publicly accepted professions of their commitments to impartial justice, a process that further demonstrated the powerful generalizing and solidarizing phenomena underway. The first special prosecutor was Archibald Cox, whose Puritan and Harvard background made him the ideal embodiment of the civil religion. When Nixon fired Cox for asking the courts to challenge the president's decision to withhold information in October 1973, there was a massive outpouring of spontaneous public anger, which newspaper reporters immediately dubbed the "Saturday Night Massacre."

Americans seemed to view Cox's firing as a profanation of the attachments they had built up during the Senate hearings, commitments to newly revivified sacred tenets and against certain diabolical values and tabooed actors. Because Americans had identified their positive values and hopes with Cox, his firing made them fear pollution of their ideals and themselves. This anxiety caused public outrage, an explosion of public opinion during which three million protest letters were sent to the White House over a single weekend. These letters were labelled a "flash-flood," a metaphor which played on the pre-crisis signification of Watergate: the polluted water of the scandal had broken the river gates and flooded surrounding communities. The term "Saturday Night Massacre" similarly intertwined deeper rhetorical themes. The "St. Valentine's Day Massacre" was a famous mob killing during the 1920s in gangland Chicago. "Black Friday" was the day in 1929 when the American stockmarket fell, shattering the hopes and trust of millions of Americans. Cox's firing, then, produced the same kind of symbolic condensation as dream symbolism, but on a mass public scale. The anxiety of the citizenry was deepened, moreover, by the fact that pollution had now spread directly to the very figure who was supposed to hold American civil religion together, the president himself. By firing Cox, President Nixon came into direct contact with the molten lava of sacred impurity. The pollution Watergate carried had now spread to the very center of American social structure. While support for Nixon's impeachment had gone up only a few points during the Senate hearings, after the "Saturday Night Massacre" it increased by fully ten points. From this flashflood came the first congressional motions for impeachment and the instauration of the impeachment process in the House of Representatives.

Another major expansion of pollution occurred when the transcripts of White House conversations secretly taped during the Watergate period were released in April and May 1974. The tapes contained numerous examples of presidential deceit, and they were also laced with presidential expletives and ethnic slurs. Once again, there was tremendous public indignation at Nixon's behavior. By his words and recorded actions he had polluted the very tenets which the entire Watergate process had revivified: the sacredness of truth and the image of America as an inclusive, tolerant community. The symbolic and structural centers of American society were further separated, with Nixon (the representative of the structural center) increasingly pushed into the polluted, evil side of the Watergate dichotomies. This transcript convulsion helped define the symbolic center as a distinct area, and it demonstrated that this center was neither liberal nor conservative. Indeed, most of the indignation over Nixon's foul language was informed by conservative beliefs about proprietary behavior and civil decorum, beliefs which had been flagrantly violated by Nixon's enemies, the Left, during the polarized period which preceded the Watergate crisis.

The impeachment hearings conducted by the House Judiciary Committee in June and July of 1974 marked the most solemn and formalized ritual of the entire Watergate episode. It was the closing ceremony, a rite of expulsion in which the body politic rid itself of the last and most menacing source of sacred impurity. By the time of these hearings the symbolization of Watergate was already highly developed; in fact, Watergate had become not only a symbol with significant referents but a powerful metaphor whose self-evident meaning itself served to define unfolding events. The meaning structure associated with "Watergate," moreover, now unequivocally placed a vast part of White House and "center" personnel on the side of civil pollution and evil. The only question which remained was whether President Nixon himself would officially be placed alongside them as well.

The House hearings recapitulated the themes which appeared in the Senate hearings one year before. The most pervasive background debate was over the meaning of "high crimes and misdemeanors," the constitutional phrase which set forth the standard for impeachment. Nixon's supporters argued for a narrow interpretation which held that an officer had to have committed an actual civil crime. Nixon's opponents argued for a broad interpretation which would include issues of political morality, irresponsibility and deceit. Clearly, this was a debate over the level of system crisis: were merely normative, legal issues involved, or did this crisis reach all the way to the most general value underpinnings of the entire system? Given the highly ritualized format of the hearings, and the tremendous symbolization which had preceded the committee's deliberations, it hardly seems possible that the committee could have adopted anything other than the broad interpretation of "high crimes and misdemeanors."

This generalized definition set the tone for the hearings' single most distinctive quality: the ever-recurring emphasis on the members' fairness and the objectivity of its procedures. Journalists frequently remarked on how congressmen rose to the sense of occasion, presenting themselves not as political representatives of particular interests but as embodiments of sacred civil documents and democratic mores. This transcendence of wide partisan division was echoed by the cooperation among the Judiciary Committee's staff, which in fact had actually set the tone for the committee's formal, televised deliberations. Key members of the staff had, in the 60s, been critics of establishment activities like the Vietnam War and supporters of anti-establishment movements like civil rights. Yet this partisan background never publicly surfaced during the vast journalistic coverage of the committee's work; even right-wing conservatives never made an issue of it. Why not? Because this committee, like its Senate counterpart one year before, existed in a liminal, detached place. They, too, operated within sacred time, their deliberations continuous not with the immediate partisan past but with the great constitutive moments of the American republic: the signing of the Bill of Rights, the framing of the Constitution, the crisis of the Union which marked the Civil War.

This aura of liminal transcendence moved many of the most conservative members of the committee, Southerners whose constituents had voted for Nixon by landslide proportions, to act out of conscience rather than political expediency. The Southern bloc, indeed, formed the key to the coalition which voted for three articles of impeachment. These final articles, revealingly, purposefully eschewed a fourth article, earlier proposed by liberal Democrats, which condemned Nixon's secret bombing of Cambodia. Though this earlier article referred to a real violation of law, it was an issue that was interpreted by Americans in specifically political terms, terms about which they widely disagreed. The final three impeachment articles, by contrast, referred only to fully generalized issues. At stake was the code that regulated political authority, the question of whether impersonal obligations of office can and should control personal interest and behavior. It was Nixon's violation of office obligations which made the House vote his impeachment.

After Nixon resigned from office, the relief of American society was palpable. For an extended period the political community had been in a liminal state, a condition of heightened anxiety and moral immersion which scarcely allowed time for the mundane issues of political life. When Vice-President Ford ascended to the presidency, there was a series of symbolic transformations which indicated ritualistic reaggregation. President Ford, in his first words after taking office, announced that "our long national nightmare is over." Newspaper headlines proclaimed that the sun had finally broken through the clouds, that a new day was being born. Americans expressed confidence in the strength and unity of the country. Ford himself was transformed, through these reaggregating rites, from a rather bumbling partisan leader into a national healer, the incarnation of a "good guy" who embodied the highest standards of ethical and political behavior.

Before continuing with the symbolic process after this reaggregation, I would like to return, once again, to the fact that modern rituals are never complete. This incompleteness represents the impact of relatively "autonomous" social system forces which Durkheim's sociological idealism made it impossible to consider. Even after the ritual ceremony which consensually voted articles of impeachment and the ritual renewal with President Ford, poll data reveal that a surprising segment of American society remained unconvinced. Between 18 and 20 per cent of Americans did not find President Nixon guilty, either of a legal crime or of moral turpitude. These Americans, in other words, did not participate in the generalization of opinion which drove Nixon from office. They interpreted the Watergate process, rather, as stimulated by political vengeance by Nixon's enemies. The demographics of this loyalist group are not particularly revealing. They were of mixed education and from every class and occupation. One of the few significant structural correlations was their tendency to be from the South. What did, apparently, really distinguish this group was their political values. They held a rigid and narrow idea of political loyalty, identifying the belief in God, for example, with commitment to Americanism. They also held a deeply personalized vision of political authority, tending much more than other Americans to express their allegiance to Nixon as a man and to his family as well. Finally, and not surprisingly, this group reacted much more negatively than other Americans to the left-wing social movements of the 1960s. The fact that they were committed to a polarized and exclusivist vision of political solidarity reinforced their reluctance to generalize from specifically political issues to general moral concerns. Such generalization would have involved not only criticism of Nixon but the restoration of a wider, more inclusive political community. In voting for Nixon they had supported a candidate who promised to embody their backlash sentiments and who had appeared, during his first years in office, inclined to carry out their wishes for a narrow and primordial political community.

The period of social reaggregation after Watergate's liminal period – the closure of the immediate ritual episode – raises, once again, the problem of the dichotomizing nature of Western social theory, for it involves the relationship between such categories as charisma/routine, sacred/ profane, generalization/institutionalization. On the one hand, it is clear that with Ford's ascension a much more routine atmosphere prevailed. Institutional actors and the public in general seemed to return to the profane level of goal and interest conflict. Political dissensus once again prevailed. Conflicts over the inflationary economy captured the news for the first time in months, and this issue, along with America's dependence on foreign oil, loomed large in the autumn, 1974, congressional elections.

According to the theories of routinization and specification, or institutionalization, the end of ritualization ushers in a new, completely post-spiritual phase, in which there is the institutionalization or crystallization of ritual spirit in a concrete form. The most elaborated theory of this transition is found in the works of Smelser (1959, 1963) and Parsons (Parsons and Bales 1955:35–132). In these works, post-crisis structures are described as evolving because they are better adapted to deal with the source of initial disequilibrium. Generalization is ended, then, because of the "efficiency" with which newly created structures deal with concrete role behavior. Now, to a certain extent, such new and more adaptive institution building did occur in the course of the Watergate process. New structures emerged that allowed the political system to be more differentiated, or insulated, from interest conflict and which allowed universalism to be more strongly served. Conflict-of-interest rules were developed and applied to presidential appointments; congressional approval of some of the president's key staff appointments, like Director of the Office of Management and Budget, was instituted; a standing Special Prosecutor's Office was created, the attorney-general being required to decide within thirty days of any congressional report on impropriety whether a prosecutor should actually be called; finally, federal financing of presidential election campaigns was passed into law. There were, in addition, a range of more informally sanctioned institutional innovations: the post of "chief of staff" became less powerful; the doctrine of "executive privilege" was used much more sparingly; Congress was consulted on important matters.

Durkheim and Weber would tend to support this dichotomous picture of crisis resolution. Weber, of course, saw most political interaction as instrumentally routine. The transition from charisma (Weber 1978:246–55) was preceded by structural innovation on the part of the leader's self-interested staff and triggered automatically and conclusively by the leader's death. Durkheim's understanding is more complex. On the one hand – and this, of course, is the problem with which we began our inquiry – Durkheim saw the non-ritual world as thoroughly profane, as non-valuational, as political or economic, as conflictual, and even in a certain sense as non-social (Alexander 1982:292–306). At the same time, however, Durkheim clearly overlaid this sharp distinction with a more continuous theory, for he insisted that the effervescence from rituals continued to infuse post-ritual life for some time after the immediate period of ritual interaction. Once again, I believe that this profound empirical insight can be understood only by reconceptualizing it, specifically by using it to critique and reorient the generalization–specification theory of the Parsonian tradition.

Though the crisis model of generalization–specification has been taken from functionalist analysis, the notion of generalization as ritual has been drawn from Durkheim. The analysis of social crisis presented here, therefore, has given much more autonomy to symbolic process than would a purely functionalist one. Generalization and ritualization are not engaged, in my view, purely for psychological or social-structural reasons – either because of anxiety or the inefficiency of social structures – but also because of the violation of ardently adhered to moral beliefs. Symbolic processes, therefore, occur as much to work out issues on this level as to provide more efficient structures for addressing specific, "real" disequilibriating problems. It is for this reason that ritualization is succeeded not by merely structural change but also by continued cultural effervescence. The recharged antinomies of the cultural order, and the emotional intensity which underlies them, continue to create moral conflict and, often, to support significantly different cultural orientations.

As compared, for example, to the aftershocks of the Dreyfus Affair, the effervescence of Watergate must be understood in terms of relative cultural unity. "Watergate" had come to be viewed – and this is extraordinarily significant in comparative terms – not as an issue of the Left or the Right but rather as a national issue about which most parties agreed. There were, it was universally agreed, certain "lessons of Watergate" from which the nation had to learn. Americans talked incessantly in the period between 1974 and 1976 about the imperatives of "post-Watergate morality." They experienced it as an imperious social force which laid waste to institutions and reputations. "Post-Watergate morality" was the name given to the effervescence from the ritual event. It named the revivified values of critical rationality, anti-authoritarianism, and civil solidarity, and it named the polluted values of conformity, personalistic deference, and factional strife. For several years after the end of liminality,

Americans applied these highly charged moral imperatives to group and interest conflict and to bureaucratic life, demanding radical universalism and heightened solidarity at every turn.

For the adult population, therefore – the case seems to have been somewhat different for children – the effect of Watergate was not increased cynicism or political withdrawal. Quite the opposite. Ritual effervescence increased faith in the political "system" even while the distrust it produced continued to undermine public confidence in particular institutional actors and authorities. Institutional distrust is different from the delegitimation of general systems per se (Lipset and Schneider 1983). If there is trust in the norms and values which are conceived as regulating political life, there may actually be more contention over the wielding of power and force (cf. Barber 1983). In this sense, political democracy and political efficiency may be opposed, for the first lends itself to conflict while the second depends on order and control.

In the immediate post-Watergate period, a heightened sensitivity to the general meaning of office and democratic responsibility did indeed lead to heightened conflict and to a series of challenges to authoritative control. Watergate became more than ever before a highly charged metaphor. No longer was it simply a referent for naming events which "objectively" occurred but a moral standard which helped "subjectively" to create them. Members of the polity, inspired by its symbolic power, sought out sinful behavior and tried to punish it. The result was a series of scandals: "Koreagate," "Winegate," "Billygate," to mention only a few. The giant explosion of Watergate into the American collective conscience vented a series of aftershocks of populist anti-authoritarianism and critical rationality. Some discussion of these follows.

(1) Almost immediately after the reaggregation ceremonies, there unfolded in close succession a series of unprecedented congressional investigations. Nelson Rockefeller, Ford's vice-presidential nominee, was subjected to a long and sometimes tendentious televised inquiry into the possible misuses of his personal wealth. Enormous televised investigations were also launched by the Congress into the secret, often anti-democratic working of the Central Intelligence Agency (CIA) and the Federal Bureau of Investigation (FBI), institutions whose authority had previously been unquestioned. This outpouring of "little Watergates" extended well into the Carter administration of 1976–80. Carter's chief assistant, Bert Lance, was forced out of office after highly publicized hearings that badly impugned his financial and political integrity. Each of these investigations created a scandal in its own right; each followed, often down to the smallest detail and word, the symbolic model established by Watergate.

(2) Whole new reform movements were generated from the Watergate spirit. The emergence of a Society for Investigative Reporting represented the fantastic growth of morally inspired, critical journalism among journalists who had internalized the Watergate experience and sought to externalize its model of critical reporting. Federal crime investigators – lawyers and policemen – formed white-collar crime units throughout the United States. For the first time in American history prosecutorial resources were significantly shifted away from the conventionally defined, usually lower-class, "enemies" of society to high-status office holders in the public and the private domain. Inspired by the Watergate model, it became the established, *a priori* conviction of many prosecutors that such office holders might well commit crimes against the public. By ferreting them out and prosecuting them, these legal officers would maintain the moral alertness of all authorities to the responsibility of office as such.

(3) In the months subsequent to reaggregation, authority was critically examined at every institutional level of American society, even the most mundane. The Boy Scouts, for example, rewrote their constitution to emphasize not just loyalty and obedience but critical questioning. The judges of the Black Miss America beauty pageant were accused of personalism and bias. Professional groups examined and rewrote their codes of ethics. Student-body officers of high schools and universities were called to task after little scandals were created. City councillors and mayors were "exposed" in every city, great and small. Through most of these controversies, specific issues of policy and interest were not significantly considered. It was the codes of office themselves which were at stake.

These concrete, institutional events, in other words, were actually motivated by the continuing "religious" struggles within post-Watergate culture. This connection is further demonstrated by the continuation in that period of even more specific Watergate-related themes. There were continuous assertions, for example, that America was morally unified. Groups which had been previously excluded or persecuted, most particularly those associated with the Communist Party, were publicly cleansed. I have already mentioned that those institutions most responsible for political witch-hunts, particularly the FBI, were reprimanded for their un-Americanism. Alongside this there occurred a more subtle outpouring from the collective conscience: books, articles, movies and television shows appeared about the immorality and tragedies associated with "McCarthyism," all painting persecuted fellow-travellers and communists in a sympathetic and familiar light. The anti-war movement assumed, through this same retrospective figurational process, a respectable, even heroic light. No doubt inspired by this rebirth of community, leaders of New Left underground organizations began to give themselves up, trusting the state but particularly the American opinion-making process to give them a fair hearing.

Through it all the vividness of Watergate's impure symbols remained strikingly intact. Trials of the Watergate conspirators generated large headlines and great preoccupation. Their published confessions and *mea culpas* were objects of intensely moral, even spiritual dispute. Richard Nixon, the very personification of evil, was viewed by alarmed Americans as a continuing source of dangerous pollution. Still a source of sacredness, his name and his person were forms of "liquid impure." Americans tried to protect themselves from this polluting lava by building walls. They sought to keep Nixon out of "good society" and isolated in San Clemente, his former presidential estate. When Nixon tried to buy an expensive apartment in New York, the building's tenants voted to bar the sale. When he travelled around the country, crowds followed to boo him, and politicians shunned him. When he reappeared on television, viewers sent indignant, angry letters. Indeed, Nixon could escape this calumny only by travelling to foreign countries, though even some foreign leaders refused to associate with him in public. For Americans, there was an extraordinary fear of being touched by Nixon or his image. Such contact was believed to lead to immediate ruin. When President Ford pardoned Nixon several months after assuming office, Ford's honeymoon with the public abruptly ended. Tarnished by this (however brief) association with Nixon, he alienated such a large body of the electorate that it cost him the subsequent presidential election.

The spirit of Watergate did eventually attenuate. Much of the structure and process which had stimulated the crisis reappeared, although it did so in a significantly altered form. Nixon had ridden a backlash against modernity into office, and after his departure this movement against liberal and inclusive secularism continued. But this conservatism now emerged in a much more anti-authoritarian form. Social movements like the tax revolt and the anti-abortion movement combined the post-Watergate spirit of critique and challenge with particularistic and often reactionary political issues. Ronald Reagan was swept into office on many of the same backlash issues, yet with Reagan, too, there continued to be a noticeable post-Watergate effect. For if Reagan was even more conservative than Nixon, he was committed to carrying out his reaction against the Left in a democratic and consensual way. This commitment may not have been a personal one, but it was enforced unequivocally by the public mood and by the continuing vitality of the potential counter-centers to presidential power.

Not only did the rightward movement of American politics reappear, but the authoritarianism of the "imperial presidency" regained much of its earlier force. As the distance from Watergate increased, concrete economic and political problems assumed greater and greater importance. Foreign crises, inflation, energy problems – the American people focused more and more on solving these apparently intractable "goals." These generated demands for specificity and efficacy, not for generalized morality. Given the structure of the American political system, these demands for efficacy necessitated a strong executive. The concern about the morality of authority became increasingly blunted by demands for strong and effective authority. Jimmy Carter began his presidency by promising the American people, "I will never lie to you." He ended it by making a strong presidency his principal campaign slogan. By the time Reagan became president, he could openly disdain some conflict-of-interest laws, re-employ some of the lesser-polluted Watergate figures, and move to wrap executive authority once again in a cloak of secrecy and charisma.

These later developments do not mean that Watergate had no effect. The codes that regulate political authority in America had been sharply renewed, codes which even when they are latent continue to affect and control concrete political activity. Politics in America had simply, and finally, returned to the "normal" level of interests and roles. If, however, "Watergate" had not happened, or had not happened in the same way, the American political system would be incalculably different.

III

In the first part of this chapter I maintained the importance of Durkheim's later, "religious" sociology. At the same time, I argued that it should be accepted more as an empirical theory of specific social processes than as a general theory of societies. In the second section I explored what these specific social processes are with reference to the Watergate crisis in the United States, placing the religious sociology within a more general theoretical and empirical framework. In this concluding section, I would like to focus briefly on the status of this later religious theory in a more general and abstract way.

There are three dimensions of Durkheim's later religious theory: morphology, solidarity, and classification. Each of these dimensions refers to a different empirical element in Durkheim's later work, yet, at the same time, Durkheim often conflates and reduces each element to the other. Each of these three elements, moreover, becomes the focus for independent strands of the Durkheimian tradition after Durkheim's death. Before a satisfactory cultural sociology can be developed, these traditions must be brought back together, the elements of each reconceptualized and analytically intertwined (see Alexander 1984).

Durkheim's theory of classification related purely to the organization of symbols, and his major contribution in this regard is to suggest that the antipathy between sacred and profane presents a fundamental structure of symbolic organization. Certainly the structuralism of Lévi-Strauss (1966) represents the foremost contribution to expanding, systematizing and applying this classificatory scheme.[8] But because of its purely cognitive focus, structuralism ignores the manner in which such bifurcating classification is oriented not simply to mind but to affect and society. These emphases can be brought into the abstract schema of structuralism by reinvoking the actual terms "sacred" and "profane." Sacred symbols are not simply one side of an abstract dichotomy. They are the focus of heightened affect, reflecting the emotional desirability of achieving the good. The opposite, antagonistic side of Durkheim's classification system must, however, also undergo further reconstruction. As Caillois (1959 [1939]) first demonstrated, Durkheim often confused the profane-as-routine with the sacred-as-impure. It is necessary, therefore, to develop the threefold classification of pure–sacred/impure–sacred/profane. Mary Douglas (1966), building upon notions of taboo, has expanded Durkheim's original understanding in a similar way, demonstrating that every symbolization of sacred purity is classified with an impure element which is given enormous polluting power. Because the fear of pollution is motivated by psychological anxiety and is directed, as well, to deviant social forces and groups, this revised understanding allows Durkheim's classificatory theory to be set forth in a manner that avoids the idealist and abstract implications of structural theory.

Yet the theory of symbolic antagonism must be complemented by other theories of symbolic classification. Symbols are also powerfully organized by myths, by narratives that assemble and reassemble symbols into dramatic forms. Eliade (1959) has elaborated mythical organization in historical and archaeological ways. Ricoeur has developed perhaps the most elaborate contemporary phenomenology of mythical organization, particularly in his work (Ricoeur 1967) on the symbolism of evil. But more present-oriented myth analyses must also be explored, for example the work of Henry Nash Smith, *Virgin Land* (1970), which builds upon Levy-Bruhl to explore how myths about the Yeoman Farmer helped guide the Western movement of the American nation.

Neither myth nor structural analysis address the issue of temporality, the actual historical development which often occurs within the realm of symbolic classification itself. Here, I believe, lies the contribution of Weber and others in the German Idealist school. In his account of the movement from this-worldly mysticism to this-worldly asceticism (1978:541–635), Weber systematically demonstrated the evolution of religious ideas about salvation. Troeltsch (1960 [1911]) followed up Weber's contribution by demonstrating historical evolution in ideas about individual autonomy. Jellinek's writings (1901 [1885]) on the origins of the Declaration of the Rights of Man represent another significant, if less known, work in this genre, one indeed which later inspired Weber himself. Among contemporaries, Bellah's (1970 and Bellah and Hammond 1980) theory about the comparative evolution of "civil religions" is the most significant secular transformation of Weberian ideas, although Walzer's (1965) work on Puritanism and the English Revolution and Little's (1969) on Puritanism and law are also exemplary.

This historical dimension of the Weberian approach to symbolic organization feeds into the Parsonian-functionalist concentration on values. "Values" refers to explicit cognitive ideas about the meaning of social structure. Value analysis has often functioned as a cover for the reduction of culture to social structure, and it has also tended to produce a fragmentary description of culture as composed of discrete and unconnected units of meaning. It need not do so, however, particularly if it is combined with the thematic approach of intellectual history. Martin Wiener's (1981) analysis of the rise of anti-industrial values in English history is just such a case. Sewell's (1980) work on the value of corporatism in French working-class history is another. Viviana Zelizer's (1979) analysis of how shifting ideas related to the development of the American life insurance industry is perhaps the finest such value analysis in the functionalist tradition (see also Zelizer 1985).

Finally, as Lukes (1984) has reminded us in his recent introduction to Durkheim's writing on sociological method, any contemporary extension of Durkheimian "classification" theory must come firmly to grips with the hermeneutical and interpretive tradition. Rhetorical theories of textual analysis – so brilliantly elaborated by Geertz (1973) – must be incorporated into the tools of cultural sociology. So must the general stricture, first insisted upon by Dilthey (1976:155–263) and most recently articulated by Ricoeur (1971), that for purposes of symbolic analysis social action must be read as a text. Semiotics, both as literary method and as social theory, can be incorporated into cultural sociology only in this way (cf. Sahlins 1976 and Barthes, e.g. 1983).

Yet Durkheim's analysis of solidarity is just as significant, I believe, as his theory of symbolic organization. He leads classification to solidarity through his ritual theory, hence it is not only solidarity but ritual that symbolic structuralism ignores.[9] Ritual theory provides the social process and action for symbolic classification; solidarity provides the link between ritual, symbolization, and the concrete social community. Together, ritual and solidarity allow the cultural analyst to discuss social crisis and renewal, and their relation not only to symbolic organization but to institutions and social groups.

Durkheim tied solidarity too closely to classification. Although he implied an independent power for the sacred and profane (here Lévi-Strauss' critique (e.g. 1966: 214) is wrong), he just as often explained classification merely as the reflection of solidary forms (here Lévi-Strauss was right). Not only must symbolic organization be treated as an independent dimension, but solidarity itself must be internally differentiated. The solidary renewal that ritual inevitably provides must be considered separately from the degree of its empirical reach, apart, that is, from the question of just how far such solidarity extends.[10] Both these issues, moreover – renewal and integration – must be dissociated from the unreflexive, automatic quality that accrues to them in Durkheim's original work. Not only must the initiation of ritual be treated in an historically specific way, but the course which ritualization and solidarizing processes take once they are initiated must be theorized in a manner that allows an open-ended understanding. Evans-Pritchard's (1953) demonstration of how ritual activity can re-establish the relationship between socially refracted cultural themes is a crucial early contribution to this problem (cf. Alexander 1984). More recently, Victor Turner (e.g. 1969) has made the most explicit effort to expand Durkheim's solidarity/ritual theory. Turner's generalization and abstraction of van Gennep's stages of ritual process – separation, liminality, reaggregation – is important because it allows ritual analysis to be applied outside of tightly structured domains. Liminality, and the communitas which accompanies it, can now be more clearly seen as typical responses to status reversal and instability at any level of social life. Yet Turner's work still suffers from the rigid dichotomies of Durkheim's original, particularly from the idealistic reification of solidarity and from his insistence that liminality is astructural rather than simply less specified and routinized. Sewell's detailed and historically specific description of the episodic eruption of working-class solidarity and the gradual expansion of worker cooperation avoids these problems while maintaining a close, if implicit, faithfulness to the central core of Durkheim's work. Sally Moore's (1975) insistence on the processual and contingent within ritual process, by contrast, tries to push contemporary ritual analysis toward the flux and flow of social life.

Finally, there is the problem of morphology. For Durkheim, morphology is social structure. Yet, though he insisted that classification and solidarity must be linked to morphology, once he abjures the morphological determinism of his early work he never gets anywhere near telling us how such a link might take place. One problem is that his theoretical dichotomies force him to work with a correspondence theory of interrelationship. A more multidimensional stance, by contrast, would make morphology the continuous referent for a symbolizing process which simultaneously refers to the personality and cultural orders and which is governed, as well, by aesthetic-expressive considerations of continuity and form. Most contemporary work on culture and social structure, however, recapitulates Durkheim's mistake, what Sahlins (1976) describes – in reference to Marx – as giving morphology temporal if not ontological priority over symbolization. This is especially true, for example, in the later work of Mary Douglas (Douglas and Wildavsky 1982), which describes pollution symbols as if they were mere reflections of core-group/out-group relations. Turner makes much the same mistake in his discussion of solidarity, which is invariably described as propelled by concrete social arrangements without any prior relationship to cultural codes. Sewell, too, derives his French workers' initial ideas about solidarity from the purportedly "real" structures of their economic life.

To avoid this false prioritizing, one must keep in mind Parsons' insistence that there is only an *analytical* (never empirical or historical) differentiation between culture and social system. Structural components are never without symbolic internalization or institutionalization, nor are symbolic classifications ever without some element of socialized form.[11] To capture this analytic point empirically is to acknowledge that every structural event, and even every specific social value, exists within a very broad matrix of cultural tradition. Until recently, this matrix has been religion, and morphological analysis which separates material from religious structure does so at its peril. Walzer's (1965) analysis of the interrelation of class, Christianity, education, political exile and social change remains the most successful analysis of interrelation of which I am aware.

But the problem of morphology extends beyond the problem of inter-relationship alone. It is based as well on the very difficulty of conceptualizing morphology itself. Durkheimian theory has had a very underdeveloped sense of the nature of social structure. One must turn to the functionalist and Weberian traditions to find a more complex and dynamic referent for symbolization and solidarity. Only after this referent is discovered can the most interesting substantive processes of contemporary symbolization be studied – for example, the Weberian problem of authority – and can questions like the degree of ritual integration finally be addressed. It has been a working hypothesis of this chapter that the ability to reconstitute solidarity in social crises is related, on the one hand, to the degree of social structural differentiation and, on the other, to the degree to which a given culture defines symbolic authority in universalistic terms.

If social science today is to develop a cultural theory it must build on Durkheim's "religious " sociology. If it is to do this, however, it must reconstruct this later writing in a serious and ambitious way. I have tried, in the present chapter, to lay out some of what this reconstruction entails and to offer an extended example of what such a reconstructed theory might look like in action.

Notes

1 These figures are drawn from the 1972–4 panel survey taken by the American National Election Study conducted by the University of Michigan's Institute for Social Science Research.

2 In developing this scheme, I have relied on – in addition to Shils and the other Durkheimians whose work I have already mentioned – Douglas (1966), Keller (1963), and Eisenstadt (1971), among others.

3 I am drawing here upon my reading of the televised news reports on Watergate-related issues available in the Vanderbilt Television Archives in Nashville, Tennessee.

4 I am drawing here, of course, on Lévi-Strauss (e.g. 1966), but reworking this structuralist scheme in a moral and affective, i.e. Durkheimian, direction (see my Introduction, above).

5 This observation is based on a systematic sampling of national news magazines and televised news reports from 1968 through 1976.

6 That Nixon struggled against television in order to prevent ritualization underscores the peculiar qualities of this medium's aesthetic form. In his pioneering essay, *What Is Cinema?*, André Bazin (1958) suggested that the unique ontology of cinema, as compared to written art forms such as novels, is realism. Bazin meant not that artifice is absent from cinema but that the end result of cinema artifice gives the unmistakable impression of being real, life-like, and "true." The audience cannot distance itself from talking and speaking images as easily as it can from static, impersonal literary forms. It seems to me that this forceful realism is as true for television, particularly documentary and news television, as for the classic cinema, though in this case the medium of contrast is newspapers rather than novels. Thus, ever since its appearance after the Second World War, political leaders have sensed that to command the medium of television, with the hidden artifice of its *mise-en-scène*, means that one's words will possess – in the public's mind – the ontological status of truth.

In this sense, Nixon's struggle against televising the hearings was a struggle to contain information about the Senate hearings within the less convincing aesthetic package of newsprint. He and his supporters sensed that if the televised form were to be achieved, the battle already would be partly lost.

This insight from the philosophy of aesthetics should, however, be modified in two ways. On the one hand, I will suggest in the following discussion that because live television coverage of news events is contingent, the realism of the Senate hearings was necessarily uncertain. The "possession" of the Watergate *mise-en-scène* – the play-by-play of the hearings – was far from determined.

My previous discussion, on the other hand, indicates that Bazin's aesthetic dictum must be modified in another sociological way as well. Television, even "factual" television, is a medium that depends on influence, and the willingness to be influenced – to accept statements of fact at face value – depends on trust in the persuader. The degree to which factual television is believed – how and to what degree it achieves the ontological status to which it is, as it were, aesthetically entitled – depends on the degree to which it is viewed as a differentiated, unbiased medium of information. Indeed, the analysis of poll data from the period suggests that one of the strongest predictors of support for impeachment was the belief that television news was fair. It follows that one of the primary reasons for the failure to accept Watergate as a serious problem – let alone Nixon's culpability – before the 1972 election was the widespread perception that the media was not independent but part of the vanguard modernist movement, a linkage which was, of course, strongly promoted by Vice-President Spiro Agnew. Because of the processes I have described, however, between January and April 1973 the media gradually was rehabilitated. Feelings of political polarization had ebbed, and other key institutions now seemed to support the media's earlier reported "facts." Only because the medium of television now could draw upon a fairly wide social consensus, I believe, could its messages begin to attain the status of realism and truth. This shifting social context for the aesthetic form is critical, therefore, for understanding the impact of the Senate hearings.

7 The figures in these last two paragraphs are drawn from the poll data presented in Lang and Lang (1983: 88–93, 114–17). Appropriating the term "serious" from the polls, however, the Langs do not sufficiently differentiate the precise symbolic elements to which the designation referred.

8 For an example of the best recent work in this tradition, see Sahlins (1976).

9 Benjamin Kilbourne, my colleague at UCLA, has commented that structuralism reads like *The Elementary Forms of the Religious Life* without its third book! 10 I believe that Lukes (1975) was getting at this separation in another way in his important piece on neo-Durkheimian treatments of ritual life.

11 While the latter point is often denied by Sahlins (1976), his analysis of food symbolism as structured by the value placed on human life actually demonstrates its truth.

References

Alexander, Jeffrey C. 1982. *The Antinomies of Classical Thought: Marx and Durkheim*. Berkeley and Los Angeles: University of California Press.
1984. "Three Models of Culture/Society Relations. The Watergate Crisis in

the U.S." *Sociological Theory* 2:290–314. Reprinted in Alexander, *Action and its Environments.* New York: Columbia University Press, 1988.

 1987. "Action and Its Environments." In J. C. Alexander, B. Giesen, R. Münich and N. Smelser, eds., *The Micro-Macro Link.* Berkeley and Los Angeles: University of California Press.

Barber, Bernard. 1983. *The Logic and Limits of Trust.* New Brunswick, NJ: Rutgers University Press.

Barthes, Roland. 1983. *The Fashion System.* New York: Hill and Wang.

Bazin, André. 1958. *Qu'est-ce que le cinéma?* Vol. 1. Paris: Editions du Cerf.

Bellah, Robert N. 1970. "Civil Religion in America." In R. B. Bellah, *Beyond Belief,* pp. 168–89. New York: Harper and Row.

Bellah, Robert N. and Phillip E. Hammond. 1980. *Varieties of Civil Religion.* New York: Harper and Row.

Caillois, Roger. 1959 [1939]. *Man and the Sacred.* New York: Free Press.

Dilthey, Wilhelm. 1976. *Selected Writings.* Cambridge: Cambridge University Press.

Douglas, Mary. 1966. *Purity and Danger: An Analysis of the Concepts of Pollution and Taboo.* London: Penguin.

Douglas, Mary and Aaron Wildavsky. 1982. *Risk and Culture: An Essay on the Selection of Technical and Environmental Dangers.* Berkeley and Los Angeles: University of California Press.

Durkheim, Emile. 1938 [1895]. *The Rules of Sociological Method.* New York: Free Press.

 1958 [1895–6]. *Socialism and Saint-Simon.* Yellow Springs, Ott: Antioch.

 1951 [1897]. *Suicide. A Study in Sociology.* Trans. John A. Spaulding and George Simpson. Glencoe, Ill: Free Press.

Eisenstadt, S. N. 1971. *Political Sociology.* New York: Basic Books.

Eliade, Mircea. 1959. *The Sacred and the Profane.* New York: Harcourt, Brace.

Evans-Pritchard, E. E. 1953. "The Nuer Concept of the Spirit in its Relation to Social Order." *American Anthropologist* 55:201–41.

Friedrichs, Carl J. 1964. *Transcendent Justice.* Durham, NC: Duke University Press.

Geertz, Clifford. 1973. *The Interpretation of Cultures.* New York: Basic Books.

Jellinek, Georg. 1901. [1885]. *The Declaration of The Rights of Man and of Citizens: A Contribution to Modern Constitutional History.* New York: Holt.

Keller, Suzanne. 1963. *Beyond the Ruling Class.* New York: Random House.

Lacroix, Bernard. 1981. *Durkheim et le politique.* Paris: PUF.

Lang, Gladys and Kurt Lang. 1983. *The Battle for Public Opinion.* New York: Columbia University Press.

Lévi-Strauss, Claude. 1966. *The Savage Mind.* Chicago: University of Chicago Press.

Lipset, Seymour Martin and William Schneider. 1983. *The Confidence Gap.* New York: Free Press.

Little, David. 1969. *Religion, Order, and Law.* New York: Harper and Row.

Lukes, Steven. 1975. "Political Ritual and Social Integration." *Sociology* 9:289–308.

1984. Introduction. In E. Durkheim, *Rules of Sociological Method*. London: Macmillan.

Moore, Sally F. 1975. "Uncertainties in Situations: Indeterminates in Culture." In Moore and Barbara Myerhoff, eds., *Symbol and Politics in Communal Ideology*, pp. 210–39. Ithaca, NY: Cornell University Press.

Parsons, Talcott and Robert F. Bales, eds. 1955. *Family, Socialization, and Interaction Process*. New York: Free Press.

Parsons, Talcott and Neil J. Smelser. 1957. *Economy and Society*. New York: Free Press.

Ricoeur, Paul. 1967. *The Symbolism of Evil*. Boston: Beacon.

1971. "The Model of the Text: Meaningful Action Considered as Text." *Social Research* 38:529–62.

Sahlins, Marshall. 1976. *Culture and Practical Reason*. Chicago: University of Chicago Press.

Sewell, William H., Jr. 1980. *Work and Revolution in France*. New York: Cambridge University Press.

Shils, Edward. 1975. *Center and Periphery: Essays in Macrosociology*. Chicago: University of Chicago Press.

Smelser, Neil J. 1959. *Social Change in the Industrial Revolution*. Chicago: University of Chicago Press.

1963. *Theory of Collective Behavior*. New York: Free Press.

Smith, Henry Nash. 1970. *Virgin Land*. New York: Vintage.

Tiryakian, Edward A. 1967. "A Model of Societal Change and Its Lead Indicators." In Samuel Z. Klausner, ed., *The Study of Total Societies*, pp. 69–97. New York: Praeger.

Troeltsch, Ernst. 1960 [1911]. *The Social Teachings of the Christian Church*. Chicago: University of Chicago Press.

Turner, Victor. 1969. *The Ritual Process: Structure and Anti-structure*. Chicago: Aldine.

Walzer, Michael. 1965. *The Revolution of the Saints*. Cambridge, MA: Harvard University Press.

Weber, Max. 1978. *Economy and Society*. Berkeley and Los Angeles: University of California Press.

Wiener, Martin J. 1981. *English Culture and the Decline of the Industrial Spirit, 1850–1980*. New York: Cambridge University Press.

Zelizer, Viviana. 1979. *Morals and Markets*. New York: Columbia University Press.

1985. *Pricing the Priceless Child*. New York: Basic Books.

Index

American Federation of Labor (AFL), 78, 79, 83
anthropology, symbolic and cultural studies in, 1, 8, 9
Aquino, C., 59
authority, 191

Barthes, R., 5, 6, 164
Bellah, R., 7, 8, 140–1, 148, 218
Berger, P., 140
Bernstein, B., 16n, 17n, 112
Billington, J., 60n
Blau, P., 102–3
Bloor, D., 4, 124n
Bouglé, C., 3

Caillois, R., 16n, 31, 192, 217
Carter, J., 216
Catholic Church: Durkheim's attitude toward, 59; and Nicaraguan revolutionary movement, 54, 55, 58; and Philippines revolutionary movement, 59–60; and Polish revolutionary movement, 54–5, 58
center, 195; and Watergate, 197, 198, 199, 201
civil religion: American, 203; Bellah on, 7–8, 140–1; Bellah versus Habermas on, 140–1; and celebrations, 161, 163, 181–3; cult of the individual as, 145, 147, 148; Durkheim on, 141, 145; Hammond on, 8; Luhmann on, 149n; Müller on, 14
classification, Durkheim's theory of, 192, 216–19
codes, 5; language, 112
collective conscience, Durkheim's notion of, 110, 142, 143
collective representations: Durkheim's notion of, 142, 143; Watergate as, 197

"communitas," Turner's notion of, 9, 70, 71, 74
community: in Durkheim, 143, 148; creation of, 30, 50, 51
conflict, social: in celebrations, 162, 164–6; and "communitas", 71; and generalization, 192; industrial, 73; and liminality, 12, 86
conquests, in media events, 168, 169, 170
consensus, social: celebrations of, in media events, 161, 163–4, 165–6; and Durkheimian religion, 30; and Watergate, 195, 196, 198
contests, in media events, 168, 169, 170
coronations, in media events, 169–70
Cox, A., 207

dedifferentiation, 45, 51–2
democracy, and Durkheim, 145–6
density, Durkheim's notion of, 114
differentiation, 45, 51, 142, 143, 146
Dilthey, W., 16n, 218
division of labor, in Durkheim, 94, 142, 145
Division of Labor, 49, 93, 94, 102, 108, 110, 112, 143, 144
Douglas, M., 4, 9, 15n, 66, 71, 217, 220

Edelman, M., 136
effervescence: Durkheim's notion of, 27, 49, 62, 188; and Parsons, 62; in revolutionary movements, 27, 49, 57, 58; in Watergate, 212–13
Elementary Forms, 3, 11, 26, 44, 45, 47–50 *passim*, 61n, 96–8, 108, 110, 112, 143
Eliade, M., 49, 217
Evans-Pritchard, E., 219

Filloux, J., 10